NATIONALISM AND ETHNIC CONFLICT

Other Books in the Current Controversies Series:

NATIONALISM AND ETHNIC CONFLICT

David L. Bender, *Publisher*
Bruno Leone, *Executive Editor*

Bonnie Szumski, *Managing Editor*
Katie de Koster, *Senior Editor*

Charles P. Cozic, *Book Editor*

CURRENT CONTROVERSIES

Cover photo: © T. Hornbak/Impact Visuals

Library of Congress Cataloging-in-Publication Data

Nationalism and ethnic conflict / Charles P. Cozic, book editor.
   p. cm. — (Current controversies)
   Includes bibliographical references and index.
   ISBN 1-56510-080-8 (lib. : alk. paper) — ISBN 1-56510-079-4
(pbk. : alk. paper)
   1. Ethnic relations. 2. Nationalism. 3. Culture conflict. [1. Nationalism.
2. Ethnic relations.] I. Cozic, Charles P., 1957-   . II. Series.
GN496.N37   1994
306.8—dc20   93-19854
                                   CIP
                                   AC

Printed on
recycled paper

Contents

Bosnian Muslims and Croats living in Bosnia-Herzegovina and Croatia initiated violence against Serbs living there. Serbs have the right to defend their homes and villages in these lands, this Serb journalist and soldier asserts. In the Balkan war, Serbia has been unjustly shunned by the world as a pariah.

No: Ethnic Conflict Is Not Justified

Cruel violence such as murder, rape, and torture is an ugly political tool that defiles all of the Arab world. Perhaps no other Arab nation has utilized such violence more devastatingly than Iraq, which pillaged Kuwait and has sought to exterminate its own Kurdish population. Tragically, many Arab intellectuals and leaders do not condemn such violence.

Chapter 3: What Are the Causes of Ethnic Conflict?

Chapter 4: Should Nations Intervene in Ethnic Conflicts?

Case Study: The Balkans

Nations Should Intervene in the Balkans

for maintaining peace and security and to pledge to confront aggression against other members, using military force if necessary.

Ethnic revolts and ethnic partitioning of nations are the major causes of today's (and probably tomorrow's) armed conflicts. Readily available weapons—from small arms to missile systems—facilitate these uprisings and stymie efforts to suppress them. Reducing arms production and sales, as well as the number of weapons already deployed, would be a major step toward preventing violent ethnic conflict.

Democracy in America has successfully fostered mutual respect among the nation's ethnic groups. Nation-states beset by ethnic conflict could alleviate such tensions by emulating America's brand of democracy.

Much of the world's warfare and unrest stems from the failure to resolve the problems of ethnic groups and stateless nationalities. One way to keep ethnic grievances from erupting into violence is to empower ethnic groups by granting them authority over various cultural and legal issues.

Group dialogue sessions among diverse and influential private citizens from both sides of an ethnic conflict can help resolve differences and prevent violence. These participants, who are more likely to make progress than government negotiators, could positively change the ways their own ethnic groups regard each other.

Foreword

By definition, controversies are "discussions of questions in which opposing opinions clash" (Webster's Twentieth Century Dictionary Unabridged). Few would deny that controversies are a pervasive part of the human condition and exist on virtually every level of human enterprise. Controversies transpire between individuals and among groups, within nations and between nations. Controversies supply the grist necessary for progress by providing challenges and challengers to the status quo. They also create atmospheres where strife and warfare can flourish. A world without controversies would be a peaceful world; but it also would be, by and large, static and prosaic.

The Series' Purpose

The purpose of the Current Controversies series is to explore many of the social, political, and economic controversies dominating the national and international scenes today. Titles selected for inclusion in the series are highly focused and specific. For example, from the larger category of criminal justice, Current Controversies deals with specific topics such as police brutality, gun control, white collar crime, and others. The debates in Current Controversies also are presented in a useful, timeless fashion. Articles and book excerpts included in each title are selected if they contribute valuable, long-range ideas to the overall debate. And wherever possible, current information is enhanced with historical documents and other relevant materials. Thus, while individual titles are current in focus, every effort is made to ensure that they will not become quickly outdated. Books in the Current Controversies series will remain important resources for librarians, teachers, and students for many years.

In addition to keeping the titles focused and specific, great care is taken in the editorial format of each book in the series. Book introductions and chapter prefaces are offered to provide background material for readers. Chapters are organized around several key questions that are answered with diverse opinions representing all points on the political spectrum. Materials in each chapter include opinions in which authors clearly disagree as well as alternative opinions in which authors may agree on a broader issue but disagree on the possible solutions. In this way, the content of each volume in Current Controversies mirrors the mosaic of opinions encountered in society. Readers will quickly realize that there are many viable answers to these complex issues. By questioning each author's conclusions, students and casual readers can begin to develop the critical thinking skills so important to evaluating opinionated material.

Current Controversies is also ideal for controlled research. Each anthology in the series is composed of primary sources taken from a wide gamut of informational categories including periodicals, newspapers, books, United States and foreign government documents, and the publications of private and public organizations. Readers will find factual support for reports, debates, and research papers covering all areas of important issues. In addition, an annotated table of contents, an index, a book and periodical bibliography, and a list of organizations to contact are included in each book to expedite further research.

Perhaps more than ever before in history, people are confronted with diverse and contradictory information. During the Persian Gulf War, for example, the public was not only treated to minute-to-minute coverage of the war, it was also inundated with critiques of the coverage and countless analyses of the factors motivating U.S. involvement. Being able to sort through the plethora of opinions accompanying today's major issues, and to draw one's own conclusions, can be a complicated and frustrating struggle. It is the editors' hope that Current Controversies will help readers with this struggle.

"Not since Nazi Germany have extremist right-wingers been more popular, their messages more hateful, and the ensuing ethnic violence more deadly."

Introduction

During his ascent to the dictatorship of Nazi Germany, Adolf Hitler mastered the use of propaganda, raising both the public's hatred of non-Aryans and its loyalty to himself and the Nazis. In many speeches, Hitler aimed his propaganda at Germany's sparse Jewish population in order to scapegoat them as agents of cultural and economic decline. In his book *Mein Kampf*, the "bible" of the Nazi party, Hitler wrote, "By defending myself against the Jew, I am fighting for the work of the Lord. In every mingling of Aryan blood with that of lower peoples, the result was the end of the cultured people." Hitler's strategy succeeded. His anti-Semitic cultural and religious propaganda inflamed many Germans' deep hatred of Jews and sparked a reign of terror against them.

Today, many extremist right-wing leaders and politicians, bent on building or keeping political power, spout Hitler-like propaganda to fan ethnic hatred and violence and to blame minorities for domestic problems. In turn, followers who embrace their leaders' rhetoric vent their pumped-up ethnic hatreds in a mounting spiral of violence. As the American socialist New Union party explains:

> To get the people to fight for their respective rulers' interests, the politicians and warlords stoke ethnic hatred through propaganda about invented atrocities committed by the other side. Then the same characters go out and actually commit atrocities in supposed retribution for the atrocities they claimed were done by their opponents. The cycle of violence and murder then escalates and develops a life of its own.

Events in the war-torn former Yugoslavia illustrate how propaganda can ignite ethnic fighting. As Yugoslav-born religious studies professor Paul Mojzes writes, "Even the most cursory reading of the politicians' statements indicates that each [ethnic] side liberally provoked the other. The name-calling was belligerent, the speeches and articles untruthful and incendiary. All lie[d] massively." As a result of bitter ethnic hatred, hundreds of thousands of Croats, Muslims, and Serbs have been killed or wounded and more than three million have been left homeless.

Tragically, this brutal type of ethnic hatred and violence seems to be intensifying around the world. In many European countries, for example, experts argue that not since Nazi Germany have extremist right-wingers been more popular, their messages more hateful, and the ensuing ethnic violence more deadly. Today, many right-wing leaders use propaganda to foment ethnic hatred toward people of color, immigrants, and other minorities.

Recent Immigrants: In Germany, for example, where more than fifteen million foreigners have immigrated since 1980, neo-Nazis echo Hitler's propaganda and exploit fears that the immigrant wave will ruin Germany's culture and economy. Neo-Nazi skinhead violence against Turkish and other immigrants has become so widespread that Germany has banned some neo-Nazi political parties for cultivating xenophobia. According to German novelist Gunter Grass, "The most dangerous thing is, we have [skinheads] in government. They think the same way as the young kids who shave their heads and carry swastikas and demonstrate. They encourage these ideas and brutal actions."

Rooted Minorities: But immigrants are not the only victims of ethnic propaganda. Ethnic groups with traditional roots—Muslims in the Balkans and India, Gypsies and Jews in Europe, indigenous tribes in Africa and South America, and other minorities—are also threatened. Like the Jews in Nazi Germany, the tiny minority of Gypsies, or Romanies, in Hungary are victims of persecution and government propaganda. In an attack that author Paul Hockenos declares "clearly alludes to the Gypsy community, if not all people of non-Magyar ethnicity," Hungarian ruling party vice president Istvan Csurka wrote: "We must end the unhealthy practice of blaming Skinheads for all that is bad among the youth, while leniently acknowledging other sicknesses, crimes, and cultural crimes. We can no longer recoil from the fact that there are also genetic reasons behind degeneration." Hockenos charges that in many statements like this, "the ruling [party] has complicitly fueled aggression and resentment against people of color." For when right-wing leaders wield their power in government and the media, the objects of their hatred find it difficult to combat propaganda and ethnic violence.

Ethnic conflicts or wars are never completely resolved unless they end in genocide. Ethnic hatreds thus tend to simmer, often ready to erupt when demagogues preach racist lies. But although propaganda can be an extremely persuasive message that creates the type of strife discussed in *Nationalism and Ethnic Conflict: Current Controversies*, it is never predestined to succeed and many ethnic groups have rejected its emotional appeal. Nations committed to peace can take solace in this fact as they attempt to strengthen ethnic relations within their own borders and around the world.

Chapter 1

Is Nationalism Beneficial?

Nationalism: An Overview

by Peter Alter

About the author: *Peter Alter is deputy director of the German Historical Institute in London and a professor of modern history at the University of Cologne in Germany.*

Nationalism is a political force which has been more important in shaping the history of Europe and the world over the last two centuries than the ideas of freedom and parliamentary democracy or of communism. The roots of modern nationalism are to be found in late eighteenth-century Western Europe and North America, whence it subsequently spread to the whole of Europe and eventually to all parts of the world. Alongside socialism, it was one of the two "main currents of thought of the nineteenth century" (thus the German historian Friedrich Meinecke). In the twentieth century, nationalism has had unparalleled successes, its importance growing by leaps and bounds in Europe directly before and after the First World War, and then, particularly after the Second World War, in Asia and Africa.

Emancipation or Oppression

The plethora of phenomena which may be subsumed under the term "nationalism" suggests that it is one of the most ambiguous concepts in the present-day vocabulary of political and analytical thought. The programme of an insurgent movement in the Balkans in the nineteenth century or in Africa in the twentieth, just to give two examples, may as easily be classified under the category of nationalism as may the oppression of one people by another. It has been—and continues to be—part of the make-up of both imperialism and anti-imperialism. It can be associated with forces striving for political, social, economic and cultural emancipation, as well as with those whose goal is oppression.

In the nineteenth and twentieth centuries, large multinational states which had emerged during the course of history, such as the Ottoman or Habsburg Empires, were split asunder in the name of nationalism, and were succeeded by a large number of small separate states. In the last century and a half, new states such as Greece, Italy, the German Reich, Czechoslovakia and Poland were proclaimed in the name of nationalism. Nationalist interests were among the driving forces behind the colonialist expansion of the European powers as they created overseas empires in Asia, Africa and other parts of the globe. Between 1918 and 1945, nationalism became synonymous with intolerance, inhumanity and violence. Wars were fought and heinous crimes perpetrated in its name. It inspired the violent expulsion of people from their homelands, and justified campaigns of territorial conquest. For individuals and whole peoples alike, nationalism signalled danger, restrictions on liberty, and not infrequently a threat to their very survival. The policies of extermination pursued by the National Socialists during the Second World War are the most horrifying examples. And yet at the same time, nationalism could just as often engender hopes for a free and just social order; indeed for many it equated with liberation from political and social discrimination.

> *"Nationalism . . . conceals within itself extreme opposites and contradictions."*

Concealed Contradictions

It is clear that nationalism, so convenient a label and justification for many developments, conceals within itself extreme opposites and contradictions. It can mean emancipation, and it can mean oppression: nationalism, it seems, is a repository of dangers and opportunities. It has so many different forms and "national" variations that it is often argued whether they can all be accommodated under the one roof. Only with reference to a concrete historical context can we say what the term actually does or should signify. An initial conclusion could run like this: *nationalism* does not exist as such, but a multitude of manifestations of nationalism do. In other words, it is more appropriate to speak of *nationalisms* in the plural than of *nationalism* in the singular. This still leaves the issue of whether the various nationalisms the world has witnessed since the late eighteenth century nevertheless possess common formal and substantial structures, and whether they can be traced back to comparable historical geneses.

Current linguistic usage defines "nationalists" as people whose actions or reasoning gives indiscriminate precedence to the interests of one nation (usually their own) over those of other nations, and who are prepared to disregard those others for the sacrosanct honour of their own nation. A modern German encyclopedia defines nationalism as an "exaggerated and intolerant form of thought in relation to a nation." In other words, it has negative connotations, suggesting an extreme ideology, and is judged in more or less moral terms. The term is used to brand forms of collective yearning and aggression arrogantly posturing in the name of a nation. By contrast, "the national interest" and "a sense of national pride" are wholly laudable, since they are felt to refer to clearly legitimate concerns which do not inevitably conflict with the nationalism of other peoples. The underlying idea in this case is that equality exists between various

19

nationalisms, and their frequently competing claims can be settled through peaceful compromise.

As a way of avoiding the frequently pejorative term "nationalism," the older word "patriotism"—love of one's homeland—is used. In eighteenth-century Europe it bore the notion of an emotional attachment to a landscape, a dynastic state or a ruler. A love of one's country was combined with universal human ideals; it was easy to be both a patriot and a citizen of the world. Then from the nineteenth century onwards, the meaning of patriotism shifted to allegiance to the nation and the nation-state, and came to be synonymous with nationalism and national consciousness, though it fact it was more and more rarely used as such. Later it resurfaced as a contrast to nationalism, which by now was increasingly being associated with expansionism. As the Dutch historian Johan Huizinga once put it, patriotism now referred to "the will to maintain and defend what is one's own and cherished." Unlike nationalism, patriotism has virtually never had the effect of an aggressive political force. For this reason, the historian Hans Kohn, who together with Carlton Hayes can be regarded as the doyen of the modern study of nationalism, has justifiably called it a "purely vegetative group feeling."

The term "nationalism," whose earliest mention can be found in a work of 1774 by the German philosopher Johann Gottfried Herder, did not begin to enter into general linguistic usage until the mid-nineteenth century.

> *"Unlike nationalism, patriotism has virtually never had the effect of an aggressive political force."*

But today arguments still rage over what nationalism really is. Even the academic world, which has been studying nationalism for decades, has failed to agree on a generally acceptable definition. The same is true of the concepts of "nation" and "nationality." In essence, the range of definitions that have been offered merely reflect the multiformity that nationalism has assumed in historical and political reality since the late eighteenth century. Since new hybrids of nationalism are constantly being thrown up in words and deeds, in the definition and study of the phenomenon, the depth of the student's experience continues to be equally important as the weight he or she gives to the components that, by general consensus, must be present in any given nationalism. These common structural components, or features, of nationalism include: consciousness of the uniqueness or peculiarity of a group of people, particularly with respect to their ethnic, linguistic or religious homogeneity; emphasizing of shared sociocultural attitudes and historical memories; a sense of common mission; disrespect for and animosity toward other peoples (racism, xenophobia, anti-Semitism).

Greater Status

The American political scientist Karl W. Deutsch, whose work has enriched research into nationalism to an extraordinary degree since the 1950s, has consequently defined nationalism as "a state of mind which gives 'national' messages, memories, and images a preferred status in social communication and a greater weight in the making of decisions." In Deutsch's opinion, a nationalist devotes greater attention to those messages which "carry specific symbols of nationality, or which originate from a specific national source, or which are couched in a specific national code of language or culture." This definition, which emphasizes intensive social communication as the pre-condition for feelings of national identity, is not entirely watertight, however, for it considers only some, albeit important, aspects of nationalism.

> *"New hybrids of nationalism are constantly being thrown up in words and deeds."*

A definition must necessarily be more comprehensive if it hopes to cater for all the forms of nationalism the nineteenth and twentieth centuries have witnessed: the nationalism of peoples which possess a state, and the nationalism of those which do not. The Bohemian-born sociologist and historian Eugen Lemberg comes a great deal nearer to the mark. In the framework of a "sociological theory of nationalism," he characterizes nationalism as a "system of ideas, values and norms, an image of the world and society" which makes a "large social group aware of where it belongs and invests this sense of belonging with a particular value. In other words, it integrates the group and demarcates its environment." Lemberg goes on to list the nuclei around which the group's awareness of its own location can crystallize: "shared language, origins, character and culture, or common subordination to a given state power."

Lemberg's definition of nationalism as an ideology capable of integrating large social groups has been refined by Theodor Schieder, who holds nationalism to be a *specific* integrative ideology which "always makes reference to a 'nation' in one sense or another, and not *merely* to a social or religious type of group." This broad conception will be adopted here: nationalism, such as it has appeared since the American and French Revolutions, will be understood as both an ideology and a political movement which holds the nation and the sovereign nation-state to be crucial indwelling values, and which manages to mobilize the political will of a people or a large section of a population. Nationalism is hence taken to be a largely dynamic principle capable of engendering hopes, emotions and action; it is a vehicle for activating human beings and creating political solidarity amongst them for the purposes of achieving a common goal.

Highest Loyalty

In accordance with this definition, nationalism exists whenever individuals feel they belong primarily to the nation, and whenever affective attachment and loyalty to that nation override all other attachments and loyalties. It is not status group, nor religious conviction, nor a dynasty or a particularistic state, nor a physical landscape, nor genealogical roots, not even social class which determine the supra-individual frame of reference; the tenet of Enlightenment philosophy—that the individual is principally a member of the human race and thus a citizen of the world—no longer holds: individuals perceive themselves, rather, as members of a particular nation. They identify with its historical and cultural heritage and with the form of its political life. The nation (or the nation-state) represents the site where life is led, and endows existence with meaning both in the present and the future. . . .

Liberal Nationalism

The great variety of roles nationalism has played in specific historical contexts can serve as a starting point for a typology classifying these diverse forms systematically into two main groups or basic types: Risorgimento [resurrection] nationalism and integral nationalism. Though it runs the risk of oversimplifying matters, this kind of historical, functional-based typology treats nationalism as a value-free, analytical category and tries to get away from moral judgements of "good" and "evil." Notwithstanding the generalizations it entails, it is of considerable value as a heuristic device for describing and explaining the complex phenomenon of nationalism.

In order to gain an overall, keynote grasp of Risorgimento nationalism . . . it can for the moment be defined as an emancipatory political force that accompanies the liberation both of new social strata within an existing, formerly absolutist western European state, and of a people that has grown conscious of itself in opposition to a transnational ruling power in east-central Europe. Risorgimento nationalism, frequently referred to as "liberal nationalism," "genuine nationalism," or "nationalism in its original phase," serves as a medium for the political fusion of large social groups, the formation of nations and their self-identification in the national state. The ultimate goal of Risorgimento nationalism, whose historical model is nineteenth-century Italian nationalism, is liberation from political and social oppression. It comprises unmistakable elements of a liberal ideology of opposition. It is a protest movement against an existing system of political domination, against a state which destroys the nation's traditions and prevents its flourishing. Its adherents stress the right of every nation, and with it the right of *each* and *every* member of a nation, to autonomous development, for in their minds, individual freedom and national independence are closely connected. The national movement in early nineteenth-century Germany, for instance, therefore campaigned for civil freedoms too. On 27 January 1822, the Greek constitutional national assembly, which sat in Epidaurus, issued a declaration to the peoples of Europe. It read:

> *"Nationalism exists whenever individuals feel they belong primarily to the nation."*

> The war which we are carrying on against the Turk is not that of a faction or the result of sedition. It is not aimed at the advantage of any single part of the

Greek people; it is a national war, a holy war, a war the object of which is to reconquer the rights of individual liberty, of property and honour,—rights which the civilized people of Europe, our neighbours, enjoy today; rights of which the cruel and unheard of tyranny of the Ottomans would deprive us—us alone—and the very memory of which they would stifle in our hearts.

Influential prophets of liberal Risorgimento nationalism, such as the German Johann Gottfried Herder and the Italian Giuseppe Mazzini, believed that peoples so evidently different in language and character also had unique duties to perform for humanity: each of them had a mission. Their philosophy could be traced directly to French nationalism in the late eighteenth and early nineteenth centuries, for French revolutionaries again and again justified their nationalism in terms of their mission to propagate the universal human ideals of liberty, equality and fraternity throughout Europe. . . .

Integral Nationalism

Integral nationalism, the counter-type to Risorgimento nationalism, is encountered under various titles. Radical; extreme; militant; aggressive-expansionist; derivative; right-wing; reactionary; excessive: these are just a few of the more common adjectives attaching to the term, and clearly show that a generally accepted nomenclature for the typology of nationalism does not exist, even among professional academics. The term "integral nationalism" will be preferred here, despite some reservations. It was coined by the French writer Charles Maurras, one of the most influential intellectual founding-fathers of this type of nationalism. Maurras propagated nationalism as a substitute religion culminating in a mystical cult of the earth and the dead that made absolute demands of the individual. Integral nationalism casts off all ethical ballast, obligating and totally subordinating the individual to one value alone, the nation. *"La France d'abord,"* "My country, right or wrong," "You are nothing, your people everything," are the kinds of moral commands to which integral nationalism binds the faithful and with which it legitimizes the use of physical violence against the heretic and minorities.

> *"French revolutionaries . . . propagate[d] the universal human ideals of liberty, equality and fraternity."*

In complete contrast to Risorgimento nationalism, which proceeds from the notion that all nationalisms and the claims of all national movements are equal, integral nationalism defines the one nation as the Absolute. It is not justified by its followers in terms of service for a higher cause; the cult of the nation becomes an end in itself. In place of the humanistic ideas of a Herder or a Mazzini, the skimpy philosophical foundation of integral nationalism is provided by Charles Darwin's theory of natural selection and the doctrine of the survival of the fittest. As far as the prophets of integral nationalism are concerned, what goes for animals and individuals must also go for races and nations. The nation that proves itself as the strongest and fittest in a hostile and competing world shall gain the upper hand and ultimately survive. While for Herder and Mazzini the awakening of nations meant the unfurling of a new world order, for integral nationalism it merely exacerbates the battle for all against all. Hence Risorgimento nationalism is qualitatively totally different. This is also true with respect to individuals: Benito Mussolini and Adolf Hitler represent a type of nationalist quite distinct from Alexander Ypsilanti [a Greek independence movement leader] or Mazzini.

At Others' Expense

Exponents of integral nationalism are prepared unscrupulously to assert the interests of their own nation at the expense of others. The interests themselves are defined and interpreted by the foremost political figure, the "leader." "Il duce ha sempre ragione"—the leader is always right—as was said in Italy in the 1920s and 1930s. Absolute devotion to the nation became the guiding principle of Fascist education. The existence of other nations was questioned, or even denied. In integral nationalism, slogans about national supremacy, and the superiority of one's own nation, replaced the maxim of national self-determination that in the decades after the French Revolution had given such enormous dynamism to Risorgimento nationalism. It is as if at a certain historical juncture a boiling point is reached, and nationalism enters into a new chemical state; the pattern of values and norms that had obtained hitherto shifts to a new paradigm. What is now "ethical" and morally justified is whatever serves the nation and its power; for that higher purpose injustice, even crime, is acceptable. Here lie the roots of relentless persecution and violation of the law, of expansionist foreign policy and the unbridled ambitions of a "master race" seeking *Lebensraum* [living space], of the compulsory expulsion of people from their homelands and of genocide that have been perpetrated in the twentieth century in the name of the nation. . . .

There are good grounds for regarding integral nationalism as the offspring of the "genuine" form of Risorgimento nationalism—hence the term "derivative" nationalism. Integral nationalism can take root in any people, and it is possible roughly to indicate under what circumstances this may happen. The nation-state—the goal of Risorgimento nationalism—provides the framework for its development. In simple terms, integral nationalism is only possible in a world of established nation-states. It represents an ideology that asserts the interests of one nation-state in a ruthless and expansionist manner. . . .

> *"Integral nationalism . . . legitimizes the use of physical violence against . . . minorities."*

The new system of nation-states was as incapable of guaranteeing a peaceful world order as the order it has replaced. Instead, the nation-state served to delineate a framework within which emancipatory and "legitimate" nationalism metamorphosed into the conservative, indeed reactionary ideology of integration that represents nationalism as it is normally understood today. This form of nationalism, whose ultimate goal seems to be to mobilize those parts of society constituting the "nation" to protect the domestic status quo against internal and external enemies, tends, unfairly, to obscure the earlier movements for national independence that emerged in Europe in the nineteenth and twentieth centuries. Historical experience over two centuries has shown this if nothing else: the undeniable formal and functional transformation that nationalism undergoes from a rather progressive "left-wing" body of thought into a predominantly "right-wing" ideology of integration opposed to internationalism, liberalism and socialism, is not the inevitable consequence of Risorgimento nationalism or any other form of nationalism apostrophized as "legitimate" that might precede it; neither does this development in different nations exhibit the same pattern, time scale or intensity. The possibility of this happening is, however, present in every society that conceives of itself as a nation. The specific political and social context determines whether, and in which way, integral nationalism might evolve.

Nationalism Can Be Beneficial

by Lynne Jones

About the author: *Lynne Jones is a psychiatrist and writer who has lived and traveled extensively in Eastern Europe and the former Yugoslavia. She is the author of the book* States of Change: A Central European Diary.

"Nationalism is currently the main motor of history," British journalist Neal Ascherson stated at a talk in the autumn of 1991. And even the most cursory reading of the media would bear this out. The multinational post-Communist states are disintegrating; native peoples throughout the Americas are gaining a new assertiveness in challenging the legacy of Columbus; Germans are asking for self-determination in the Italian South Tyrol; and a poll in Scotland showed that half of those interviewed wanted Scotland to be fully independent while a further 27 percent wanted more powers handed over from Westminster.

To anyone interested in the psychological aspects of nationalism at the present moment, two things are immediately striking. The first is that it is not a unitary phenomenon either in the form it takes or in its meaning for the individual. Secondly, our responses in the West to its emergence in Eastern Europe have been remarkably unified in their condemnation. In fact, our negative construction is one of the forces that helps to foster some of nationalism's most damaging manifestations.

The Negative View

Nationalism east of the Elbe has a form of pariah status among Western liberals and the left. It is currently a catch-all term for all sorts of ugliness: xenophobia, national chauvinism, racism, anti-Semitism, authoritarianism, fascism, and ethnic hatred. So much so that I found myself shocked by the blandness and seeming neutrality of the *Oxford English Dictionary* definition: "devotion to one's nation; a policy of national independence."

The negative view is understandable, given the historical legacy of two world

From Lynne Jones, "Nationalism and the Self," *Peace and Democracy News*, Winter 1992/1993. Reprinted with permission.

wars and long periods when nationalism has indeed been associated with all of these things. Moreover, wrapping up all the negative developments that have occurred in the post-Communist world since 1989 in this manner in some way seems to lessen the frustration and disappointment that 1989 did not turn out quite the way we hoped. There is apparently not going to be a neat "end of history," no welcome home to the secure garden of liberal capitalism. Instead we contemplate chaos, poverty, conflict, diversity, confusion, potential nuclear catastrophe, and as one American ambassador was heard to complain, far too many new names to learn. Never mind our own role in the arms race, never mind that we suggested the economic remedies that are failing to work. This dreadful muddle cannot be our fault—it must be theirs. Nationalism is to blame. And interestingly the most strident complaints about nationalism come from those nations whose hegemonic position as large or small empires removes the need for any assertion of independence or self-determination on their part, yet whose own political behavior seems fixated on national identity and national superiority. . . .

The trouble with any stereotype is that it obscures complexity, determining the direction of any further search for information, thus in some senses becoming self-fulfilling. The pejorative uses of the term nationalism ignore for example its role in promoting democracy, in enhancing a sense of identity and respect for difference, and in enabling people to acquire a sense of community that encourages social justice and mutual aid. I do not think that this is simply a semantic problem solved by an agreement that the word nationalism has undergone a historical shift of meaning since the nineteenth century and should now only be used to define the negative phenomena. One cannot simply wipe out the ambiguity of language in such an Orwellian manner. The presence of ambiguity demonstrates a psychological, political, and social reality that does exist.

> *"The pejorative uses of the term nationalism ignore for example its role in promoting democracy."*

No Direct Correlations

Moreover, in giving nationalism this pejorative meaning, the negative phenomena are themselves oversimplified: fundamentalism, chauvinism, authoritarianism, fascism, racism, anti-Semitism, and ethnic conflict do not always occur in clusters associated with nation-building. They are problems in themselves that need full understanding if they are to be successfully confronted. This complexity is well illustrated by the findings of a recent Times Mirror poll in which 13,000 people were interviewed in Britain, across the continent, and in the U.S. What the poll shows is that one cannot make direct correlations between an uncritical commitment to the nation, strong feelings of patriotism and, for example, negative attitudes to minorities, anti-Semitism, and the desire for censorship.

The unhelpfulness of this conflation of ideas is also well illustrated by the discussions over the origins of the war on the territory of former Yugoslavia. The cause of the war is cited in innumerable articles as nationalism/ethnic hatred. Certainly thousands of people are being killed, some by the most brutal atrocities, and millions more displaced, largely because they are of the wrong ethnic group. Ethnic hatred has played an ever-increasing role in this war, and its legacy will cloud the future for years to come. Understanding the psychological processes of stereotyping, dehumanization, projection, and denial make it easier to understand how this might happen, as does understanding the mechanisms by which aggression becomes more likely when legitimacy is provided by a group with shared social norms. But ethnic hatred has little explanatory power as a cause. It does not explain why Serbs and Croats fought side by side in the defense of Vukovar while castigating the Croatian government for its betrayal of them; nor why Bosnia's independence is currently defended against desperate odds by an alliance of Muslims, Serbs, and Croats who totally reject the media description of them as "Muslim forces."

> *"Nationalism developed a strong association with self-determination and the desire to escape from empire."*

By labeling what is happening in this pejorative way, by making the term nationalism synonymous with ethnic hatred, and by squeezing it into an inappropriate historical stereotype, the Western powers failed to observe that these were new forms of nationalism and differed from republic to republic. The most chauvinist and aggressive nation was not asking for recognition at all but wanted to maintain its status as a hegemonic power. Slovenia and Croatia, tired of domination by Belgrade, were trying to escape one federation in order to join another, seeing sovereignty as the step that made integration into Europe possible. Bosnia wanted to be an independent nation-state in order to preserve ethnic heterogeneity and human rights. . . .

Individual and Collective Struggles

Erik Erikson argues that individual psychology can only be understood within its historical context; the historical struggles of a period help explain individual psychology, and individual psychological struggle helps to explain collective struggle. The two are intermeshed in such a way that they define each other. Nationalism particularly demonstrates how changes in individual identity and concepts of self resonate with, that is, are both determined by and help to determine, historical change. The notion of communism as a refrigerator from which ancient animosities have emerged intact does not stand up. In both Eastern Europe and the Soviet Union national feeling was actually fostered by both state authorities and opposition movements for different ends and in different ways.

In an excellent essay on this subject, George Schopflin points to the way Stalinism, through its attack on the major affective bonds of community, manifest in family, religion, and workplace, actually intensified the importance of nationhood for the majority of society as a symbol of the familiar and continuity with the past. Not surprisingly therefore, "nationalism became one of the repositories of social autonomy" and a vehicle for the democratic aspirations of the opposition. In Eastern Europe particularly, nationalism developed a strong association with self-determination and the desire to escape from empire. This sometimes took a chauvinist form but was more often connected with a demand for human rights and an outward-looking internationalist perspective, as demonstrated by the dialogues and solidarity between the Czech, Polish, and Hungarian opposition.

The program of "Freedom and Peace," a Polish anti-conscription movement of the late 1980s, conveys this combination of nationalist and anti-chauvinist sentiment. Its rejection of the military oath of allegiance to the fraternal armies of the Soviet Union and its emphasis on the struggle for national independence in Poland are combined with support for the rights of ethnic minorities in Poland, an internationalist perspective on the need for peace, condemnation of the death penalty, and an active condemnation of anti-Semitism, racism, and intolerance. And one can identify similar combinations in the programs of emerging youth movements in Hungary, Czechoslovakia, and Slovenia. . . .

National Identity and Concepts of the Self

The self is that bundle of memories, ideas, thoughts, feelings, beliefs, talents, hopes, and fears by which we characterize ourselves and differentiate ourselves from others. For psychological well-being, the perceived public self should feel coherent and should match our private sense of ourselves. What others recognize us to be is enormously important in helping us to define ourselves. Recognition is part of the process of socialization. As we grow up our sense of self matures, helped by reciprocal interaction with family, peer groups, work colleagues and so on. There is an increasing orientation outward toward a social, public world and need for recognition from it. One could argue that the normal adult self needs access to some form of public space for healthy psychological development. It is certainly true that membership in a group with relatively limited access to such space or access so disadvantaged that it is burdensome, as is the case, for example, for many women, is associated with a higher incidence of psychiatric morbidity.

"What others recognize us to be is enormously important in helping us to define ourselves."

The other important thing to say about the self is that there is increasing recognition that it is a far more fluid and malleable structure than we thought and that this fluidity is a direct result of particular historical forces at work today. Kenneth Gergen identifies this fluidity as postmodern. Robert Lifton calls it proteanism and also identifies a rigid and fundamentalist response to these same forces. Proteanism he defines as a psychological "flexibility, multiplicity, and fluidity," characterized by "restless experiments, and odd combinations of involvements" that can occur either sequentially or simultaneously. . . .

> *"One can see . . . constricting and totalizing tendencies in the nationalist chauvinist or racist self."*

Lifton suggests that proteanism, which increases our capacity for creativity and survival, is one response to threatening historical forces. One important aspect of its creative potential is that by developing the capacity to hold multiple value patterns within ourselves we also increase our capacity for empathy, that is awareness of how the other thinks and feels. He also points out that proteanism can manifest itself in a negative way. There is obviously the danger of superficiality, fragmentation, or the complete breakdown of coherence that one sees in multiple personality disorder, a diagnosis that is becoming increasingly common. However, there is "another side to the historical coin, that of the constricted, totalized or fundamentalist self." The same historical forces that produce the protean self can result in a closing down of the self, a closing down, however, that "is itself largely a reaction to the perceived dangers of proteanism," that is, against the confusion of formlessness and chaos and its own desire to open out. Lifton illustrates this by drawing on his own work with American fundamentalists to show how openness and pluralism are perceived as danger and sin, and skepticism and doubt as the failure to acknowledge an eternal moral truth. "The fundamentalist self clings to a fixed structure of absolute purity and virtue that can never be; the quest is for unification within and without and above all a sense of control over that which cannot be controlled." Consequently, there is rarely equilibrium. The fundamentalist self "tends to be engaged instead in a continuous struggle against ever-present evil including especially the evil of its own deep ambivalences." Lifton also describes the psychological appeal of violence to both the fragmented protean state, "where the sense of self can only take shape by living out a pattern of violence in accordance with others' expectations," and to the fundamentalist, where "by destroying designated enemies one can reassert one's own claim to absolute ethical and even scientific truth."

The Struggle Against "Ever-Present Evil"

One can see the same constricting and totalizing tendencies in the nationalist chauvinist or racist self. A declaration by the Vatra Romaneasca Federation (VRF), a fascist party in Romania, exemplifies the desire for control: "We are the sole owners in our country, in the sense that the existence and activity of the Romanian national minorities must be kept under supervision in all regions"; the desire for purity and unity: "Gypsies and other scum still defile the holy Romanian soil. Unite so that we can drive them out of the country"; and the call for violence as a means of purification: "Don't be afraid to fight and shed their dirty blood! The hairy apes have nothing to do in our dear homeland. . . . The federation regards as its principal task to apply in practice the different forms and methods of intimidation. In this way it is impossible that the holy Romanian land will not be purified of its shameful blemishes with the emigration of these elements."

This fundamentalist search for purity through violence can also be seen in the Yugoslav Army's ruthless and senseless bombing of Croatia. Zarko Puhovski, a Croatian professor of philosophy, described it in the following way: "It is almost as if the army were trying to exorcise an evil spirit and can only do so by burning the body of Croatia to free the soul." . . .

By contrast, Poland seems to have avoided the worst excesses of chauvinism. I would suggest that this is directly related to the slow process of democratic transformation and to the fact that the country had an institutionalized, pluralistic, and open opposition. The importance of this is not that the majority were politically active—most people were not—but that a public space existed in which one could participate as oneself and be recognized as participating, without the damaging effects of doubling [expressing public and private beliefs that are opposite]. This might mean reading occasional underground literature, listening to Radio Free Europe, singing patriotic hymns in church, or going to rock concerts, or it might simply be not showing any support for the government. All of these acts would increase one's sense of coherence and integration as well as the chances of a creative opening out of the self in the face of change.

> *"Poland seems to have avoided the worst excesses of chauvinism."*

Flexibility and Understanding

What also emerges from my research is that the opposition was strongly characterized by a protean fluidity and flexibility. This was clearly related to the ad hoc quality of opposition life, which was often characterized by the absence of any formal job, dependence on informal networks of social support, and a constantly changing pattern of daily activity, be it writing articles, meeting, travelling, organizing, or spending time in jail. The relation between lifestyle and self is obviously reciprocal. One chooses such a life if it suits one, and living it further determines one's sense of self. None of the activists in my study had pursued any one occupation for more than two years at a time. One, for example, had in the space of seven years gone from medical student to art historian to probation doctor to magazine editor to TV journalist to parliamentary candidate. He did not perceive this as inconsistent or superficial, and when I asked him how he described himself to himself, said "I am at a crossroads." Others responded similarly with phrases like "in transition," reinforcing the picture of fluidity.

31

I am not denying the existence of fundamentalism in Poland, both in the opposition and in society at large. In his essay, "Maggots and Angels," Adam Michnik challenges the manicheanism of some of his colleagues and emphasizes the need for tolerance, understanding, and compromise, fearing that these would be difficult to achieve. However, it was Michnik's evolutionary strategy of compromise that brought about change, rather than any head-on conflict between the forces of good and evil.

> *"People on the whole want to feel that they are part of a political community which shares their interests."*

At the institutional level in Poland today, Stanislav Tyminski notwithstanding, fundamentalism has not prevailed. Boleslaw Tejkowski, the leader of the most extreme nationalist party, is currently being prosecuted for racism.

There are other hopeful signs: national independence has allowed Poles to stop perceiving themselves as victims and to publicly acknowledge responsibility for past crimes committed by the Polish state. Lech Walesa made a much-publicized trip to Israel and, speaking in the Israeli Knesset, asked for forgiveness for Poland's role in the Holocaust. An unequivocal condemnation of anti-Semitism has been made by the Polish Catholic Church and there are the beginnings of dialogue between Poles and the Ukrainian minority. The ability to acknowledge guilt and responsibility, even when it is that of a previous generation, and the capacity to forgive past crimes without an endless demand for retribution, as with the acceptance of the Soviet apology for the Katyn massacre, denote an openness and flexibility that bodes well.

Making national generalizations is problematic. In Poland and Romania both the protean and fundamentalist selves exist at all levels of society. Which tendencies dominate at the institutional level appears to a large extent to determine whether and in what way the country is perceived as nationalist.

The Persistence of Nationalism

Nationalism is not going away. On the contrary, there is another historical force at work that is likely to increase its importance even more: the growth, and through immigration, shifting distributions, of population. People on the whole want to feel that they are part of a political community which shares their interests and concerns and in which their voices can be heard should they wish to speak. The modern state as it grows in size and complexity is less and less able to serve this function, especially for minority groups. Moreover, political centralization may be encouraged for ideological reasons, as, for example, under the Thatcher government in Britain. The result can be a growing political apathy and alienation and a slide into authoritarianism by default, or it can be the demand for a breakdown into smaller units in order to have some control over one's own political destiny.

Which unit should one choose? The family and local community are certainly too small; the nation, with its visible markers of culture, language, and shared history, seems to be the main choice. It does not have to be a harmful or chauvinistic choice. It is the smaller nations rather than the larger multinational states who seem most keenly aware of the need for integrated efforts on ecological and economic matters, and it is many of the smaller nations with their past experience as minorities who seem most aware of the need for supranational bodies to oversee the rights of their own minorities.

An Evolving Phenomenon

Nationalism is a continually evolving phenomenon with complex roots. Its varied face is just one aspect of the varied response of the self to historical forces at work, not only in Eastern Europe but globally, that is, to those feelings of threat and possibility that come from an awareness of rapid historical change and the growing fragility of our planet, reinforced by our instant access to images and information from every part of the globe.

The effect of these forces in Eastern Europe is in part determined by the nature of Communist society, the degree to which it allowed flexibility and plurality, the access it afforded to some kind of public space and the pace of the transition to democracy, abrupt transition being more dislocating and threatening than slow change. By reframing the problem as one aspect of the relationship between the self and history it may be easier to see the continuities between what is happening in the East and in the West. Nation can be one aspect of identity that enhances our sense of self, adds to our enjoyment of difference, in-

> *"Nation can be one aspect of identity that enhances our sense of self."*

creases our possibility for participation in public life, and enriches the world community, or it can be a constricting, "ill-fitting shirt" to which all else is reduced at the cost of any sense of self at all. Which way it continues to develop in each case depends not only on the past but on our response to it now, that is, the tendencies towards fundamentalism and proteanism within ourselves.

Nationalism Is Vital to Democracy

by Ghia Nodia

About the author: *Ghia Nodia is head of the political philosophy department at the Institute of Philosophy in Tbilisi in the republic of Georgia.*

The collapse of communism in Eastern Europe and the former Soviet Union has led simultaneously to dramatic new gains for liberal democracy and to a resurgence of nationalism. Many analysts appear to regard these as contradictory phenomena, inasmuch as they consider nationalism to be fundamentally antidemocratic. I believe that this is a superficial view that distorts our understanding of what is happening in the postcommunist countries and elsewhere as well. In any case, the experience of the anticommunist revolution requires us to rethink not only the relationship between nationalism and democracy, but also many of the other basic ideas on which modern civilization is grounded.

Dim View of Nationalism

The first major attempt at such a rethinking appeared on the very cusp of the great change when Francis Fukuyama's meditation on the "end of history" was published in the summer of 1989. Fukuyama's main idea, later developed at book length, was that the disintegration of communism left the idea of liberal democracy standing alone, with no viable ideological competitor in sight. Thus the posthistorical stage of human development, boring though it may be, has arrived, and there is no threat to the reign of liberal democracy.

Although I generally agree with Fukuyama's analysis, I do not share his mostly negative assessment of the role of nationalism in the advent, spread, and victory of liberal democracy. To put it simply, Fukuyama (despite occasional equivocations) agrees with the predominant Western view that democracy and nationalism are mutually hostile. If one wins, it can do so only at the other's expense. Democracy, moreover, has become a term linked to adjectives like "good," "civilized," "progressive," "rational," and so on, while nationalism is

From Ghia Nodia, "Nationalism and Democracy," *Journal of Democracy*, October 1992. Reprinted by permission of the Johns Hopkins University Press.

associated with "backwardness," "immaturity," "barbarism," "irrationality," and the like. Given these valuations, Fukuyama's presumption that "irrationalist" nationalism does not present a viable alternative to democracy, and that history has thus come to a safe end, marks him as an optimist. Meanwhile, pessimists like Shlomo Avineri argue that nationalism, not liberal democracy, is the real successor to communism, which means that history will continue.

> *"Democracy never exists without nationalism. The two are joined in a sort of complicated marriage."*

But what if nationalism and democracy are not two separate things? What if nationalism is a *component* of the more complex entity that is called "liberal democracy"? In raising these questions, I mean to suggest that the idea of nationalism is impossible—indeed unthinkable—without the idea of democracy, and that democracy never exists without nationalism. The two are joined in a sort of complicated marriage, unable to live without each other, but coexisting in an almost permanent state of tension. Divorce might seem the logical solution to a Western liberal horrified by the twentieth century's experience of European nationalism, but this option stands revealed as nothing more than wishful thinking once real political forces are taken into account.

The manner in which the collapse of communism and the breakup of the Soviet empire occurred tends to demonstrate the validity of my approach. Conversely, the failure of mainstream Western political science to keep pace with developments in the postcommunist East is at least partly due to the West's one-sided understanding of nationalism and its relation to democracy.

Social Science Considerations

This one-sidedness flows largely from Western social science's tendencies toward both economic determinism and value-laden judgments. When it is presumed that social developments cannot be explained in a really "scientific" way unless they can be traced to economic conditions, it is only a small step to the modern instrumentalist doctrine according to which nations and nationalisms emerge as a result of 1) industrialization and 2) mass manipulation undertaken by elites pursuing their own (ultimately economic) interests. This "scientistic" attitude, however, does not prevent many of the very same scholars who assume it from using "democracy" and "nationalism" as valuative rather than descriptive terms. Democracy is cast in the hero's role, and is not supposed to have anything in common with the nationalist villain.

Of course, no social scientist can completely avoid value preferences. I myself, for instance, agree with Winston Churchill that democracy is a very bad political system with one very good justification: all the others are worse. Still, the valuative attitude is incompatible with the theoretical one. As a theorist, I cannot be interested in whether nationalism is "good" or "bad"; what is important is that it exists. On the other hand—and here I agree with Fukuyama—social reality does not depend solely on objective data; subjective human attitudes that defy all attempts at reductionism can and do exist. This is a truth that we ought to keep in mind as we try to understand the relationship between democracy and nationalism. . . .

The Logic of Democracy

At the core of democracy is the principle of popular sovereignty, which holds that government can be legitimated only by the will of those whom it governs. This general principle has to be distinguished from democratic *procedures*, which are intended as devices for discerning what the people really will. The main procedure is, of course, elections. Other sets of procedures help to safeguard democracy by restraining elected rulers through such measures as the separation of powers, limits on reelection, special requirements for constitutional amendments, and so on.

Democracy is supposed to be a highly *rational* enterprise. Its debt to the rationalist philosophical tradition can be easily seen in the notion of the social contract, which conceives of society as the construct of free and calculating individuals bent on maximizing their own interests. Democracy is a system of rules legitimated by the will of the people; it is presumed that the people will generally choose what seems to be in their best interest.

Thus anything that seems insufficiently rational, be it irrationalist philosophy or irrational human sentiments, is commonly understood as contrary to the idea of democracy. Nationalism is only one example of an "irrational" phenomenon that supposedly cuts against the democratic grain. By arguing that there is a necessary and positive link between nationalism and democracy, I am of course flying in the face of this common understanding. . . .

Since the idea of democracy is universal, it would only be logical for the principle of popular sovereignty to be embodied in a worldwide polity. But this assumes that the democratic transition should be worldwide in the first place, and that the people themselves want it that way. History bears out neither of these assumptions. Democracy has always emerged in distinct communities; there is no record anywhere of free, unconnected, and calculating individuals coming together spontaneously to form a democratic social contract *ex nihilo*. Whether we like it or not, nationalism is the historical force that has provided the political units for democratic government. "Nation" is another name for "We the People."

> *"I cannot be interested in whether nationalism is 'good' or 'bad'; what is important is that it exists."*

Traditional European nationalism tried to formulate objective marks of nationhood that would enable any given unit of people to provide a rational justification of its demand for "self-determination." These could include language, common origin, historical tradition of statehood, or the like, and could—or so it was hoped—place the democratic edifice on a completely rational foundation. There would exist universally valid objective criteria defining a "fair" distribution of territory among peoples; groups or individuals with doubts about their membership in a given nation could find just and impartial standards for resolving them. But the actual history of nationalisms, to say nothing of the theoretical critiques offered by scholars like Hans Kohn and Ernest Gellner, has shown that such objective and universal criteria are unattainable. The development of premodern ethnic communities into modern nations has always been mediated by historical contingencies and conscious political effort; there simply are no God-given or naturally preordained national borders.

However much this discovery may have undermined nationalism's claim to provide universally valid rational criteria, it did not change nationalism's function of molding democratic (i.e., self-determining) political communities. The criteria by which nations are distinguished from one another may not pass the test of universal objective validity, but the political cohesion necessary for democracy cannot be achieved without the people determining themselves to be "the nation."

Irrational Nationalism

The less than fully rational character of the nationalist principle can shake the foundations of democracy and even give rise to bloodshed. In the absence of universally valid criteria of nationhood, conflicts arise which are not always susceptible to fair and rational solutions. It is hard to find even an island nation that has not had some sort of territorial dispute with its neighbors. The typical means of resolving such conflicts is war. Many nations must deal with ethnic minorities who are distrusted as potential traitors and who in turn view the majority as would-be oppressors. There are different means of resolving these problems: radical "final" solutions like genocide or expulsion; gradualist solutions like assimilation; or compromise solutions, like various schemes for communal or regional autonomy within a federal state. Only rarely can solutions be reached without pain and violence, which is why so many supporters of modern democracy devoutly wish to avoid the nationalist principle. Wishes, however, cannot dictate reality.

Attempts to deny the reality and significance of nationalism often stem from a reluctance to admit that the democratic enterprise, supposedly the epitome of rationality, rests unavoidably on a nonrational foundation.

> *"Nationalism is the historical force that has provided the political units for democratic government."*

The early stages of democracy-building make it especially clear that a nonrational act of political definition (determining who belongs to "We the People") is a necessary precondition of rational political behavior. The failure to recognize this kept most Western intellectuals from understanding what was really happening in (or rather to) the Soviet Union during *perestroika*. Their

> *"The less than fully rational character of the nationalist principle can . . . give rise to bloodshed."*

warnings about nationalism as a major obstacle to democratic reform ignored the truth that all *real* democratic movements (save the one in Russia proper) were at the same time nationalist. Leaders from independence-minded republics were asked what they hoped to gain economically from independence, while the would-be nations themselves saw sovereignty as an end in itself rather than as a mere means to prosperity.

Democracy and Liberalism

The interdependence between democracy and nationalism expresses itself in still another way. Modern democratic regimes, no less than modern nations, are artificial constructs. Premodern democracy was tied exclusively to the *polis*, the classical city-state. This democracy was essentially commensurate with human personality: the site of the democratic enterprise was small, and citizens dealt with one another face-to-face. Modern democracy extends far beyond such intimate boundaries, and so requires citizens to develop a sense of community that is based less on their unaided senses and more on the human mind or imagination. For the most part, modern nations and modern democracies alike are too large to do without this "imagined" quality. . . .

Most denunciations of nationalism in the name of democracy are actually denunciations of nationalism in the name of *liberalism*. By liberalism, I mean that doctrine which holds individual human liberty to be the foremost political value. Nationalism, on the other hand, gives preference to collective claims based on race, culture, or some other communal identity. Liberalism champions a person's right to *choose*, while nationalism gives pride of place to something that does not depend on personal choice.

The controversy, however, is about more than value preferences. The basic liberal critique of nationalism is that the nation is "unreal" ("imagined," "created," "concocted," etc.), while the individual human person is completely "real." Closely tied to this view is the notion that the individual (the bearer of inalienable rights) is "rational," while the nation is "irrational." Nations are held to be irrational and unreal because, as we saw earlier, there exist no universally objective criteria of nationhood. . . .

So far, we have said nothing to contradict the conventional wisdom that liberalism and nationalism are mutually exclusive principles between which one must choose. Let us ask, then, whether there is not some *positive* link between liberalism and nationalism, as well as between the idea of nationhood and that of human personality. That both ideas are tied to the historical epoch of modernity is no accident. Their relation is not only mediated by "objective" mechanisms of modernization; the real connection between them should be traced back to the modern paradigm of thought, from which liberal ideology stems.

At the center of the modern paradigm is the concept of the autonomous human personality. The bearer of a unique and transcendent value (in Kant's terms, it is always the end and should never become a means), this personality is only willing to follow rules endorsed by its own decision (self-determination). Although this idea is often said to have necessarily atheistic implications, it flows historically from the Christian tradition. In principle, moreover, it is possible for an autonomous human being to affirm the existence of an absolute divine order even while maintaining that the interpretation of that order and the application of its precepts to specific cases belong finally to the reason and moral conscience of the individual rather than to any community or institution.

The concept of nationhood also has an intrinsic link to this idea of personality, which is what distinguishes modern self-conscious nationalism from primordial ethnicity. The essence of ethnicity lies in its extension of the idea of *family* to the macrosocial level. Community is "imagined" as a big family stemming from the same ancestor. When a nation "imagines" itself, however, it sees not a family, but a unique personality with a distinct character.

> *"Nationalism gives pride of place to something that does not depend on personal choice."*

Self-Determination

National self-consciousness is patterned on the blueprint of individual human personality in two ways. First, a nation is a community of people organized around the idea of *self-determination*. A modern nation, like a modern self-conscious individual (and unlike an ancient *ethnos*), observes only those laws which it endorses for itself and rejects rules imposed by an external force. Secondly, a nation no less than an individual person requires partners for interaction and mutual recognition. Nations need other nations. A nation can understand and recognize itself only in the context of the history of humanity as such—an idea that is completely unthinkable for even the most advanced ethnic consciousness (for example, that of the ancient Greeks). The idea of nationhood is an idea of membership in humanity, and the idea of humanity as a "family of nations" has long been a mainstay of liberal nationalism.

The conceptual linkage between nationhood and personality has an important corollary. A nation demands self-determination not as an exclusive privilege, but as a way of realizing the general proposition that each nation deserves a state of its own. I do not understand why Fukuyama thinks that nationalism is by definition "megalothymic" (demanding of greater recognition), while holding that liberal individualism is by definition "isothymic" (demanding of equal recognition). Nationalism in its proper sense does not, as Fukuyama claims, "extend recognition only to members of a given national or ethnic group." This attitude is better covered by such terms as "racism" or "chauvinism." Nor does nationalism demand recognition only for *individual* members of a given national or ethnic group. What it demands is recognition for the nation *as a whole*, which means acquiring the general hallmark of nationhood: legal status as an independent state (comparable to the legal status of citizenship in the case of an individual) and acceptance as an equal member of the "family of nations." The basic idea of nationalism is at least as isothymic as that of individualist personalism, even though nations, like individuals, can become megalothymic.

Unifying Forces

Another sign of the kinship between liberalism and nationalism is that both are often criticized for the same thing: being divisive. The atomized individualism associated with liberalism divides the community, it is said, while nationalism divides humanity. Both accusations are accurate in a sense, but both overlook the record of practical achievement which shows liberalism and nationalism to be the most effective *unifying* forces known to history.

Liberal individualism is emotionally divisive, but only liberal societies have achieved stable civil peace, while "warm" communal ideologies often end up fomenting bloodshed. Attempts to unite the world in the name of universalist doctrines like Christianity (I mean Christianity as a *political* force) and communism have only led to international hostilities. Although plenty of blood has been shed for the sake of "national interests," the first organization to embrace almost the whole world is called the United Nations (not the Universal Church or the Communist International), and it is based on isothymic nationalism ("respect for national sovereignty," "inviolability of borders," etc.). The general principles of nationalism still seem more widely accepted around the globe than those of liberalism or any other ideology. The part of the world that invented nationalism—Western Europe—has also outrun all other regions in defining new patterns of international unity. Europe has reached this unprecedented degree of comity not by neglecting nationalism, as many believe, but by cultivating its isothymic aspect. Independent states voluntarily give up more and more of their sovereignty *because* it is respected. The movement from megalothymia to isothymia is possible not only on the individual but also on the national level.

> *"The essence of ethnicity lies in its extension of the idea of family to the macrosocial level."*

The Liberal Dilemma

Although most liberals since World War II have denounced nationalism as a barbarous atavism, the classical liberals of the nineteenth century harbored more complicated attitudes. On the theoretical level, nothing in the liberal principle requires an acceptance of the principle of nationhood at all, for to a true liberal the autonomous human person is *the* decisive unit of analysis. The liberal attitude toward nationalism, however, is mediated by the liberal attitude toward the *state*.

All states unavoidably involve some sort of domination or repression—things that liberals naturally dislike. They regard the state as a necessary evil, acceptable only because its absence is even worse for the individual. Thus do liberals make their peace with the state—the only force capable of preventing the war of all against all and guaranteeing individual rights. . . .

Peoples themselves, when it is up to them, always begin building democracy by creating independent nation-states that may wind up being less friendly to personal freedom than the *ancien régime* was.

Nowadays the People, having turned into the middle class, no longer seem very dangerous. Still, liberals reject nationalism more strongly than ever. Why?

There are, of course, various reasons for this. The role played by nationalist extremism in our century's two horrific world wars has had a powerful impact. The decolonization of the post-World War II period made "national self-determination" a predominantly Third World problem, thus reinforcing the liberal tendency to associate nationalism with "backwardness.". . .

The best available counterbalance

> *"The record . . . shows liberalism and nationalism to be the most effective* unifying *forces known to history."*

to the nationalism that lives in the past and fixates on old grievances and old ambitions is an alternative version of the nationalist sentiment that makes it a point of national honor to join the civilized world as an equal and dignified member. A sense of isolation from the comity of nations can be much more painful than any concrete sanction. The civilized world provides adequate (even if imperfect) models not only of flourishing market economies, but of regimes that have struck a real and working balance among the forces of democracy, liberalism, and nationalism. The power of these examples to help the fledgling democracies of the postcommunist world should not be underestimated.

Nationalism Sustains Cultural Diversity

by Isaiah Berlin, interviewed by Nathan Gardels

About the authors: *Isaiah Berlin is a well-known political philosopher and a fellow at All Soul's College in Oxford, England. He is the author of several books, including* Karl Marx *and* The Crooked Timber of Humanity. *Nathan Gardels is the editor of* New Perspectives Quarterly *magazine.*

NPQ: According to Harold Isaacs, author of *Idols of the Tribe*, today we are witnessing a "convulsive ingathering" of nations. Open ethnic warfare rages in Yugoslavia. The Soviet Union has been rent asunder by resurgent nationalist republics.

The new world order built from the rubble of the Berlin Wall has already gone the way of the Tower of Babel. What are the origins of nationalism? Whence this ingathering storm?

Berlin: The Tower of Babel was meant to be unitary in character; a single great building, reaching to the skies, with one language for everybody.

The Lord didn't like it.

There is, I have been told, an excellent Hebrew prayer to be uttered when seeing a monster: "Blessed be the Lord our God, who introducest variety amongst Thy creatures." We can only be happy to have seen the Soviet Tower of Babel collapse into ruin, dangerous as some of the consequences may turn out to be—I mean, a bitter clash of nationalisms. But, unfortunately, that would be nothing new.

Nationalism's Power

In our modern age, nationalism is not resurgent; it never died. Neither did racism. They are the most powerful movements in the world today, cutting across many social systems. . . .

Non-aggressive nationalism is another story entirely. I trace the beginning of that idea to the highly influential eighteenth-century German poet and philosopher Johann Gottfried Herder.

From Nathan Gardels' interview of Isaiah Berlin, "The Ingathering Storm of Nationalism," *New Perspectives Quarterly*, Fall 1991. Reprinted by permission of *New Perspectives Quarterly*.

Herder virtually invented the idea of belonging. He believed that just as people need to eat and drink, to have security and freedom of movement, so too they need to belong to a group. Deprived of this, they felt cut off, lonely, diminished, unhappy. Nostalgia, Herder said, was the noblest of all pains. To be human meant to be able to feel at home somewhere, with your own kind.

> *"Herder believed in a variety of national cultures, all of which could, in his view, peacefully coexist."*

Each group, according to Herder, has its own *Volksgeist*, or *National-geist*—a set of customs and a lifestyle, a way of perceiving and behaving that is of value solely because it is their own. The whole of cultural life is shaped from within the particular stream of tradition that comes of collective historical experience shared only by members of the group.

Thus one could not, for example, fully understand the great Scandinavian sagas unless one had oneself experienced (as he did on his voyage to England) a great tempest in the North Sea.

Herder's idea of the nation was deeply nonaggressive. All he wanted was cultural self-determination. He denied the superiority of one people over another. Anyone who proclaimed it was saying something false. Herder believed in a variety of national cultures, all of which could, in his view, peacefully coexist.

Each culture was equal in value and deserved its place in the sun. The villains of history for Herder were the great conquerors such as Alexander the Great, Caesar, or Charlemagne, because they stamped out native cultures. He did not live to see the full effects of Napoleon's victories—but since they undermined the dominion of the Holy Roman Empire, he might have forgiven him.

Only what was unique had true value. This is why Herder also opposed the French universalists of the Enlightenment. For him there were few timeless truths: time and place and social life—what came to be called civil society—were everything.

The Backlash of Nationalism

NPQ: Of course, Herder's *Volksgeist* became the Third Reich.

And today, the Serbian *Volksgeist* is at war with the Croatian *Volksgeist*, the Armenians and the Azeris have long been at it, and, among the Georgians and Russians—and even the Ukrainians and the Russians—passions are stirring.

What transforms the aspiration of cultural self-determination into nationalist aggression?

Berlin: I have written elsewhere that a wounded *Volksgeist*, so to speak, is like a bent twig, forced down so severely that when released, it lashes back with fury. Nationalism, at least in the West, is created by wounds inflicted by stress. As for Eastern Europe and the former Soviet empire, they seem today to be one vast, open wound. After years of oppression and humiliation, there is liable to occur a violent counter-reaction, an outburst of national pride, often aggressive self-assertion, by liberated nations and their leaders. . . .

Today Georgians, Armenians and the rest are trying to recover their submerged pasts, pushed into the background by the huge Russian imperial power. Persecuted under Joseph Stalin, Armenian and Georgian literature survived: Isakian and Yashvili were gifted poets; Pasternak's translations of Vaz Pshavela and Tabidze are wonderful reading—but when [German foreign minister] Joachim von Ribbentrop went to see Stalin in 1939, he presented him with a German translation of the twelfth-century Georgian epic *The Knight in the Tiger Skin* by Rustaveli. Who, in the West, knew of later masterpieces?

Sooner or later, the backlash comes with irrepressible force. People tire of being spat upon, ordered about by a superior nation, a superior class, or a superior anyone. Sooner or later they ask the nationalist questions: "Why do we have to obey them?" "What right have they. . . ?" "What about Us?" "Why can't we . . . ?"

The Fallacy of Universalism

NPQ: All these bent twigs in revolt may have finally overturned the ideological world order. The explosion of the Soviet system may be the last act of deconstruction of the Enlightenment ideals of unity, universality, and liberal rationalism. That's all finito now.

Berlin: I think that that is true.

And Russia is an appropriate place to illuminate the misapprehensions of the *lumiéres.*

Most Russian westernizers who followed the eighteenth-century

> *"People tire of being spat upon, ordered about by a superior nation, a superior class, or a superior anyone."*

French thinkers admired them because they stood up to the church, stood up to reactionary tendencies, stood up to fate. Voltaire and Rousseau were heroes because they enlisted reason, and the right to freedom, against reaction.

But even the radical writer, Alexander Herzen, my hero, never accepted, for example, Condorcet's claims to knowable, timeless truths. He thought the idea of continuous progress an illusion, and protested against the new idolatries, the substitute for human sacrifice—abstractions, like the universal class, or the infallible party, or the march of history; the victimization of the present for the sake of an unknowable future, that would lead to some harmonious solution.

Herzen regarded any dedication to abstract unity and universality with great suspicion. For him, England was England, France was France, Russia was Russia. The differences neither could nor should be flattened out. The ends of life were life itself.

For Herzen, as for Herder and the eighteenth-century Italian philosopher Giambattista Vico, cultures were incommensurable. It follows, though they do not spell it out, that the pursuit of total harmony, or the perfect state, is a fallacy, and sometimes a fatal one.

Of course, nobody believed in universality more than the Marxists: Lenin, Trotsky, and the others who triumphed saw themselves as disciples of the Enlightenment thinkers, corrected and brought up to date by Marx.

If one were to defend the general record of communism, which neither you nor I would be willing to do, it would have to be defended on the basis that Stalin may have murdered forty million people—but at least he kept nationalism down and prevented the ethnic babel from anarchically asserting its ambitions. Of course, Stalin did keep it—and everything else—down but he didn't kill it. As soon as the stone was rolled away from the grave it rose again with a vengeance.

How Universalism Prevailed

NPQ: Herder was a *horizontal critic*, if you will, of the French *lumiéres* because he believed in the singularity of all cultures. Giambattista Vico also opposed the Enlightenment idea of universality but from a *vertical,* or historical, perspective.

As you have written, he believed each successive culture was incommensurable with others.

Berlin: Both rejected the Enlightenment idea that man, in every country at every time, had identical values. For them, as for me, the plurality of cultures is irreducible.

NPQ: Does the final breakup of communist totalitarianism, a creature of the ideal of universality, suggest that we are living out the final years of the last modern century?

Berlin: I accept that, almost. The ideal of universality, so deeply perverted that it would utterly horrify the eighteenth-century philosophers who expounded it, evidently lives on in some form in the remote reaches of Europe's influence: China, Vietnam, North Korea, Cuba.

NPQ: One can only imagine how differently the twentieth century would have turned out had Vico and Herder prevailed rather than the French philosophers, or Hegel and Marx; if the local soul had not been overrun by the world soul. We might have had a century of cultural pluralism instead of totalitarianism.

Berlin: How could that have happened? Universalism in the eighteenth century was the doctrine of the top nation, France. So everyone tried to emulate its brilliant culture.

Perhaps it is much more the rise of the natural sciences, with the emphasis on universal laws, and nature as an organism or a machine, and the imitation of scientific methods in other spheres, which dominated all thinking.

> *"As soon as the stone was rolled away from the grave [nationalism] rose again with a vengeance."*

Fuelled by these ideas, the nineteenth-century explosion of technology and economic development isolated the intellectual stream deriving from such non-quantitative—indeed, qualitative—thinkers as Vico and Herder.

45

The temper of the times is illustrated in a story told in one of Jacob Talmon's books. He writes of two Czech schoolmasters talking with each other around the early 1800s. "We're probably the last people in the world to speak Czech," they said to each other. "Our language is at an end. Inevitably, we'll all speak German here in Central Europe, and probably the Balkans. We're the last survivors of our native culture."

> *"Cultural self-determination without a political framework is precisely the issue now."*

Of course, such survivors are today in the saddle in many lands.

Cultural Self-Determination

NPQ: What political structure can possibly accommodate this new age of cultural self-determination, preserve liberty, and perhaps stem some of the impending bloodshed?

Berlin: Cultural self-determination without a political framework is precisely the issue now, and not only for the East. Spain has the Basques and Catalans; Britain has Northern Ireland; Canada the Quebecois; Belgium has the Flemings; Israel the Arabs, and so on. Whoever in the past would have dreamed of Breton nationalism or a Scottish national party?

Idealists like Herder evidently didn't consider this problem. He merely hated the Austro-Hungarian Empire for politically welding together incompatible elements.

In Eastern Europe they really do seem to loath each other: Romanians hate the Hungarians and Hungarians have for years disliked the Czechs in a way the Bretons can't pretend to hate the French. It is a phenomenon of a different order. Only the Irish are like that in the West.

Only in America have a variety of ethnic groups retained their own original cultures, and nobody seems to mind. The Italians, Poles, Jews, and Koreans have their own newspapers, books, and I am told, TV programs.

NPQ: Perhaps when immigrants forsake their soil, they leave behind the passionate edge of their *Volksgeist* as well.

Yet even in America, a new multicultural movement has emerged in academia that seeks to stress not what is common but what is not in the curriculum.

Berlin: Yes, I know. Black studies, Puerto Rican studies, and the rest.

I suppose this too is a bent twig revolt of minorities that feel disadvantaged in the context of American polyethnicity.

Polyethnicity was not Herder's idea. He didn't urge the Germans to study Dutch, or German students to study the culture of the Portuguese.

In Herder, there is nothing about race and nothing about blood. He only spoke about soil, language, common memories, and customs. His central point, as a Montenegran friend once said to me, is that loneliness is not just absence of others but far more living among people who do not understand what you are saying; they can truly understand only if they belong to a community where communication is effortless, almost instinctive.

Herder looked unkindly on the cultural friction generated in Vienna, where many nationalities were crammed into the same narrow space. It produced men of genius, but with a deeply neurotic element in a good many of them—one need only think of Gustav Mahler, Ludwig Wittgenstein, Karl Kraus, Arnold Schoenberg, Stefan Zweig, and the birth of psychoanalysis in this largely Jewish—particularly defenseless—society.

All that tremendous collision of not very compatible cultures—Slavs, Italians, Germans, Jews—unleashed a great deal of creativity. This was a different kind of cultural expression from that of an earlier Vienna, that of Mozart or Haydn or Schubert.

The Middle Ages

NPQ: In grappling with the separatist Quebecois, Pierre Trudeau often invoked [English historian] Lord Acton. He felt that wherever political boundaries coincided with ethnic ones, chauvinism, xenophobia, and racism inevitably threatened liberty.

Only individual constitutional rights—equal citizenship rights for all, despite ethnicity—in a federal republic could protect minorities and individuals. "The theory of nationality," Trudeau quoted Acton as saying, "is a retrograde step in history."

Berlin: Lord Acton was a noble figure, and I agree with him. Yet we have to admit that, despite Trudeau's efforts, the Quebecois are still seeking independence.

In the grand scale of things, one has to consider that, despite royal and clerical monopolies of power and authority, the Middle Ages were, in some ways, more civilized than the deeply disturbed nineteenth—and worse still, our own terrible century, with widespread violence, chauvinism, and in the end mass destruction in racial, and Stalin's political, holocausts. Of course, there were ethnic frictions in the Middle Ages, and persecution of Jews and heretics, but nationalism as such didn't exist. The wars were dynastic. What existed was the universal church and a common Latin language.

> *"Loneliness is not just absence of others but far more living among people who do not understand what you are saying."*

We can't turn history back. Yet I do not wish to abandon the belief that a world that is a reasonably peaceful coat of many colors, each portion of which develops its own distinct cultural identity and is tolerant of others, is not a utopian dream.

NPQ: But of what common thread can such a coat be spun?

In a universe of autonomous cultural worlds, each in its own orbit, where is the sun that keeps the various planets from colliding with the others?

Berlin: The idea of a center can lead to cultural imperialism again.

In Herder's universe, you didn't need a sun. His cultures were not planets, but stars that didn't collide. I admit that at the end of the twentieth century, there is little historical evidence for the realizability of such a vision.

At eighty-two, I've lived through virtually the entire century. I have no doubt that it is the worst century that Europe has ever had.

Nothing has been more horrible for our civilization. In my life, more dreadful things occurred than at any other time in history. Worse even than the days of the Huns.

One can only hope that after the peoples get exhausted from fighting, the bloody tide will subside. Unless tourniquets can be applied to stop the hemorrhaging, and bandages to the wounds so that they can slowly heal, even if they leave scars, we're in for the continuation of a very bad time.

The only nations about which one need not wring one's hands are the sated nations, unwounded or healed, such as the liberal democracies of North America, Western Europe, Australia, New Zealand, and one hopes, Japan.

Dual Civilizations

NPQ: Perhaps the two futures will live, decoupled, side by side. A civilization of the soil, so to speak, and a civilization of the satellite.

Instead of the violent splintering of nations, the sated nations will become a small world after all, with the passions of blood and soil drained away by homogenizing consumerism and mass entertainment.

Perhaps that is the price of peaceful integration. As Milan Kundera has recently written, frivolous cultures are anthropologically incapable of war. But they are also incapable of producing Picassos.

Berlin: As for that, I don't believe that only tragic events and wounds can create genius. In Central Europe, Kafka and Rilke bore wounds. But neither Racine nor Moliére nor Pushkin nor Tolstoy—unlike Dostoyevsky—bore deep wounds. And Goethe seems completely free from them. The fate of the Russian poets of our century is another, gloomier, story.

Without doubt, uniformity may increase under the pressure of technology, as is already happening with the Americanization of Europe. A great many people hate it, but it clearly can't be stopped.

"I do not wish to abandon the belief . . . [in] a world that is a reasonably peaceful coat of many colors."

As we discussed, it is possible, as in the Austro-Hungarian Empire, to have political and economic uniformity, but cultural variety.

That is what I ultimately visualize.

A degree of uniformity in the sated nations, combined with a pleasing degree of peaceful variety in the rest of the world. I admit that the present trend is in the opposite direction: sharp, sometimes aggressive, self-assertion on the part of some very minor human groups.

NPQ: What about the emergence of a new set of common values—ecological rights and human rights—that can to some degree unite all these erupting cultures without cramping their style?

> *"Frivolous cultures are anthropologically incapable of war. But they are also incapable of producing Picassos."*

Berlin: At the present, there don't seem to be accepted minimum values that can keep the world straight. Let us hope, one day, that a large minimum of common values, such as the ones you mention, will be accepted. Otherwise we are bound to go under.

Unless there is a minimum of shared values that can preserve the peace, no decent societies can survive.

NPQ: The liberal dream of cosmopolitanism, even in the sated world, is not on the agenda as far as you are concerned?

Berlin: Like Herder, I regard cosmopolitanism as empty. People can't develop unless they belong to a culture. Even if they rebel against it and transform it entirely, they still belong to a stream of tradition. New streams can be created—in the West, by Christianity, or Luther, or the Renaissance, or the Romantic movement—but in the end they derive from a single river, an underlying central tradition, which, sometimes in radically altered forms, survives.

But if the streams dried up, as, for instance, where men and women are not products of a culture, where they don't have kith and kin and feel closer to some people than others, where there is no native language—that would lead to a tremendous desiccation of everything that is human.

Nationalism Drives Self-Determination Movements

by Julius Jacobson

About the author: *Julius Jacobson is coeditor of* New Politics, *a quarterly socialist journal.*

"Nationalism" has become the "N" word. Mention it and the reactive image triggered is of socially retrograde and morally base movements marked by xenophobia, bigotry, ethnic hatred, anti-Semitism, religious fanaticism, blood-letting and of the governance of theocratic mullahs, assorted secular despots and authoritarian apparatchiks turned nationalist. This perception of nationalism as demonology is historically and politically untenable but it is not arrived at without cause. There are the chilling press accounts and televised images of mutilated victims of ethnic strife, of shattered neighborhoods, the heart-wrenching spectacle of refugees going only god knows where, the human toll of warfare within and between the newly created nations of Georgia, Armenia, Azerbaijan, Croatia, Bosnia-Herzogovina, and more. Meanwhile, a nationalistic neo-Nazi scum has risen to the political surface in what was the Communist German Democratic Republic.

A Complex Phenomenon

The affliction is not confined to the ex-Communist world. Witness Iran, where hundreds of thousands chant themselves into a mystical frenzy in support of inquisitorial nationalist leaders who have condemned a novelist to death and offered a bounty for his murder for the alleged sin of allegedly offending Allah. Meanwhile, in the more advanced capitalist West nearly 20 percent of the French voters cast their ballots for a fascist nationalist.

Viewed thus, modern-day nationalism does not make a pretty picture. But this is only a profile of nationalism; at best, an unfinished sketch of what was and remains a more complex, multifaceted and contradictory phenomenon.

The nationalism of the French Resistance cannot be mentioned in the same breath as the nationalism of Jean-Marie Le Pen's National Front. The national-ism of Polish revolutionaries in the 19th century—many of whom were to aid the Communards resist the fury of French nationalism—was antithetical to the nationalism of Pilsudski and his colonels in this century. The nationalist Ger-man revolutionary democrats (and socialists) of 1848 were hardly the forerun-ners of the National(ist) Socialists of the Third Reich.

According to the world's most prominent enlightened apparatchik, the deposed Mikhail Gorbachev, "nationalist exclusiveness" leads to "all-embracing xeno-phobic hatred" and "nationalist extremism is a serious threat to more civilized relations within and among states." (This blather, as he accepted the Ronald Rea-gan Freedom Award from the beaming and gushing Gipper whose international-ism when president took the form of petting and feeding national tyrants throughout the world.) It does take chutzpah for Gorbachev to lecture us so since we remember well how, only yesterday, his troops, with rifles, sharpened shovels and tanks fought "the threat to more civilized relations" in Armenia, Georgia, Azerbaijan, Lithuania and elsewhere. But even if we take Gorbachev's caution-ary pieties at face value there are problems with casting so wide the anti-nation-alist net. Are all nationalists also extremists today? And are those nationalists who are extremists all cut from the same satanic cloth? Don't we have to make distinctions, basic ones? For example, the dispossessed Palestinians are national-ists and many are not loathe to use extremist tactics. The Israeli authorities are no less nationalistic and even more disposed to extremism. (Rodney King-type beatings and torture of Arabs, sometimes unto death, are commonplace in Israel and the occupied territories.) In Iraq there is the nationalism and extremism of the Kurdish minority. There is also the nationalism and extremism of Saddam Hussein's despotism.

Is it rational or just in either Israel or Iraq to equate the nationalism of the op-pressed with that of the oppressor, the extremism of the victim with that of the victimizer?

The Right of National Self-Determination

No less troubling about one-dimensional and sweeping generalizations on the evils of nationalism is that they tend to sweep out of our political consciousness what has been a cardinal democratic principle of socialism—the right of national self-determination. It emerged as a principle, above all in the Marxist movement, that a na-tion—a people who have a con-sciousness of shared political, cul-

> *"Nation[s] . . . have a right to any degree of self-rule they desire, including the right to secede."*

tural and historical experiences, of a common language, myths, customs, codes, living in proximity within a larger alien, and often hostile, nation—have a right to any degree of self-rule they desire, including the right to secede and create an independent state.

It is a principle that is as relevant and just today as it was when initially formulated by Karl Marx nearly 150 years ago. It is a principle that is now largely ignored on the left, sometimes ridiculed, often selectively applied (which means that it is not treated as a principle at all).

"Lenin recognized struggles for national independence as part of the struggle against imperialism, for democracy."

Marx's early advocacy of the right to self-determination initially centered around a global European revolutionary perspective, a key element of which focused on the struggle of Polish nationalists against Czarist domination. The establishment of an independent democratic Poland was essential for the purpose of undermining the power of semi-feudal Russian absolutism, the bulwark of European reaction which was playing an aggressive role in the suppression of democratic revolutionary movements in Europe. Polish independence and the military defeat of Russia (Marx and Friedrich Engels favored war against Russia) were seen as necessary preliminary stages in the struggle for power of the European working class.

Strategic concerns with Polish independence were to be generalized into clearly enunciated Marxist principles of national rights to self-determination.

For all the differences 110 years can make it is as true today as when Engels wrote in 1882 that "It is historically impossible for a great people even to discuss internal problems of any kind seriously, as long as it lacks national independence" and that "[a]n international movement of the proletariat is possible only among independent nations.". . .

Self-Determination in Russia

Lenin recognized struggles for national independence as part of the struggle against imperialism, for democracy. Even if it meant the creation of another bourgeois state, it also meant setting the masses into motion, opening up new possibilities for building socialist forces in the newly created nation. Thus, the oppressed nationality seceding to create new national boundaries was a step necessary for the eventual removal of national barriers in an integrated socialist Europe.

What Lenin had to say about the right of self-determination for the oppressed nations held captive in Czarist Russia has remarkable currency. In one particularly powerful polemic directed against "Russian Socialists who fail to demand freedom of secession for Finland, Poland, the Ukraine, etc.," (he had in mind a number of leading Bolsheviks who shared [German Communist Party co-founder Rosa] Luxemburg's rejection of self-determination) he wrote:

> In Russia—where no less than 57 per cent, i.e., over 100,000,000 of the population, belong to oppressed nations, where those nations mainly inhabit the border provinces, where some of those nations are more cultured than the Great Russians, where the political system is distinguished by its particularly

barbarous and mediaeval character. where the bourgeois-democratic revolution has not yet been completed—the recognition of the right of the nations
oppressed by tsarism to free secession from Russia is absolutely obligatory for
Social-Democracy in the interests of its democratic and social tasks.

Correct a few figures and with a little technical editing Lenin's statement could
be published as a timely contribution to a contemporary socialist journal. It
would be noted that what was "particularly barbarous and medieval" in the political character of Czarism grew to monstrous proportions under Stalinism;
pogroms turned into mass murder and genocide, Siberian exile and prisons
turned into a concentrationary universe. During the post-Stalin era the terror sub-
sided, yet the experience of Stalinism, and the longer history of Czarist oppression in Russia, nourished irrepressible aspirations for national rights. Glasnost
only emboldened the people of the Baltics, Ukraine, Georgia, Armenia, etc. to
press harder for national rights, including the right to secede. The appetite for
national freedom could not be ap-
peased by promises to relax central
controls; they knew that even in a
loosened federation, Moscow would
still be the first among "equals."
They had seen how hypocritical, de-
ceitful and ruthless Gorbachev could
be in his failed mission to preserve at least some form of Union, with Moscow in
a privileged position.

> *"Glasnost only emboldened the people of the Baltics . . . [and other republics] to press harder for national rights."*

If it was "absolutely obligatory," as Lenin insisted, for socialists to support
the right of nations to secede from Russia (whether Czarist or socialist) in 1916,
then it was no less obligatory for democrats and socialists to support the will of
the non-Russian republics to secede from the Soviet Union at any time since.
Unfortunately, most liberals and leftists (not to mention bourgeois politicians
and their experts) believed more in self-determination for Gorbachev than in the
right of self-determination for the constituent republics of the USSR. . . .

The Double Standard

The failure of the broadly defined left to unambiguously support self-
determination everywhere was evidence that the double standard was still
operative.

The U.S. invasion of Panama was rightly denounced as a naked display of old-
fashioned imperialism, violating the democratic rights of self-determination of
the Panamanian people, even though Panama was controlled by an utterly corrupt
government dominated by a drug-dealing, homicidal dictator given to brandish-
ing machetes. And President Manuel Noriega who had just stolen an election
was despised by the majority of Panamanians who may actually have looked on
the U.S. invaders—at least initially—as liberators. Still, the invasion was condemned, as it should have been, since it violated a country's national sovereignty

and because the right of self-determination and opposition to imperialism are not dependent on our judgment of the weaker power of the victimized.

Why were there, then, so many "Hands Off Panama" placards at the time, and so few inscribed "Hands Off Lithuania" when Soviet tanks and troops killed a number of Lithuanian protesters? Unlike Panama, Lithuania was subject to a *permanent* invasion by the troops of a Soviet army of occupation and the Soviet occupiers were detested by the vast majority of Lithuanians. Unlike Panama's authoritarian government, Lithuanian leaders were bourgeois democratic and enjoyed overwhelming popular support. Why, then, so wide the opposition to U.S. imperialism and so relatively modest a concern for the plight of the Lithuanians and their right to self-determination? The difference is clearly more one of perception than geography; it is not that the U.S. left was only concerned with U.S. imperialism but that so many in the left still resisted acknowledging the realities of Soviet imperialism.

Raw Imperialism

Alexander Cockburn, for example, had his doubts about whether the Lithuanians even had the right to self-determination, and they are worth noting because I assume that what he wrote reflects the thinking of an important segment of the left. "I support Lithuania's right to self-determination. Its case is at least as strong as those that could be advanced by nationalists in Hawaii, Alaska or Mexico's stolen territory, Texas," he added, no doubt priding himself on being wickedly clever. In checking his 1906 Century Atlas, he could not even find a country called Lithuania, "only a slab of territory called West Russia." I am not up on the secessionist movement in Texas. I do know about Lithuania and can assure Cockburn that it has a long, rich history and culture, its own language and a socialist tradition. Lithuania was occupied and fully absorbed by Moscow in a raw display of imperialism. During that Soviet occupation 45,000 Lithuanians were killed or sent to Siberian camps. When the Soviet armies recaptured Lithuania after the German occupation of 1941-44 the slaughter did not abate. Within five years of their return, the Stalinist authorities deported another 265,000 Lithuanians to the Siberian camps. In just six years of Communist subjugation over 300,000 adults in a country of an estimated three million in 1946 were either killed or sent to the camps from which, we can assume, many never returned. And that was only one of three Baltic nations integrated into the totalitarian Behemoth.

> *"Why were there ... so many 'Hands Off Panama' placards ... and so few inscribed 'Hands Off Lithuania'?"*

Independence has often been accompanied by, or resulted in, appalling levels of violence but here, too, there has been a selective judgmental response. For example, winning Indian independence was a wrenching experience accompanied by escalating warfare between Moslem and Hindu taking a toll far greater than that of the tragic violent conflict between Armenians and Azeris. Yet, few progressives have suggested that the right of self-determination for the peoples of India should never have been exercised, that it would have been better had India remained a jewel in the British crown. Contrast that with the attitude of so many who point to ethnic violence, or its potential, in the former republics of the Soviet Union as proof enough that whatever merit there is to the principle of self-determination elsewhere, it was wrong for the historically oppressed republics to exercise their rights to sovereignty.

> *"Few progressives have suggested that . . . it would have been better had India remained a jewel in the British crown."*

The Nation, for example, mourned the disintegration of the Soviet Union: ". . . the democratic [!] distribution of resources, participatory [!] government and the institutional regulation of privilege are at least possible in a single state of many provinces[!]. . . ." It is bad enough that Stalin labeled the subjugated nations of the internal empire "republics" but this is the first time we have seen nations such as Ukraine reduced to a "province." (A "province" approximately as large in size and population as the "province" of France.) Apparently, it is easier to deny the right of self-determination of a province than of a nation such as India. It also makes it possible to believe that had these "provinces" settled for a more loosely organized "single state" it would have been "at least possible" to eventually enjoy a "democratic distribution of resources" and even "participatory government." The peoples of these "provinces" knew better; that such pie in the sky was not in the offing at all if they sacrificed the exercise of their right to secede and remained in the more loosely Soviet "single state.". . .

Self-Determination: Not a Blank Check

Rosa Luxemburg was guilty of a polemical excess when she argued that the right of national self-determination implied that every region in Germany with its own spoken dialect could claim the right to secede. If successful, she said, that would mean turning back the clock of history, with Germany regressing into a number of mutually hostile, warring feudal regions. As polemic this might have been effective. As argument, it had no merit. The right of self-determination is not determined by differences in dialect.

Similar objections (especially regarding the former republics of the Soviet Union) are made today. Where will it all end? There are national minorities within national minorities and once the process of dismemberment begins, if all minorities which demand statehood are acceded to, that might mean not 14 new states but 24, maybe more, as people who speak different dialects, have special grievances, regional concerns, etc. put in their bid for secession on grounds of rights of self-determination.

Undoubtedly there is a problem, and a serious one. Ukraine, for example, is not a homogeneous state by any means. It includes ethnic minorities which will increasingly insist that they have rights of nationhood. And there is the possibility of civil strife there since it is evident that the Kravchuk leadership does not know (or want to know) the difference between rights of self-determination and the rites of national chauvinism.

Avoiding Ethnic Violence

There are distinct peoples within Ukraine who do qualify as a nation and are entitled to secede and form new states if that is what they want. That this would mean three or four additional states in Ukraine is no necessary obstacle to social and economic progress, and certainly reduces the possibilities of ethnic violence.

More than that where it is unclear—in Ukraine or elsewhere—about whether or not a demand of a particular minority for secession is legitimate it is better to accede to the demand for independence than to resist it and thereby leave open the possibility of inter-ethnic violence.

This does not suggest that all who might conceivably claim the right to statehood are entitled to it. That would be reducing the concept of self-determination to an absurdity. Specific groups might be entitled to special rights and compensation because of past and perhaps ongoing injustices, and ethnic minorities could legitimately demand some level or other of social or cultural autonomy and support for their institutions but that does not necessarily mean the right to secede from a state with major territorial concessions to create a new nation.

It is argued that the debate about the right of self-determination a century or so ago has little relevance to the modern world. In a world of transnational corporations and in a Europe that is progressively moving in the direction of greater economic integration than was thought possible, carving a number of independent sovereign states out of the former Soviet Union is retrogressive. Why erect new national boundaries in the East when such barriers are being overcome in the West?

The notion that the nation-state is an antiquated concept is also a selective one. Some of us in the left look upon the integration of European

> *"The right of self-determination is not determined by differences in dialect."*

states with reactionary governments as a mixed blessing. But even if we believe that integration opens up progressive possibilities and calls for enthusiastic endorsement, that should not cast doubt on the moral, political and economic propriety of creating new nations out of the single Soviet state. Nationhood may be an antiquated notion in the West but it is a novel and necessary experience for the long repressed peoples of the East. After all, West European "internationalism" presupposes the existence of nations and a parallel internationalist development in the East presupposes that nations there must first be constructed as sovereign entities.

56

There is also the assumption that creating many states out of one empire implies a breakdown of the economic order. This overlooks the fact that in the Soviet empire economic order had already broken down and there was little reason to believe that a reformed, more loosely organized Soviet Union could overcome the social contradictions inherent in the system.

Economic relationships among the former republics obviously have to be continued but these contacts can be just as well maintained, perhaps more rationally and productively, by independent states rather than by republics still subject to often irrational bureaucratic central controls. Moreover, if European union is not to be restricted to the advanced West but to extend to continental levels on a healthy permanent basis, attaining that objective requires independent national entities in the East. . . .

Struggles for Democracy

If there is to be revival of socialism—no less essential today than when it had a substantial presence—it is incumbent on socialists to be engaged in and supportive of all struggles for democracy. For the fate of socialism is inextricably linked with the growth and expansion of political, social and economic democracy. This, in turn, means that socialists must struggle against empire and for the right of all subjugated peoples to create independent democratic nations. Exercising the right of self-determination represents a major democratic advance, increasing the possibilities for socialist revival. That should be axiomatic for socialists today.

Liberal Nationalism Can Benefit Ethnic Groups

by Yael Tamir

About the author: *Yael Tamir is a senior lecturer in philosophy at Tel Aviv University in Israel. Tamir, author of the book* Liberal Nationalism, *is a founding member of the Israeli peace organization Peace Now and is active in the civil rights movement in Israel.*

As we entered the final quarter of the twentieth century, there was a widespread assumption that the age of nationalism was over, that we were on the threshold of a postnational era. It is now clear that this assumption was wrong. National movements are regaining popularity, and nations that had once assimilated and "vanished" have now reappeared. Estonians, Latvians, Corsicans, and Lombards awake from the long slumber that communist regimes or Western European nation-states had forced upon them, flex their muscles, and set out to march under the banner of national independence.

End of an Era

Unfortunately, such attempts to turn back the historical clock are often marked by bloodshed and violation of the rights of neighboring nations. In their enthusiasm to regain their national identity and acquire recognition and self-respect, national activists often overlook the changes that have taken place in the surrounding political, economic, and strategic circumstances, and fail to realize that ethnocentric national slogans have become obsolete. The era of homogeneous and viable nation-states is over (or rather, the era of the illusion that homogeneous and viable nation-states are possible is over, since such states never existed), and the national vision must be redefined.

At first glance, the task of redefining nationalism might seem unpromising from a liberal perspective. The national tradition, with its emphasis on belonging, loyalty, and solidarity, would seem to be fundamentally opposed to the liberal tradition, with its respect for personal autonomy, reflection, and choice. Indeed, some would argue that liberals should engage in a struggle against the national phenomenon, offer a universalist alternative, and rely on persuasion and education to eradicate national feelings.

Such an enterprise might be justified were we to agree that national aspirations are inherently evil and there is nothing in them that merits our respect. Karl Popper, in what is probably the best-known attack on nationalism, endorsed such a view when he claimed that nationalism is akin to a revolt against reason and the open society—that it appeals "to our tribal instincts, to passion and to prejudice, and to our nostalgic desire to be relieved from the strain of individual responsibility which it attempts to replace by a collective or group responsibility."

Mediating Disparate Beliefs

But there are problems with the liberal tendency to describe nationalism as resting merely on irrational (some say primitive) fears of the stranger, as motivated by a morally irrelevant attraction to what is familiar and similar, or as simply giving expression to an unscrupulous desire for power. National existence may instead be founded on a range of perceptive understandings of the human situation, of what makes human life meaningful and creative, as well as a set of praiseworthy values. No doubt there are inherent tensions between certain national values and those of the liberal tradition. But the two modes of thought are not irreconcilable at all points, and the existence of tensions does not imply that we must engage in the ultimate pursuit of one set of values at the expense of the other. A theory of liberal nationalism renounces such absolute solutions, above all by seeking to mediate between the nationalist belief that individuals are the inevitable product of their culture, and the liberal conviction that individuals can be the authors of their own lives. . . .

In the modern era, nation-builders have not always acknowledged the role of choice in sustaining national identity. Insisting that their nation is a natural community shaped entirely by history and fate, they compulsively search for ancestral origins to which the new nation might "return," cling to even the faintest testimony of historical continuity, and advance patently false claims locating the nation's roots in a distant past. By emphasizing the link to the past, nation-builders try to play down the fact that their nation is the outcome of a bureaucratic decision or an international agreement and that its national consciousness is only beginning to take shape. Nevertheless, in their attempts to project their idea of a real nation—a group sharing a common denominator based on history, culture, language, and rituals—they express values that are central to national life generally: the urge for continuity, the desire to see at least some parts of social life as unchanging and invariant, and the need for a locus of identification.

> *"National activists . . . fail to realize that ethnocentric national slogans have become obsolete."*

59

Liberal nationalism does not oppose such sentiments. To the contrary, it recognizes that many elements of the nationalist ethos, although unacknowledged, have long been fused into liberal thought. For example, the liberal conception of distributive justice is particularistic and applies only within well-defined, relatively closed social frameworks, which favor members over nonmembers. The same applies to the liberal conceptions of membership and political obligations. These conceptions simultaneously embody two contradictory images of the political community: that of a voluntary association and that of a community of fate. Liberal nationalism, in its understanding of national and personal identity, embodies a similar contradiction, arguing that although cultural choices are neither easy nor limitless, cultural memberships and moral identity are not beyond choice.

> *"[Liberalism and nationalism] are not irreconcilable at all points."*

The Nature of Cultural Membership

In the past, the version of nationalism that places cultural commitments at its center has usually been perceived as the most conservative and anti-liberal form of nationalism. Cultural nationalism, it has been argued, preaches the establishment of closed societies, favors the authoritarian uniformity of state and faith, and fosters xenophobia.

But although liberal nationalism emphasizes the role of culture in constituting nations, it does not claim that individuals can find true freedom and expression only through complete identification with the community. From a national perspective, a painter working in the solitude of his atelier, the poet writing to his loved one, and the athlete competing in a sports event strive for the pinnacle of their own individual achievements, even as they contribute to the advancement of their own particular nations. Moreover, if we accept Raymond Williams' claim that "culture is the ordinary"—the language we teach our children, the bedtime stories we tell them, the lullabies we sing to them—then the meaning of most of our daily actions transcends their particular and direct function. The ability to turn an everyday act into a source of national pride is one of the most appealing aspects of nationalism. It contextualizes human actions, no matter how mundane, making them part of a continuous creative effort whereby culture is made and remade.

In placing reflection, choice, and internal criticism at its center, liberal nationalism rejects the notion that nationalism must necessarily, in Gordon Graham's words, "exalt the idea of the nation above all other ideas." It is true that nationalism implies a morality of community—a belief that we are justified to some degree in favoring the interests of fellow members over those of nonmembers. However, liberal nationalism recognizes that modern individuals belong to a complex network of memberships, and therefore argues that a morality of community need not be as xenophobic as it might appear at first glance.

For example: I see myself as an Israeli, but I am also a member of an academic community and therefore committed to the notion of academic freedom. I therefore have a duty to support Palestinian colleagues in their struggle to re-open the universities closed by the Israeli Army in the West Bank. Obviously, the duty to defend academic freedom is a general duty, but the fact that I am a member of the academic community and share this membership with members of other nations intensifies my duty to defend their interests. Hence, I am less troubled by the fact that brokers at the Israeli stock exchange failed to organize a sit-down strike in solidarity with Palestinian academics, than by the fact that no Israeli university has officially done so.

Liberal nationalism insists upon fostering national ideals without losing sight of other human values against which those ideals ought to be weighed. It celebrates the particularity of culture together with the universality of human rights. In this sense it differs radically from organic interpretations of nationalism, which assume that the identity of individuals is totally constituted by their national membership, and that the personal will is "truly free" only when submerged in the general one. It is a direct descendant of the cultural pluralism of Johann von Herder and the liberal nationalism of Giuseppe Mazzini.

Self-Determination and Individual Liberty

The demand for a public sphere in which the cultural aspects of national life come to the fore constitutes the essence of the right to national self-determination. In the past, the full exercise of this right has often been identified with the creation of a homogeneous nation-state. Many nineteenth-century liberals favored the establishment of such states because, in Hugh Seton-Watson's words, they believed that "individual liberty and national independence or unity would go together," and that liberal principles generally could best be implemented in a unitary state. "Free institutions are next to impossible in a country made up of different nationalities," argued John Stuart Mill. "Among a people without fellow-feeling, especially if they read and speak different languages, the united public opinion, necessary to the working of representative government, cannot exist."

However, as Mill had already noted in 1861, there are major difficulties in implementing the national ideal of a state for each nation. The most prominent obstacle is the geographic one: there are areas of the world

> *"Many elements of the nationalist ethos . . . have long been fused into liberal thought."*

where members of different nations are so closely intermingled that it is impossible to grant each an independent nation-state.

This would have been particularly true in light of the interpretation of national self-determination prevailing in Mill's time and extending into the Wilso-

61

nian era. National self-determination was perceived, Eric Hobsbawm writes, as a stage in the social evolution of human units as they developed from "family and tribe to county and canton, from the local to the regional, the national and eventually the global." As long as national self-determination was expected to be part of a linear process of historical evolution leading to increasingly larger social units, the idea that it should be granted not just to

> *"A morality of community need not be as xenophobic as it might appear at first glance."*

unifying national movements, but also to groups wishing to *secede* and create their own small, homogeneous national units, was ruled out a priori (though Mill himself made some exceptions). Thus, even in Western Europe, the cradle of nationalism, many citizens continue to see themselves as members of national minorities living in a state that does not fly their flag.

Independence or Rights

The nineteenth-century hope that individual liberty and national independence would go together has also failed to materialize. In fact, the yearning for national self-determination is different from, and may even contradict, the liberal democratic struggle for civil rights and political participation. History shows that individuals often desire to secure status and recognition for their nation even at the cost of relinquishing their civil rights and liberties.

The U.N. Human Rights Committee has viewed the realization of the right to national self-determination as an essential condition for the effective guarantee and observance of individual rights. But members of nations granted national self-determination can, and indeed have, set up regimes that restrict the human rights of their fellow nationals, while individuals sometimes enjoy a full range of civil rights even when not governed by their fellow nationals. Members of national minorities who live in liberal democracies—the Quebecois and the Indians in Canada, the aborigines in Australia, the Basques in France—are not deprived of their right to political participation or their freedoms of speech, press, assembly, and association, although they may feel marginalized and dispossessed because they are governed by a political culture and political institutions imprinted by a culture not their own.

Individuals wish to be ruled by institutions informed by a culture they find understandable and meaningful. When they are able to identify their own culture in the political framework, when the political institutions reflect familiar traditions, historical interpretations, and norms of behavior, individuals come to perceive themselves as the creators, or at least the carriers, of a valuable set of beliefs. Fortunately, the right to a public sphere where one's national culture may find expression may be achieved through a variety of political setups, including federative and confederative arrangements, local autonomies, or the establishment of national institutions. Were the creation of a separate nation-state the only way of realizing the right to national self-determination, its implementation would remain the privilege of only a fortunate few.

The Universality of National Rights

Liberal nationalism holds that because national rights rest on the value that individuals attach to their membership in a nation, all nations are entitled to equal respect. The justification of national rights is thus separated from the glorious or tormented past of each nation, from its antiquity, or from its success in attaining territorial gains. Because liberal nationalism is predicated upon a commitment to the existence of national groups as such, it insists that a nation can affirm its identity without disregarding the dignity and value of other nations.

This conception is well expressed in the writings of the Polish revolutionary Kazimierz Brodzinski, who insisted that national egoism, wherein each nation regarded itself as "the goal and center of everything," had to be replaced with a liberal perspective. Brodzinski's writings convey the extraordinary combination of particularistic pride and universal commitment typical of the progressive-romantic version of liberal nationalism prevalent in mid-nineteenth-century Europe:

> the Polish nation alone (I say it boldly and with patriotic pride) could have a foreboding of the true movement of the moral universe. It has recognized that every nation is a fragment of the whole and must roll on its orbit and around the center like the planets around theirs.

Brodzinski promoted the idea of the brotherhood of nations, which shared a sacred duty to be mutually helpful in the struggle for freedom and international justice. It is in this spirit that Mazzini addresses his fellow Italians:

> A people, Greek, Polish, Circassian, raises the banner of the Fatherland and of Independence, fights, conquers, or dies for it. What is it that makes your hearts beat at the story of its battles, which makes them swell with joy at its victories, and sorrow over its defeats? . . . And why do you eagerly read the miracles of patriotic love recorded in Greek story, and repeat them to your children with a feeling of pride, almost as if they were stories of your own fathers?

Ethnocentric nationalists, who rely on arguments exclusively related to one particular nation, rule out a universal justification of national rights and lose the ability to hold a meaningful dialogue with members of other nations. This limitation is one that the tradition of liberal nationalism seeks to overcome.

> *"There are major difficulties in implementing the national ideal of a state for each nation."*

Recent versions of nationalism seem to lend little credibility to the liberal nationalist position I have offered. Witness the bloody struggles in Yugoslavia, the violent clashes between Sikhs and Hindus in India, and the frequent outbursts of ethnic hatred within and between the new republics of Eastern Europe. A cursory glance at the surrounding reality could easily lead to the conclusion that liberal nationalism is a rather esoteric approach.

Yet there are reasons to think otherwise. Since the end of the Second World War, independent nation-states have agreed to restrict their autonomy, and cross-national economic cooperation—involving the development of joint policies, effective regulations, and continuous coordination—seems to have become the order of the day. Some observers assume that such cooperation will necessarily lead to a postnational world. But one can imagine nations enjoying the right to national self-determination along with the benefits accruing from membership in broader political alliances—especially if, as liberal nationalism proposes, the aspiration of creating an independent state for each nation is replaced with more modest solutions, such as local autonomies or federative or confederative arrangements.

Many of Europe's small nations, which failed to establish independent nation-states, look forward to European unification. The Corsicans, Basques, Catalans, and Irish nationalists assume that, as a self-professed multinational entity, the EC [European Community] will not seek to shape a homogeneous cultural community, nor will it follow the undesirable tradition in which international organizations include only states. The EC could become a community of nations that openly recognizes the diversity of its constitutive units.

> *"Liberal nationalism holds that . . . all nations are entitled to equal respect."*

On the other hand, as technological development and economic prosperity increasingly depend on cross-national associations, assimilation is, more than ever, a feasible option. This could mean that the real test for cultural and national affiliations has arrived. Will national groups accede to pressures to melt together into a larger culture, or will they be motivated to invest in the preservation of their own cultural heritage, their language, their distinctiveness?

Individuals may, in the future, choose to surrender their particularities and assimilate into one international culture. But the need for mediating communities makes this scenario unlikely. As Mazzini rightly argued, "the individual is too weak and Humanity is too large."

Nationalism Impedes Progress

by Ernest Erber

About the author: *Ernest Erber, a scholar of social change theory, is a profes-*
sional planner specializing in national and international economic planning.
He has been a writer, educator, and organizer for democratic socialist groups
for many years.

The current proliferation of civil strife of every conceivable type throughout
the world seems to be accentuated by a barbaric cruelty and disregard of human
life that surpasses anything experienced since the Holocaust. To be informed of
organized and politically motivated mass rape; of the cold-blooded slashing of
throats of prisoners; of wanton and repeated shelling of civilian populations in
their homes, suggests a form of mega-madness that defies clear comprehension,
even with the most skillful use of the analytic tools that are customary to historical and/or socio-political investigation.

But if we are to adhere to a belief in rationalism and if we are to continue to
utilize scientific method, it leaves us no alternative but to assume that, in the
last analysis, all human social conduct is subject to comprehension, even
though our best answers might be less than complete and, possibly, be the
source of new questions.

A Historical Backdrop

I base my view of the current status of nationalism, the right to self-
determination and the nation-state, upon observations of the ever-changing institutional and ideological framework which gives them meaning. Seeing current
events against this historical backdrop facilitates separating reality from appearance and provides a basis for improved theoretical generalization.

I begin by setting down my views on our subject matter in the form of these
propositions:

(a) that the nation-state, together with the principle of national sovereignty, is in historical decline, as it is increasingly subordinated to big-power pressure for world order as exercised through the United Nations and other international bodies;

(b) that the right of national self-determination will be reduced, especially by challenging the workability of separation in every case, with ethnic minority rights generally becoming subsumed under the growing umbrella of human rights;

(c) that nationalism plays an increasingly reactionary role, with ever fewer occasions for reappearing as an historically progressive force.

These propositions reflect an effort to read and interpret historical change as it affects the subjects under consideration. The most salient impressions that influence my historical and theoretical interpretations are the following:

1. The *Nation-State* is a relatively recent phenomenon in Western civilization, dating mainly from the 19th century. It was propelled into prominence by the shock wave of the French Revolution (and its Napoleonic extension) as these unloosed a tide of popular demand for self-rule that pressed upon the passé dynastic system (Hapsburgs, Ottomans, Romanoffs, Hohenzollerns) as it fought to replace it with the revolutionary concept of one nationality, one language, one culture, one state—the theoretical preconceptions for ethnic-cleansing.

The Rise of Nation-States

2. *World Order*, of one form or another and existent in actuality or theory, subordinated lesser powers (clans, tribes, city-states, nations) within Western civilization for some two thousand years, beginning with the Roman Empire and ending with the wars unleashed by the Reformation. As the uni-centered world order gave way to the system of "balance of power," there ensued an interregnum of several centuries without dominant world order, during which the struggle to create nation-states increasingly dominated European political theory and practice and dealt hammer blows to the old dynastic empires.

3. *Nationalism*, as political doctrine and movement for the creation of nation-states, emerged early in the 19th century. Its articulation began with German intellectuals who aimed to create a German nation-state out of the kingdoms, duchies, city-states and feudal localism under which Germans lived. The philosopher and poet Johann von Herder gave a semblance of theory to nationalism. To quote Isaiah Berlin: "Herder virtually invented the idea of belonging. He believed that just as people need to eat and drink, to have security and

> *"Nationalism plays an increasingly reactionary role . . . reappearing [less often] as an historically progressive force."*

freedom of movement, so too they need to belong to a group." Herder gave nationalism the concept of *Volksgeist*, which later became *Nationalgeist*, the mystical "spirit" of a people and nation. Though Herder was deeply non-aggressive and denied the superiority of one people over another, his imagery and symbolism fired ever more aggressive forms of nationalism in Germany and in many other countries and, eventually, formed a powerful motif in Nazism. Though much pedantic investigation has gone into definitions of nationalism on the basis of common language, culture, territory, history, etc., most nationalist movements were inspired by, and reflected, "geist," i.e., a popular spirit that gave vent to discontent born of grievances that were rooted in a sense of disfranchisement, inequality and impoverishment, especially when those so affected could identify a common enemy or enemies as the source of their troubles.

Nationalism and Socialism

4. *Socialism* came into existence in the same period as nationalism and in response to the same set of circumstances, viz., the revolutionary changes resulting from the uprooting and destruction of the thousand-year-old feudal order by the combined impact of the Enlightenment, the Industrial Revolution, the French Revolution, individualism and the spreading network of capitalist socio-economic relations, made visible by the new culture of urbanization. It is only with great effort that we, as creatures of the 20th century, can comprehend the shock effect upon contemporaries of *The Great Transformation* (to borrow the title of Karl Polanyi's book that so vividly describes it) in living through the replacement of feudalism's economic, political, social and cultural institutions and of its belief and behavior systems. Aftershock is still apparent in the adjustment problems of the most advanced nations, while the full force of the shock wave is still rolling through the less developed parts of the world, in keeping with the law of uneven development. And nationalism and socialism are still seeking to provide their separate answers to the unresolved consequences of this upheaval.

> *"Most nationalist movements were inspired by . . . a popular spirit that gave vent to discontent."*

5., 6. *Nationalism and/or Socialism.* The "great transformation" caused universal expectations that poverty, ignorance and oppression would soon be replaced by abundance, education and freedom, made possible by the new industrial system's mass production of wealth. But when life changed only in form for most people, and not in content, they became receptive to new explanations of the source of their ills and new programs for solutions. Both nationalism and socialism offered answers that echoed each other's appeal. Both decried the injustice of domination and exploitation of the weak by the strong. Nationalists said, "Patagonia for the Patagonians!" And "Out with our imperial oppressors!" Socialists said, "Workers of the world unite!" And "Let's begin in this workshop." The truth appears to be that most wage workers saw some merit in both appeals, nationalism and socialism. Or, socialism *and* nationalism. After all, they *were* Patagonians (even if it had never occurred to them to be proud of that until they heard a nationalist speaker say that Patagonian is one of the world's great languages—though few of them spoke it—and that three centuries ago the fearless Pata, founder of their nation, had led their forefathers in a great battle that routed the arrogant Argentini-ans). And developing a fierce hatred for their oppressors made them feel good; they straightened their backs and held their heads high and gave the name "Pata" to their next born.

> *"Crude misuse of socialist imagery succeeded in winning followers for the Nazis."*

But then again, they *were* wage workers and they felt that they were underpaid and overworked and the fact that they worked for a Patagonian did not make that easier to bear. That he was an exploiter was his problem, not theirs. They were class-conscious (but proud) Patagonians and had nothing against Argentinian wage workers. If they could have it all, they would like to get rid of their Patagonian boss—*and* their Argentinian governor.

(For those workers who had both a boss and a governor—king, president, etc.—of their own nationality, national pride took the form of patriotism, and as they marched on the picket line they carried their national flag and denounced their boss as "unpatriotic.")

Disguised Nationalism

7. *Nationalism in "Socialist" Garb.* Soon some nationalist politicians got the idea of featuring "socialism" as an add-on to their nationalism; substituting for the international class struggle of the workers the national struggle of the oppressed nationalities against their oppressors. Typical of such ideological amalgamations was the Czechoslovakian National Socialist Party founded by Thomas G. Masaryk, first president of Czechoslovakia. The most blatant example, of course, is Adolf Hitler's choice of name in founding the National Socialist Workers Party, proclaiming that true socialism is the community of all Germans as expressed by the German nation in its struggle against world capital, represented by Jewish money and the victors of World War I. Even such crude misuse of socialist imagery succeeded in winning followers for the Nazis among the jobless millions. The appeal of Nazism (and fascistic movements generally) is a mixture of extreme nationalism and populism (e.g., anti-international capital, anti-big business monopolies, etc.), an aspect that distinguishes it from traditional conservatism.

8. *"Communism" in Nationalist Garb.* After Joseph Stalin proclaimed in 1924 that socialism could be achieved within the Soviet Union without requiring the help of revolutions in the advanced nations, the strategy of the Soviet government and the Communist International shifted to stressing aid to nationalist movements everywhere, but especially in the underdeveloped and undeveloped countries, in order to strengthen Soviet defense against the world imperialist threat by undermining the latter with colonial and nationalist pressures. Since strengthening world socialist revolution was no longer the prime Soviet

aim, Soviet policy indulged in wrapping itself in all-out nationalist garb, assuming correctly that it is easier to use nationalism in attracting oppressed minorities than to feature socialism. Communists everywhere became indistinguishable from nationalists. In the face of the Nazi threat in the 1930s, Moscow, in angling for military alliances with the West, jettisoned the last vestiges of its Communist program abroad in favor of "people's fronts" designed to create patriotic public opinion that would pressure the governments of England, France, the United States and other Western nations into adopting a pro-Soviet and anti-Nazi foreign policy, in behalf of which the Communist parties proclaimed their patriotic allegiance to their countries and advised their nationalist allies in the colonial world to call off their struggles against the colonial powers.

A Cold War Legacy

Following World War II and for the 40 years of the Cold War that ensued, Moscow conducted countless campaigns of "national liberation" throughout the third world in the name and spirit of undisguised and unbridled nationalism, including "wars of liberation," accentuating ethnic, racial and national feelings and manipulating them for Soviet foreign policy purposes, diverting the valid discontent of the economically exploited into nationalist political channels. Today the map of the world is spotted with several scores of locations where the residue of this shameless policy continues to fester in hate-filled violence that erupts in ethnic, religious and nationalist clashes conducted by leaders and cadres trained in the Stalin School of Cynical Nationalism, as exemplified by the Communist apparatchik Slobodan Milosevic, and his so-called Socialist Party of Yugoslavia. . . .

9. *Cold War Aftermath.* We have lived through a half century dominated by two sets of madmen who were engaged in brinkmanship once likened to two antagonists maneuvering against each other with lighted matches in hand in a basement room with gasoline sloshing up to their ankles. Our "world order" was approvingly described as "mutual terror," one aspect of which consisted of placing huge stocks of highly sophisticated weaponry in the hands of governments and insurrectionary movements wherever it promised to tip the balance of power, including nuclear arms. With one superpower apparently out of the contest, presently, and the Cold War considered to be over, those in possession of armaments (or still tapped into a supply source) throughout the world now feel free to use them for more local goals, e.g., though the Communists are out of power in

> *"Moscow conducted . . . 'wars of liberation,' accentuating ethnic, racial and national feelings."*

Afghanistan, the accumulated stockpiles of both Russian-made and American-made arms are used by Afghans to blaze away at each other. But more than arms supplies are a factor. The political battle lines designed in Moscow and in

Washington remain in place. The C.I.A.'s network of communications is still operative. Moscow's might also be. Strings are still being pulled and puppets are still responding. And nationalist feelings remain the buttons most easily pushed.

Accommodating Nationalism

10. *Populism*, that variegated pool of valid grievances and ignorant prejudices, provides a constantly rewarding place for nationalist anglers of all types, including racists, religious fanatics, ethnic hate-mongers, etc., to cast their baited lines. But populist discontent, expressing an awareness of systemic injustices, however unclearly comprehended, also represents the most likely receptivity to the socialist message. For in the overarching historical sense, populism is the state of mind that reflects the massive, cumulative disappointment of many generations with the outcome of "The Great Transformation"—the bitter truth that the new status quo turned out to be a rigged lottery with few winners and many losers. This deep mass of discontent—influenced by history's lessons, but at a glacial pace and slipping backward from time to time—remains the source of both promise and threat.

Because the socialist promise is currently identified with the Stalinized Soviet societies that have been overthrown by those who experienced life within them, the socialist message has little or no appeal.

> *"[Populism] provides a constantly rewarding place for nationalist anglers . . . to cast their baited lines."*

Deep-seated discontent, anger and need-satisfaction connects more easily with a nationalist ("own-group") rationale for attacking short-range, nearby targets, viz., social groupings perceived as "better-off," if only moderately so (owning automobiles, apartments, houses, television sets, good furniture, etc.); and/or those considered to be (or threatening to become) oppressors or competitors; and/or those identified with undesirable change—disruptive "modernizers," alien life-stylists, and worshippers of false gods; and/or those seen as "corrupt;" and/or those seen as "tools of Western culture." And their aggressions make news from Bosnia, India, Egypt, ex-Soviet Georgia (and ex-Soviet other places), Somalia. etc.

11. *New World Order*. Among the many disservices which the recent and unlamented President George Bush perpetrated was to promise a "new world order," thereby quickly turning this concept into a laughing stock. His performance is to be regretted, because the world badly needs a new order; it simply cannot continue to exist without one. The United Nations is, obviously, not a new world order, but it does provide a beginning framework for one. And undergirding the UN are several dozen special-purpose international agencies that provide additional frameworks related to such problem areas as space, ocean floor, communications, hunger, health, monetary policy, trade, etc. Their

prospects are uncertain. Capitalism and its imperialist format are not hospitable to international regulation. Nor are Soviet-type systems (one of which is China). Yet much progress has been made, however grudgingly, spurred on by a mutual need for survival. But every inch of progress has been won by overcoming national sovereignty. The problems of nuclear proliferation, global ecological sustainability, world hunger, overpopulation, and, increasingly, basic human rights can be mitigated only by deeper inroads upon national sovereignty.

As we come to the end of the 20th century, the democratic left should see the nation-state, separatist self-determination and nationalism as road blocks to the progress, if not the survival, of humanity. We should begin with fierce opposition to all forms of nationalism—theory, doctrine, politics and movement. It has outlived whatever usefulness it had and, like an unburied corpse, its continued presence contaminates the body politic wherever it is tolerated.

Nationalism Threatens Peace in Europe

by Daniel Singer

About the author: *Daniel Singer is the European correspondent for the weekly magazine* The Nation.

The specter haunting Europe today, as it approaches the twenty-first century, is the ghost of nineteenth-century nationalism. It sends shivers down spines everywhere on the no longer formally split but still deeply divided Continent. In eastern Europe, the collapse of the Stalinist empire, followed by the fragmentation of the Soviet Union itself, has provided scope for the resurrection of local nationalisms. Since the alleged purpose of the whole operation is to reverse the course of recent history, this revival of nation-states is logical, even if it does not make much sense. In western Europe, where history has developed more in line with what was expected and the boundaries of the nation-state are being blurred, rejection of the alien, of the other, is spreading from Brussels to Vienna; the racist Jean-Marie Le Pen is no longer the odd man out. Is there some link between these two dangerous trends?

From Communism to Nationalism

Recent developments in central and eastern Europe are probably easiest to understand. The Stalinist regime had been thrust upon these countries, even if it was imposed by the Red Army liberating them from the Nazis. The discarding of "communism" in 1989 was at the same time a rejection of Russian domination. Since then, the new regimes, while enjoying their newly found independence, have been fast discovering its economic limitations. But, as discontent is rising and the governments do not dare to rebel against the iron rule of the International Monetary Fund, they must seek scapegoats. Putting the blame on the "commies" can work for a while, and attacks against "aliens," within or without national frontiers, are a classical substitute for solutions.

On the face of it, the evolution of the former Soviet Union is more difficult to grasp, since nationalism was supposed to have been uprooted there by seventy years of socialism and equality of national groups. The plain answer is that there was no more equality than there was socialism. The Russification of the outlying republics was no more acceptable because it was practiced by a Georgian tyrant and the ruthless dictation from Moscow no more bearable because it was disguised in Marxist mumbo jumbo. Nationalism was never uprooted in the Soviet Union. In Russia itself it was at times extolled and at other times suppressed. In the other republics it was always driven underground. There it festered. When *perestroika* unleashed pent-up discontents and *glasnost* allowed their expression, nationalism came back with a vengeance. . . .

The simultaneous revival of primitive capitalism and the nation-state in eastern Europe fits into an established pattern and points to the past (nationalism there was described as an "infantile disorder," to use Lenin's expression in another context, of the transition to capitalism). On the other hand, the revival of xenophobia and racism in a western Europe of vanishing frontiers does not fit that pattern and is a pointer to the future.

The New Wave of Xenophobia

Admittedly, the nation-state has not disappeared in western Europe. Indeed, General Charles de Gaulle showed how effective an instrument it could be in the hands of a determined ruler. Nevertheless, the deal struck in 1992 with I.B.M. by the French company Groupe Bull, the state-owned company picked by the general himself to counter the American computer invasion, confirmed how difficult it is for a medium-sized state to resist economic encroachment on its own. The road from Maastricht, the Netherlands (site of the conference on unification), however tortuous and full of pitfalls, will lead western Europe to some form of federation. Why is this gradual lifting of frontiers accompanied by a big boost for xenophobic parties in elections in Austria, Belgium, Italy and Switzerland; by violent attacks against immigrants throughout Germany; by another advance for Le Pen's National Front in France's regional elections?

The one answer that can be dismissed at once is the prevailing one that the foreign population in western Europe has exceeded the so-called "threshold of tolerance," beyond which the host country rejects any newcomers. France, where this new wave of xenophobia reached a political level, is an old country of immigration, and the share of foreigners in its population, and in its labor force, is exactly the same today as it was before the last war. Indeed, the proportion of immigrants in

> *"The revival of xenophobia and racism in a western Europe of vanishing frontiers . . . is a pointer to the future."*

western Europe was roughly the same twenty years ago as it is today, and it was perfectly bearable. It was only after 1975 and the rise of unemployment that it began to be described as intolerable. The phenomenon is thus not due to any population "threshold" but to an economic crisis.

Immigrant labor massively entered the European economy in the 1960s and early 1970s, that is to say, in the second phase of the unprecedented expansion that changed the face of western Europe. Indeed, manning the assembly lines and filling jobs that were dirty, difficult, monotonous or dangerous, the immigrant workers were a key element in that economic miracle. By standing on the backs of these people, the natives could climb the ladder to the higher-skilled, white-collar jobs. Everything was fine until the mid-1970s, when the deep structural crisis altered the mode of production and lowered the demand for unskilled immigrant labor. Then it was discovered that the provisional had become permanent, that the "guests," as the Germans euphemistically called them, had come to stay.

The Foreigner as Culprit

Not that it was possible to get rid of them rapidly in any case. The natives were not rushing to fill their unrewarding jobs. But the foreigner could now, once again, be painted as the culprit, responsible not only for rising unemployment but also for overcrowding, insecurity, the decline in social services—in short, for all the social evils concealed during the period of rapid growth and now revealed by the economic crisis. That aliens are scapegoats is illustrated all the time. In the epidemic of immigrant-bashing in Germany, there were many more cases in the east, where foreigners are few, than in the west, where they are more numerous. And the argument is carried *ad absurdum* by Poland's anti-Semitism without Jews. Jingoism is not a reflection of the number of immigrants. It is a symptom of a deeper sickness in society.

> *"[Increasing xenophobia] is . . . not due to any population 'threshold' but to an economic crisis."*

August Bebel, one of the founders of German social democracy, described anti-Semitism as the "socialism of fools," and there is a great temptation to extend this formula to all forms of xenophobia. The snag is that the recent waves of jingoism are not very "national socialist" in their propaganda. Nearly all the movements have had anti-Semitic undertones and quite often a weak spot for the Nazis, but they do not echo the allegedly anticapitalist slogans of their predecessors from the 1930s. A Le Pen can vituperate against the Brussels bureaucracy, but he cannot attack the Nazis' *bête noire*, the "Jewish-American plutocracy," and at the same time describe himself, as he does, as a sort of French Ronald Reagan.

This significant shift cannot be explained simply by the fact that socialism today is unfashionable. It is largely due to a difference in the economic context. Although unemployment in western Europe is now roughly three times higher than it was twenty years ago, it has not reached the proportions of the prewar

Depression, nor is the fate of its victims comparable. Although discontent is high, workers are not flocking en masse to Le Pen and his equivalents. The danger for western Europe is not an immediate takeover by various National Fronts. The threat lies in the gradual extension of the disease: the spread of racism and the weakening of class solidarity, sapping society's capacity for resistance should a really catastrophic slump bring back another bout of the deadly epidemic.

> *"Jingoism is not a reflection of the number of immigrants. It is a symptom of a deeper sickness in society."*

What connection is there between this creeping xenophobia in the west and the potentially more explosive jingoism of eastern Europe, where economic tensions are already reaching the breaking point? The first link is obvious now that Europe's great divide has been formally abolished. Until the last war eastern Europe was a great provider of immigrants for western Europe, as well as for the United States. Deprived of this source, the advanced countries of northwestern Europe had to look to the south for labor, first to Italy, Spain and Portugal, then to Turkey or, across the Mediterranean, Africa.

Now that western Europe is no longer mobilizing its army of labor, it is faced with two waves of recruits, one coming from the south, the other from the east. In Poland, the pioneer on the road to capitalism, the percentage of jobless has already reached double figures and keeps on rising. As Russia follows its "shock therapy," the figure one will have to play with will approach not 3 million but 30 million unemployed. No wonder that the countries of the Common Market are now trying to formulate a joint immigration policy. With the Berlin Wall dismantled, can they erect a new economic iron curtain along the Oder-Neisse line?

Ominous Nationalism

There is a deeper link between the revival of nationalism in the two halves of Europe. It is the simultaneous disappearance of a socialist alternative. Oversimplifying, one may say that nineteenth-century nationalism had two versions. The first, stemming from the American and French revolutions, was rationalist and universalist, trying to carry its values to the world at large. Socialism, promising not only to lift frontiers but also to give social content to the otherwise empty slogans of liberty and equality, was, in a sense, its heir. The other version, sponsored by German thinkers, was based on blood, kith and kin, and a historic tradition played to the tune of the *Nibelungen*. Now that the heritage of the former has been temporarily discredited through Communist crimes and social democratic surrender, the latter, darker side of nationalism is now dominant.

The error of those who proclaim the "end of history" is to assume that the collapse of the neo-Stalinist empire, and with it, however unfairly, the socialist dream, heralds the smooth advance of classical capitalism. It is true that capital now supplies the only universal model, with its McDonald's, its television serials and, more important, its system of management and exploitation. Yet, as it spreads across the planet, it squeezes, marginalizes and antagonizes growing numbers. Unless a new socialism that is cured of the disease of centralism and its overemphasis on growth provides those millions with democratic solutions—control over their economic as well as their political life—they will inevitably turn to the dangerous mixture of race, religion and ethnicity, a mixture that, incidentally, is not only for Muslim consumption. Which brings us back to the beginning: Until a resurrected, reinvented socialism inspires the people with hope and vision, and their rulers with genuine fear, the specter that is haunting Europe from Paris to Moscow will be the specter of nationalism.

Nationalism Oppresses Working Classes

by *New Unionist*

About the author: New Unionist *is a monthly publication of the New Union Party, a socialist political party based in New York City.*

Fascism is nationalism in its most extreme form. It came to power in Germany in the 1930s in the social breakdown of the Great Depression.

The Nazis offered the German people shelter from the storm through their mystic ideology of "blood and soil." They claimed the conflicts among Germans—especially the class struggle between workers and capitalists—were caused by the evil manipulations of those of non-German blood who infiltrated themselves among the Germans.

These "outsiders" were, of course, the Jews. If the Jews were gotten rid of, the Nazis said, the German people of all classes would stop fighting each other and would be united in a common "folk community."

Hitler's Promises

Adolf Hitler gained the backing of the German capitalists not because they were terribly interested in his crackpot racial theories but because the "folk community" would mean the end of working-class resistance and the threat of an anti-capitalist revolution. Hitler promised them that the powerful German labor movement—which understood the enemy was not the Jews but the German ruling class—would be crushed by force if he were given government power.

The Nazi party gained popular support not because of the appeal of its generally incoherent political program but because of the psychological relief it offered a large segment of the German population. Its rallies were less political meetings than mass rituals of magic. Through their staging, lighting, music and the excited oratory of Hitler, people who felt fearful, alienated and isolated by capitalism's individualistic and materialistic culture could experience a sense of return to a "natural" community of "blood and soil."

From "Labor Solidarity Answer to Suicidal Nationalism," *New Unionist*, April 1993. Reprinted with permission.

By surrendering their intellect and critical rationality to the force of nationalistic rituals, these people emotionally regressed to the dependency and powerlessness of childhood. This emotional regression gave them the sense of security they longed for. As dependent children they could accept the authority of a supreme father figure, the all-powerful Leader, Hitler, whom they promised to obey without rebellion in return for his protection against the dangers of the world.

Of course, when they returned to the real world the next day, it was back to all the evils of capitalist society they had escaped only in their imagination. Though the Nazis railed against "Jewish capitalism" in their propaganda, the real political purpose of fascism was to save capitalism. Once in power, Hitler destroyed the unions and workers' parties as promised, enforced wage ceilings and revived German industry with government public-works and armaments spending.

The people's anger, resentment and hatred over the exploitation and humiliation they experienced under capitalism were now directed by the Nazis away from the German capitalists who profited from the system. They were directed against, first, the Jews within Germany, and then against the foreign *"untermenschen"* of Poland, Russia and other countries eyed by Hitler for conquest in the economic interest of German capitalism.

Nazism saved German capitalism at the same time it marshalled the people's passion to destroy the source of their torment in the service of the very capitalism that was that source.

Defusing the Struggle

While not all nationalist movements are explicitly fascist—often they claim to be "socialist"—they all share the same political purpose of defusing the internal class struggle of the nation and redirecting that energy against foreign "enemies."

The same rule applies to the nationalisms of peoples historically oppressed by the nationalisms of other nations.

The nationalism of the Jews is known as Zionism. The early Zionists used blood-and-soil terminology to describe their ideology until the Nazis' use of it made it unpalatable for Jews.

But the content remained: Jews could not escape oppression unless they had their own land and their own explicitly Jewish state, that is, a state with a racially determined citizenship. Moreover, that land had to be the ancestral home of the Jews—Palestine—because of a mystical bond they had with that soil: it was promised to them by God.

> *"Once in power, Hitler destroyed the unions and workers' parties as promised."*

The Holocaust obviously lent weight to the Zionist appeal. But the establishment of the State of Israel hasn't guaranteed safety for the Jews. In fact, since the land was forcibly seized from the Palestinians who owned and occupied it, the creation of Israel has resulted in a state of constant war with the Palestinians and Arab states.

Israeli nationalism serves to keep the Israeli working class in harness because the ruling class can say Jews have to be united to avoid being destroyed by the hostile Arabs.

Poverty is spreading rapidly in Israel. But as long as the workers' anger is directed against the Palestinians, they can't effectively fight the Israeli capitalism that exploits

"Israeli nationalism serves to keep the Israeli working class in harness."

them. And nationalist politicians stoke the hatred by their lying claim that the Jews' problems would be solved by expelling the Palestinians, an ironic echo of the Nazis' demand for the expulsion of the Jews from German life.

In any case, the idea that Israel is an independent state in which the Jews can realize their redemption is an illusion. Israel couldn't exist if it weren't a dependent of the United States. Massive aid from the U.S. keeps its economy afloat while the U.S. has helped make the Israeli military one of the strongest in the world.

In exchange for the aid and political support against the just demands of the Palestinians, Israel does the U.S. government's dirty work in the Mideast, being its on-location police force to intimidate any Arab claim on U.S. oil interests. Israel also deals with South Africa and Central American dictatorships for the U.S. when Washington is politically inhibited from acting in its own behalf.

Economic Exploitation

In the same way, an ethnically pure and "independent" Croatia will exist as a political and economic flunky of Germany and France, while "independent" Serbia will survive only if it gains the protection of Russia.

The Irish have a long history of national oppression by the English. But political independence for Ireland didn't end its status as an economic colony.

Today, the economy is dominated by foreign multinationals and Ireland has among the lowest wages and highest unemployment of all the countries of Europe. As in the days of British rule, the Irish can find economic opportunity only by leaving their country. Free and independent Eire also suffers under the oppressive influence of the Vatican in matters of social policy.

So how would Northern Ireland's unity with the Republic of Ireland, which is the goal of Irish nationalists, solve the desperate conditions of Northern Ireland's Catholic workers?

Closer to home, our media whips up nationalist fervor for America when it's time to go fight to protect the oil companies' profits in the Mideast. American workers are told to "Buy American" to save their jobs. The Japanese and other foreigners are held responsible for our economic problems.

But U.S. corporations don't hesitate to leave American workers in the lurch to chase after low-wage labor in Mexico, China and Taiwan. At the same time they scream about foreign imports, American companies enter into joint production and marketing agreements with Japanese and other foreign corporations. Capitalists of every nation happily invest in each other's stocks and bonds without worrying about which national hero's picture appears on the money they "earn."

But while capitalism is international, it wants the workers to think nationalistically because keeping the workers divided and unorganized is the key to keeping the profits flowing. In today's world of international economic interdependence, nationalism is a sucker's game. It keeps people focused on imaginary foreign enemies while their pockets are being picked by their own homegrown exploiters.

American workers have no more interest in fighting Japanese or Mexican workers for jobs than Serbian and Croatian workers have in killing each other. Increased job competition forces down wages and conditions on all sides of all national borders.

Labor Solidarity

The only way for labor to protect its interests is to organize with the same international outlook and strategy the corporations have. In a world economy, labor solidarity only has meaning if it's international solidarity. National and ethnic differences are irrelevant when workers of every nation and of every ethnic background are having their wages slashed, their benefits eroded, their lives made more insecure and stressful.

Nationalism helps further the lie that there is not enough wealth to go around, that we have to fight each other over a shrinking pie.

The truth is our capacity for producing goods and services is constantly expanding, now faster than ever with computerized technologies. The problem is not that we can't produce enough to meet all people's needs. The problem is the capitalist system only allows production and distribution to take place when it's profitable for the handful of people who currently own and control industry and technology.

International labor solidarity will only make sense if it's combined with a program to replace international capitalism with international cooperation, with the workers of the world producing for their own needs under their own democratic management.

Sure, it's a big order. It means the people of the United States and the people of every other country will have to think and act for themselves as mature, intelligent adults. It means resisting the temptation to look for a

> *"Nationalism is a sucker's game. It keeps people focused on imaginary foreign enemies."*

father figure like Ross Perot to protect us (which he can't) and solve our problems for us (which he can't).

It's a big job, yes. But think about the alternative if we don't do the job.

Think about Bosnia.

Radical Nationalism Promotes Anti-Semitism

by Robert S. Wistrich

About the author: *Robert S. Wistrich teaches modern European history at Hebrew University in Jerusalem. Wistrich is the author of several books, including* Hitler's Apocalypse *and* Anti-Semitism: The Longest Hatred.

It is hardly surprising that in the years since the fall of Communism, there has been a resurgence of the old demons of nationalism and anti-Semitism on the European continent, and particularly in Central and Eastern Europe. In this part of the world, after all, problems of national identity have been acute ever since the abortive revolutions of 1848. The experience of Communist rule for four decades after World War II merely froze rather than resolved these underlying conflicts and tensions, including the anti-Semitism which between the two world wars was an integral expression of the struggle for Polish, Romanian, Hungarian, or Slovak national identity. Once that iron grip came unfastened, many of the old wounds resurfaced, alongside and in opposition to aspirations for national independence based on traditions deriving from the Western Enlightenment.

The Jewish Question

It must be remembered that after the Nazi rise to power, anti-Semitism became an official or semi-official policy in the lands of Central and Eastern Europe. This was no chance development. Ever since the late 19th century, Jews had been regarded as an alien element which had somehow succeeded in infiltrating and undermining whole sectors of the local economy, society, politics, and culture. Even when they were assimilated, Jews were often seen as being separate from the nation or *Volk*, as belonging to a distinct culture of their own, or as espousing orientations inimical to the goals favored by integral nationalists. . . .

Some elements of the "Jewish Question" clearly changed after 1945. On the eve of the Holocaust there were 8.1 million Jews—no less than 49 percent of world Jewry—in Eastern Europe, the USSR, and the Balkans. Today, even if we

From Robert S. Wistrich, "Once Again, Anti-Semitism Without Jews." Reprinted from *Commentary*, August 1992, by permission; all rights reserved.

include the European parts of Russia and Ukraine, Eastern Europe accounts for not much more than 10 percent of world Jewry. North America has displaced Eastern Europe as the major demographic reservoir of Diaspora Jewry, and Israel has taken over the role of the geopolitical core. The Jewry of Central and Eastern Europe (excluding the ex-USSR) is a decimated, pale shadow of its former self, with only the Hungarian community approaching the 100,000 mark. The great prewar Jewish communities of Poland, Romania, Germany, Czechoslovakia, and Austria, not to mention those in the Balkans and the Baltic states, were all wiped out by Hitler, and their remnants emigrated in the Stalinist aftermath. . . .

The "Jewish Question" has definitely been revived in the wake of the collapse of the Communist regimes, and has become inextricable from all the nagging issues of national identity—of what actually constitutes Polishness, Czechness, Hungarianness, etc.—that bedevil Eastern European society. We are witnessing the gory results of that larger contention today in Yugoslavia, and perhaps tomorrow in Moldova, Ukraine, Hungary, Romania, and the Balkans. Czechs and Slovaks may have united to overthrow Communism but since then, and despite the close linguistic ties between them, militant separatism has revived in Slovakia, and the Jews have been dragged into the picture. . . .

Exploiting Anti-Semitism

As for Poland, Hungary, and Romania, the elections of 1990 showed that in these countries popular anti-Semitism is still a factor that can be exploited in public life. In Hungary, the Alliance of Free Democrats (a party generally favored by Hungarian Jews) was targeted by some supporters of the victorious Hungarian Democratic Forum. One of the Forum's spokesmen, the playwright Istvan Curka, scathingly referred to a "dwarfish minority" that had forced the whole society to accept "that their truth is the only truth," and he openly blamed Jewish Communists for having destroyed the self-esteem of the Hungarian people. This was not an isolated example—although it is also the case that Prime Minister Jozsef Antall has vigorously condemned anti-Semitism, that his government has developed close ties with Israel (as have the governments of several other East European countries), and that Hungarian-Jewish life is currently flourishing. Moreover, the Hungarian Catholic Church has been more forthright in denouncing anti-Semitism than any of its counterparts in Eastern Europe. Similarly, many of the country's leading writers and intellectuals have spoken out against anti-Semitism.

"Popular anti-Semitism is still a factor that can be exploited in public life."

Things are decisively otherwise in Romania, where since the coup of December 1989 there has been a steady rise in both xenophobia and anti-Semitism, despite the fact that only about 18,000 Jews remain in the country. The nationalist opposition newspaper *Romania Mare*, with a circulation of over half-a-million, regularly features anti-Semitic articles. In April 1991, the editor claimed that too many Jews held key positions in Romania:

> The heads of TV and radio are all Jews, and in parliament it rains Jews by the bucket. It's not their fault—domination has been their style since the dawn of time—but can't they let us breathe a little, instead of trampling on us as they have been doing since 1947?

This charge has been echoed in a number of other newspapers which frequently blame the Jews for bringing Communism to Romania. Some members of the Committee for National Salvation, including the former Prime Minister, Petre Roman, have also been attacked for being of Jewish origin. The problem was further aggravated in April 1991 by a silent tribute in the Romanian parliament to the memory of the country's anti-Semitic wartime dictator, Marshal Ion Antonescu, favored ally of Hitler. Although the ex-Communist president, Ion Iliescu, dissociated himself from these tributes, he has also accused those who condemn anti-Semitism in Romania of exaggerating the situation and sullying the country's reputation. Thus the weakness of the government, combined with economic hardship, anger at the slow pace of reform, and the lack of a democratic tradition help to keep anti-Semitism alive as an outlet for popular frustrations and discontent.

> *"Since the [Romanian] coup of December 1989 there has been a steady rise in both xenophobia and anti-Semitism."*

Anti-Semitism Without Jews

All this is even more the case in Poland. According to recent surveys, in a country where there remain at most 10,000 Jews out of a population of nearly 40 million, about 30 percent of the populace hold anti-Semitic views. This has led to such grotesque absurdities as the 1990 whisper campaign against the then-Prime Minister, Tadeusz Mazowiecki, a Catholic accused of being a "crypto-Jew." (The rumors were spread by those supporting Lech Walesa for the premiership.) At the time the response by the Catholic Church and other official Polish bodies was startlingly inappropriate—a prominent Polish bishop publicly "confirmed" that not a single drop of tainted Jewish blood lurked in Mazowiecki's past. At the end of 1990, not surprisingly, there was a rash of swastika daubings on Jewish buildings in Warsaw and elsewhere, and slogans like "A Good Jew is a Dead Jew" appeared at the Umschlagplatz, the site from which in the summer of 1942 some 300,000 Warsaw Jews had been shipped to the Treblinka death camp.

Poland is perhaps the most spectacular example of the truth that anti-Semitism does not always require the presence of actual Jews in order to flourish. But it is not the only such example. Whether we are dealing with the desecration of Jewish cemeteries, mindless graffiti, pseudo-intellectual theories about a world Jewish conspiracy or "hidden" Jews in the government, this type of anti-Semitism can be detected all over Central and Eastern Europe today. It even surfaces as part of the "explanatory" mechanism behind the measures taken in some of these countries against Gypsies—who today bear the brunt of racial stereotyping and social harassment in Eastern Europe. For who but the Jews, with their well-known world conspiracy, could be behind the influx of these undesirable people?

Rise of the Radical Right

Something similar is happening in Western and Central Europe as well, where the fear of being "swamped" by unassimilable foreign cultures has given impetus to a resurgent radical Right. In France, Belgium, Germany, and Austria this new Right does and will continue to link the imaginary "Jewish Question" with the real problem of foreign immigration. For the hard-core racists of Western Europe, anti-Semitism is anyway a central pillar of their outlook, and they have no difficulty depicting the alleged threat to the white European race as part of a diabolical Jewish conspiracy against "Aryan" civilization.

Particularly relevant to any assessment of East European anti-Semitism is the situation in Central Europe, for it was here, and above all in Germany and Austria, that anti-Semitism was primarily elevated (or rather degraded) into the pseudo-science of "biological politics," and here that the conspiracy theories embodied in *The Protocols of the Elders of Zion* mixed with national humiliation after World War I, mass unemployment, and the middle-class fear of Communism to produce the most explosive anti-Jewish cocktail of all time, Hitler's National Socialist movement. Historically, ever since 1880, this has been the geopolitical core from which anti-Jewish trends elsewhere on the Continent have tended to derive inspiration and reinforcement. . . .

To be sure, publicly expressed anti-Semitism has to a large extent been delegitimized in Germany. This may help to explain why opinion surveys consistently show that German parliamentarians and national leaders hold far more favorable attitudes to Jews and Israel than do, say, their counterparts in Austria. But there is a marked gap between the attitude of German elites and the responses of the populace. Thus, a survey taken immediately after German unification showed that 58 percent of the population (East and West) believed that "it is time for Germans to put the Holocaust behind them"; 52 percent felt that Israel "should be

> *"For the hard-core racists of Western Europe, anti-Semitism is . . . a central pillar of their outlook."*

treated like any other state"; 39 percent believed that "Jews exploit the National-Socialist Holocaust for their own purposes"; and a similar percentage held that "now as in the past, Jews exert too much influence on world events." Interestingly enough, complacent and even callous attitudes seem more prevalent among West than among East Germans, at least in respect to the Holocaust.

In Austria, the radical Right has made even more spectacular gains than in Germany. In November 1991, Jorg Haider's Austrian Freedom party won 23 percent of the vote in Vienna on an anti-foreigner platform. Unlike the portly Franz Schonhüber in Germany, Haider is no Waffen-SS veteran but a charismatic, boyish forty-one-year-old who represents the new wave of yuppie-style proto-fascism in Central Europe. Though he publicly steers clear of the neo-Nazis, some officials in his own party are former members of the neo-Nazi National party of Germany, and one of his closest associates used to publish a magazine that described the Holocaust as "a lie without end." Haider himself has praised the "orderly employment policy" of the Third Reich and has eulogized the Austrian soldiers who fell in the service of the German Wehrmacht. Though Jews are not usually targeted in his electoral politics, there is no doubt that his Freedom party contains a hard core of unreconstructed anti-Semites. Since the levels of anti-Jewish prejudice have remained remarkably high in the Alpine Republic, indeed often exceeding East European levels, a suitably coded populist anti-Semitism would most likely be no barrier to electability or popularity for national politicians.

> *"Anti-Semitism since 1945 has been largely a phenomenon 'without Jews.'"*

In Central as in Eastern Europe, anti-Semitism since 1945 has been largely a phenomenon "without Jews," often diffusely directed against the imagined hidden influence and power of "world Jewry." How dangerous is it, then? In Germany as in Austria, as indeed in Hungary, Poland, Czechoslovakia, and Russia, Jews are generally less despised than certain other groups—in the German case, the favored targets are Turks, Gypsies, and "guest workers" or "asylum-seekers" in general. Thus, there would appear to be no immediate grounds for fearing that Germany will once again become a geopolitical center of anti-Semitic inspiration, incitement, or example to any of its East European neighbors. But it does seem to offer a parallel case, sharing some common features with Eastern Europe as well as exhibiting certain unique characteristics of its own.

A Tradition of Anti-Semitism

Anti-Semitism in Eastern Europe has a long history, one which predates by far the rise of modern nationalism. I have not discussed the age-old Christian antagonism to Judaism which underlies the kind of traditional anti-Semitism still to be found in Poland and Slovakia. Nor have I mentioned the extraordinarily tenacious belief in ritual murder, still alive among the more superstitious rural population in parts of Eastern Europe, or the residues of populist peasant anti-Semitism which have their roots in both religious and national sentiment in Hungary, Romania, Slovakia, Poland, and Ukraine. This peasant populism has long operated with a traditional image of the Jew as moneylender, trader, and exploiting capitalist. The change to a free market and a competitive economy in Eastern Europe, with the severe economic dislocations it is causing, provides an opportunity for a revival of this older kind of anti-Semitism which is in essence anti-capitalist and anti-entrepreneurial.

A Real Threat

But in general it is the long-suppressed nationalist and political types of anti-Semitism which seem to me more immediately significant for the post-Communist era. It would be a mistake to exaggerate the threat: what still remains of Jewish life has in many ways improved dramatically with the demise of Communism, and others are hated more than the Jews (if that is any consolation). But it would be a bigger mistake to ignore the threat, if only because anti-Semitism is nowadays more openly expressed and therefore Jews feel more insecure, especially in the former Soviet Union.

Today, popular anti-Semitism all over Eastern Europe is no longer a government policy (masquerading as propaganda against Israel, Zionism, or Judaism) but a spontaneous, often unpredictable sentiment whose bottom line is that the Jews are to blame for everything that is going wrong. However negligible the Jewish proportion of the populace in Central and Eastern Europe today, it seems that life cannot go on without the *Judaeus ex machina*. If he did not exist, then anti-Semites would have to invent him; and so they appear to be doing.

Fascist Nationalism Incites Violence Against Immigrants

by Steve Vogel

About the author: *Steve Vogel is based in Germany and writes for the* Washington Post *daily newspaper and* Army Times, *among other publications.*

Across Europe, a frightening specter of the past is raising its head. Radical right extremism, a movement once thought dead and buried in the rubble of World War II, is very much alive and on the march.

It is a movement that takes on many forms across the continent: skinhead toughs beating foreigners; angered farmers and workers radicalized by economic problems; and people in suits and ties frustrated by an ever-growing fear of immigration. It is a movement that may spell enormous problems for Europe and the world in years to come.

Attacks on Foreigners

In Germany, neo-Nazi thugs began a wave of terrifying attacks against foreigners in August 1992, burning refugee hostels and desecrating Holocaust memorials. Even more ominously, the violence was cheered on by some Germans. What's more frightening, recent polls and elections have charted a steady rise in support for this movement.

Meanwhile, the far right in France, playing on rising nationalistic sentiments, very nearly torpedoed the country's historic vote for the European Union. The xenophobic National Front, and its anti-immigrant message, continues to gain support from voters and is influential in national politics.

In Italy, some 50,000 followers of the Italian neo-Nazi party marched through Rome in October 1992, chanting fascist slogans. Visitors to some Italian towns are confronted with graffiti reading "Viva Il Duce," and a Mussolini sits in parliament—Benito's granddaughter, Alessandra, who is a member of the neofascist Italian Social Movement.

Few would say a Fourth Reich is on the rise in Europe. Stable democracies are still the rule across the continent, and most voters reject the neo-Nazis' message of hate.

Nonetheless, the European far right is advancing and drawing increasingly broad support, and has transformed the political landscape of the continent.

> *"The world was shocked by the images of rioters in Rostock being cheered on by German citizens."*

If the trend continues—and there are expectations it will—America may be confronted with a Europe with which it shares fewer and fewer democratic values.

The situation in key European countries is disturbing.

Germany: The world was shocked by the images of rioters in Rostock being cheered on by German citizens. But the violence and the sympathy it engendered are only the latest manifestations of the rise of the right.

In the spring of 1992, voters in regional elections made the radical right the third-largest party in two state parliaments. The far-right Republikaner party claims the support of 25 percent of the voters in Bavaria—the conservative southern state that gave Adolf Hitler his start. Opinion polls show the Republikaners will have enough support to enter the national parliament in 1994, threatening to disrupt the ruling coalition.

Many politicians are running scared. Despite the wave of neo-Nazi attacks, German Chancellor Helmut Kohl has refused to visit any asylum homes or firebombed Holocaust memorials. One top Kohl adviser says this is because "a symbolic act would not improve the situation," but critics say that the chancellor is afraid to alienate the far right.

"Are we going to see it happen once again in our country that people look away, or even look on, as helpless people are persecuted?" President Richard von Wiezsaecker has asked the nation. So far, the answer seems to be yes.

Extremism Elsewhere in Europe

France: Jean-Marie Le Pen and his extremist National Front have regularly won 10 percent or more of the French vote despite France's current socialist government. The National Front has become the most powerful extremist political manifestation in Western Europe since World War II.

It rants against immigrants, crime, AIDS, moral decadence and the "Eurocrats" planning European Union. These positions barely disguise its racist intent, including a complete ban on tourist visas for Africans and Arabs.

Despite these views, polls have shown nearly a third of the French people agree with Le Pen on immigration. The ruling socialists received only 16 percent of the vote in regional elections in 1992, barely better than the National Front's 14 percent.

Austria: Joerg Haider, chief of the country's Freedom Party, has made a splash with complaints about Eastern European immigrants. The party is positioning itself as an alternative to the traditional Socialist and Christian Democrats parties. There are expectations that Haider's party will pick up at least 20 percent of the vote in the 1994 elections.

Belgium: The openly anti-Semitic and authoritarian Flemish Bloc scored well in local elections held in Antwerp in 1992.

Italy: Neo-fascists have ridden a wave of strikes and protests to win growing support. "Just as 70 years ago Italy was illuminated by the revolutionary thought of my grandfather, so have we been pushed by the same ideal of restoring the pride and splendor of the past to Italy," Alessandra Mussolini told a rally of supporters in October 1992.

Disturbing Support of Hate

The common image Americans have of the European far right is one of angry mobs throwing fire-bombs or skinheads beating up foreign workers.

Only a very small percentage of the population is involved in these frightening and well-publicized incidents, and the far-right parties have more or less distanced themselves from the attacks.

"Are we going to see . . . people look away, or even look on, as helpless people are persecuted?"

What is perhaps more disturbing is the extent to which there is support, or at least sympathy, for many of their positions by a wide segment of the population.

A recent study by a Leipzig institute shows eastern German youths gravitating to the right, and anti-Semitism on the rise. Fully one-quarter of the school children agree that the German "race" should be kept pure, and racial mixing prevented.

Nationwide, almost one-third of German youths dislike foreigners, according to a study by IBM in Germany. "That for me is a frightening thought," says Gisa Schultze-Wolters, who directed the study.

In France, the National Front claims 100,000 members from nearly all social classes. The party has recently been trying to gain respectability by organizing satellite groups for farmers, police and shopkeepers, and it claims strong support from doctors. Another party on the French far right, Combat for Values, is drawing support from young, bourgeois, pro-business voters.

Indeed, across Europe the far right is getting support from a broad spectrum that includes the working class, the unemployed and the upper class. In particular, there is strong backing from what one analyst calls "the less well-off of the well-off."

Why is this happening on a continent that has been ravaged by fascism? . . .

Immigration, more than any other factor, is responsible for the growth of Europe's far right. Western Europe has been swamped in recent years with immigration from Eastern Europe, North Africa and Asia.

An estimated 1 million to 2 million people from former communist countries applied for admission into the European Community in 1992 alone.

The issue is particularly volatile in Germany, where it has served as the spark for the neo-Nazi violence. At the root of the problem is the German constitution. In an attempt to assuage the country's World War II guilt, the constitution guarantees asylum to anyone suffering political persecution.

This guarantee caused little problem for many years because of the relatively small number of applicants. But since the revolution in Eastern Europe, the country has been overrun by immigrants looking for a piece of the good life. Most are eventually turned down, but while their applications are processed, they are, according to law, given apartments and cash.

Angry Germans believe—often correctly—that foreigners are taking advantage of the system to draw expensive social benefits.

Foreigners Out

With the encouragement of the far right, economic problems are often blamed on foreigners. "Auslaender [foreigners] must get out," says Tomas Chinielewiski, a Rostock house painter. "They live better than us. They take our apartments, everything."

The movement has ridden this issue to success at the voting booth. During its successful showing in the regional elections in 1992, the German League for People and Home based its entire campaign on one word—"raus," meaning "out."

In France, Le Pen and his disciples have also made enormous use of the issue, warning that immigrants from North Africa and elsewhere are eroding the French national character. Likewise in Italy, the influx of Albanian immigrants has fired support for the right. . . .

Few observers envision the far right taking over Western European governments anytime soon. But the extremists threaten to change the face of European democracy.

"I don't think fascism is just around the corner, but what I see is the loss of democracy within the framework of existing structures," said Anton Pelinka, [director] of Vienna's Institute for Conflict Research.

Without dramatic changes in Eastern Europe and the former Soviet Union— changes that would shut off the pressure for east-to-west migration and relieve the economic situation

> *"Auslaender [foreigners] must get out. . . . They live better than us. They take our apartments, everything."*

across the continent—analysts see little chance of stemming the far right's advances.

The most likely scenario is that the entire European political spectrum will shift rightward in coming years. To stop this loss of voters, traditional conservative parties are becoming more extreme in their positions, blaming foreigners for local economic conditions, for example.

In turn, left-leaning parties, also under pressure from the voters, are abandoning liberal policies and moving to more centrist positions. For instance, in November 1992, Germany's liberal Social Democrats voted in a party congress to change 40 years of generous policies toward foreigners fleeing political persecution. The party overwhelmingly agreed to push for significantly tightened asylum laws.

Democracy Suffers

In France, the success of Le Pen's National Front also is moving the political dialogue to the right. Polls show growing support for Le Pen's call to abolish the rights of immigrants to have their families join them in France.

Le Pen is not likely to take over France, but the next government will be considerably to the right of the current government—even if it is again socialist.

The stunning success of the far right in the German regional elections threatens to dramatically change the power equation. Some Christian Democrats now want to cooperate with the Republikaners.

Needless to say, the state of politics on the continent and the far right's growing influence presents no obvious, immediate threat to America. There are no European fascists building a military machine bent on world conquest.

Nor is the movement directing its venom at the United States. It prefers to save it for oppressed peoples knocking on Western Europe's doors.

The danger to America is more insidious in nature: a decline of democratic quality and the growth of racism in Europe. The victims will be those who can least afford it—asylum seekers, migrant workers and economic refugees.

But the democratic foundations upon which the Atlantic Alliance is based—the friendship between America and Europe that changed the world—will become that much weaker.

Chapter 2

Is Ethnic Violence
Ever Justified?

Chapter Preface

Throughout history, ethnic groups have suffered mass campaigns of genocidal slaughter. Perhaps the most horrific of these campaigns was the Jewish Holocaust, in which Adolf Hitler's Nazi regime murdered an estimated 6 million Jews, two-thirds of the total in Europe, and up to 90 percent of the Gypsies in Germany and Austria. In the late 1970s, Cambodian communist dictator Pol Pot evoked comparisons to Hitler when he had more than 1 million Buddhist, educated, and minority Cambodians massacred. Both Hitler and Pol Pot mistakenly believed that eliminating entire ethnic groups would produce greater societies.

Incredibly, many of those responsible for these deaths wholeheartedly embrace the idea of genocide and openly justified their atrocities. As Adolf Eichmann, a Nazi secret police colonel executed for sending Jews to their deaths, coldly declared: "Jewry is now suffering a fate which, though hard, is more than deserved. No compassion and certainly no sorrow is called for. Every Jew is our enemy."

Tragically, similar justifications continue today. For example, much of the world has condemned Serbian president Slobodan Milosevic for the latest episode of genocidal violence—the "ethnic cleansing" of non-Serbian groups from the former Yugoslavia as part of his goal to create a greater Serbian domain. In Germany and the United States, violent neo-Nazi skinhead attacks on minorities grow in both frequency and severity. As German history scholar Elliott Neaman writes, "In comparison to previous years, this wave of violence has shown [that] the incidents have affected a greater number of areas in Germany; the violence is more dangerous." And in America, Anti-Defamation League of B'nai B'rith researcher Irwin Suall reports, "There are trends within [the skinhead movement] to move toward more serious violence."

Assertions of racial supremacy, along with radical nationalism and retribution for past injustices, are at the core of much ethnic violence. Circumstances surrounding individual conflicts, though, can be confusing. Readers can better understand these circumstances by studying specific conflicts. The authors in the following chapter analyze several examples and offer both justifications and condemnations of current ethnic violence.

Ethnic Warfare in the Former Yugoslavia Protects Serbs

by Momcilo Selic

About the author: *Momcilo Selic is a writer and journalist in Belgrade, Serbia. Selic was a war reporter in Bosnia in 1992 and volunteered in the Serb military in 1993. He was the managing editor of* Chronicles *magazine from 1987 to 1989.*

In the twilight, the machine gunner holds aloft the disassembled barrel of his weapon, his hands oily and stained, and grins at me. White-toothed, red-haired he wears his beret like a bonnet. Cocky, not too large, he laughs, then swears a heavy, loaded Serbian curse, unsparing of the Croats.

The machine gunner is a Kraina Serb: he and I are both part of a military company whose task is to defend the Serbs, and, if need be, to hurt the Croats. Both of us are preparing for a night assault on a Croat-occupied Serb village, cleaning our weapons and listening to the sergeant. The sergeant is a six-footer, dark and lanky, with the high cheekbones of an ancient Avar. He also is a Kraina native, a volunteer who has come from Serbia to defend his father's hamlet.

Croat Atrocities

In a raspy voice, the sergeant tells us of the Croat deserters he has seen sunk in concrete up to their thighs, during the 1991 war, above Dubrovnik. "They left the poor bastards," the sergeant says, "so they could perform their bodily functions, and they fed them, until we started shelling their positions. The first to die were the built-in men, screaming for the rest of them to think about God." "The hill," says the sergeant, "is mined, by them as well as us. Remember: short bursts, grenades, watch out for the trip-wires!"

The machine gunner—a living, breathing Rob Roy, of these mellower Highlands—does not hate the Croats. His family has not been touched by the Serbo-

From Momcilo Selic, "Letter from Serbia: Notes from the Front, Part 1," *Chronicles: A Magazine of American Culture*, vol. 17, no. 6, June 1993. Reprinted with permission.

Croat war, and all his relatives are present and accounted for. But he has lost friends to the Croats: some to bullets, and some to the knife, fire, and the club. The 20-odd Serb victims of the Mali Alan ambush of January 1993, for instance, were all dismembered by the Croat soldiers, some while they were still alive.

> *"[The machine gunner] has lost friends to the Croats: some to bullets, and some to the knife, fire, and the club."*

The cockade the machine gunner wears on his camouflage beret is the silver, double-headed Serbian eagle, a legacy of Byzantine times. The Croats' memories are as long as the Serbs'—to them, the Latin pillage of Constantinople was not so great an evil as the persistence of Byzantines and Serbs who remained orthodox. Though originally welcomed to Jesus by Greek emissaries, Croats have become Roman Catholics, while the machine gunner, the sergeant, and I still cling to the religion of our ancestors.

Shunned Pariahs

In Kraina, the conflict between the two Slavic peoples has entered a new stage: in Serbian, "Kraina" means "frontier," much like the American frontier of the West, or the "Ukraine" of the Rus—a region of border wars, skirmishes, over-the-line feuds and grudges, bloody all. The Croats, despite a United Nations ban on the importation of arms, have acquired German Leopard tanks and some former East German heavy weaponry; they wear American, NATO [North Atlantic Treaty Organization], or German uniforms and equipment, eat NATO rations, and use Western standard military small arms. Gone are the days of the Croat armed rebellion against the respected Socialist Federal Republic of Yugoslavia: today, it is Croatia that is a recognized state, a member of the U.N., while what is left of Yugoslavia, the Republic of Serb Kraina, and the Serb Republic of Bosnia are international pariahs, shunned by the "international community." How has all this come about?

To my red-haired, red-bearded, blue-eyed companion with his brand new Yugoslav Army PKT machine gun, it makes no difference whether foreigners recognize Serbia, the Kraina, or Serb Bosnia. He is a simple peasant soldier, like his forefathers. Holding his weapon, in the dusk before a battle, he feels himself fulfilled. Once the military frontier of Venice against the Ottoman Turks, Kraina has for centuries been the home of a Serb yeomanry whose status is not unlike that of the Russian Cossacks. Farmer-soldiers, the machine gunner's ancestors defended the West, Christendom, and the Serbs—in their mind, always inseparable—from the East, Islam, Asia, and the myriad of evils and ills as old as the first wars between the Europeans and the Turkic steppe-raiders or the desert marauders of the Near and Middle East. Kraina Serbs—a mixture of Slavs and the native Balkan Celts and Illyrians—lived in a changeless and satisfying land, tending to tasks as immutable as their vine-covered landscape.

Along crystal-clear but turbulent rivers, all emptying into the Adriatic Sea, they—Serbian Orthodox in religion—rejoiced in being what God created them: a free people on free territory, recognized as such first by Venice, then by the Kingdom of Hungary and the Empire of Austria.

That night, we did not attack our objective. Someone—a politician, or a military bigshot thinking like a politician—had decided that it was prudent not to provoke an additional outcry against Serb "aggression." The Croats, in our village, could spend that night in peace—thanks to the Kingdom of Yugoslavia, and the Communist Republic of Yugoslavia.

A History of the Region

In 1918, the victorious Serbian Army, on the winning side of World War I, entered the Austro-Hungarian province of Croatia to preserve civil peace. Western allies and the spearhead that had broken through the Salonika front defeated the Bulgarians, bringing about the capitulation of Austria-Hungary and ultimately the fall of Germany. The Serbs of Serbia were called in by the desperate Croatian Parliament to prevent a communist revolution-in-progress. The Croatian invitation was somewhat reluctant: last among all the Austrian Slavic subjects to declare independence (following the Austrian military debacle), the Croats were faced by an angry Entente, determined to treat them as a defeated nation. . . .

Through the creation of Yugoslavia, Kraina—ethnically Croatian from the 7th to the 16th century, but entirely Serb after the 16th-century Croat exodus under the Turkish onslaught—was given to Croatia, despite the record of the past four centuries and the fact that it was the *invited* Serbs who had defended it. In 1939, under Croat pressure, the government of the Kingdom of Yugoslavia incorporated Kraina into the Province of Croatia, which was given the borders of an imaginary Croatia that had never existed, in an effort to thwart exactly what came about two years later, in World War II. (It must be remembered that Croatia lost its independence in the 12th century, to the Hungarians, and never regained it, until today.) In 1941 the whole Croat nation, led by all its political factions except the communists, lined itself solidly with the Axis and fought, with commendable tenacity, together with Mussolini and Hitler against the Free World.

This may help to explain the present German, Austrian, and Italian support for Croatia, so mistakenly glorified by the Western media as a bastion of democracy and liberty in the Balkans. As in 1941-1945, today over 300,000 Croatian Serbs are refugees in Serbia, after being declared a non-nation by the 1991 Croatian constitution and after seeing hundreds of their fellow Serbs slaughtered by the sons and the grandsons of the fascist Croatian Ustashi in the first ethnic cleansing of the last 50 years, a fact rarely noticed by the Western press.

> *"The Croats, in our village, could spend that night in peace—thanks to the Kingdom of Yugoslavia."*

96

It was the Croat police's military attack upon the Serb village of Borovo Selo, near Vukovar, that in May 1991 started the Serbo-Croatian War. What the Serbs had declined to do, in the case of the 1991 Slovene armed uprising against the Socialist Federal Republic of Yugoslavia, the Croats did without compunction, shooting at their former friends and neighbors. . . .

> *"What the Serbs had declined to do . . . the Croats did without compunction, shooting at their former friends."*

During my 1993 stay in Kraina— as a volunteer—and in 1992 in Bosnia, as a war reporter, I have heard of Serbs killing Muslims, but not Croats. It should be remembered, however, that even in this war, it was the Muslims who first shot at a Serb wedding party in Sarajevo, in the summer of 1992, murdering the father of the groom. This triggered the Bosnian carnage. It was Saban Muratovic, at Visegrad in Bosnia, who over the Yugoslav airwaves threatened to blow up the Visegrad dam and obliterate everything and everybody down the Drina and the Sava river valleys. It was Alija Izetbegovic, the Muslim President of Bosnia and Herzegovina, who over those same airwaves publicly admonished the frantic Muratovic not to proceed with his plan. This was all before any Serb retaliatory actions, at the very outset of the 1992 Bosnian explosion. Personally, in Belgrade, I have talked to a father whose son—a Serb volunteer on the Croatian front— was butchered like a hog at the beginning of the Serbo-Croatian War, in 1991, and then portrayed first on Croatian TV and later on German TV as a *Croat* victim of the satanic Serbs!

It was Alija Izetbegovic who in the 1970's, in his *Islamic Declaration*, called on Muslims to take over power in Bosnia once their number surpassed 51 percent of the population. According to Izetbegovic's book, it is also the Bosnian Muslims' obligation to institute the rule of Shari'ah, or Islamic Law, in Bosnia and to turn it, perhaps, into something like the United Arab Emirates, where it is a capital crime to convert a Muslim. Nobody in the West paid any attention to Izetbegovic then, except for Amnesty International, which defended him as a prisoner of conscience.

Understanding the Past

Croatia, on the other hand, is governed by one of Josip Broz Tito's communist generals, Franjo Tudjman, who publicly said in 1991 that he was glad he was "neither Serb, nor Jewish." In his book *Historic Dead Ends*, published much after Izetbegovic's, Tudjman belittled the number of Serbs killed in World War II, claiming only 30,000 Serbs [instead of more than 600,000] died in the Jasenovac [death] camp, "mostly anti-fascist Croats" at that. To the chagrin of many Jewish groups and lobbies, Tudjman also denies the existence of Nazi extermination camps and has allowed World War II war criminals to return to Croatia, where many of them have been publicly honored for their "contributions to the Motherland."

War in former Yugoslavia *cannot* be regarded piecemeal: what happens in Kraina is an outcome of what goes on in Bosnia, and both depend on what has happened, and is still happening, in Croatia. Nothing in former Yugoslavia can be understood without a knowledge of the past, which for most former Yugoslavs is still the living present.

Had there been no Ottoman invasion of the Balkans, in all probability Balkan history would have been as uneventful as Dutch or Danish history. But the 1389 Kosovo defeat pushed the Serbs northward into what was Hungary and Croatia, while the 1526 Hungarian defeat at Mohács emptied Croatia of most of its Croat population, which escaped (sometimes) as far north as Austria. In the 17th century, the Albanians came, as Turkish troops, into the Serbian heartland of Kosovo. A parallel is often drawn between the Kosovo and Kraina cases, but there is a crucial difference: Serbs came into a largely vacated Kraina, invited there by its Hungarian, then Venetian, masters, to defend the region from the conquering Ottomans, while the Albanians descended upon Kosovo *as part of an Asiatic occupying force* and displaced—often brutally—a numerous and established Serbian population.

> **"War in former Yugoslavia cannot *be regarded piecemeal."***

But history happened, and Serbs, Croats, and Albanians became inextricably mixed. The best solution would have been a Yugoslavia, provided there was a consensus on its institution among the constituent nations. Unfortunately, there never was a consensus: Serbs wanted a Yugoslavia, as did the Slovenes and the Croats initially (so long as they could dominate it), whereas the Muslims and the Albanians had no use for a plan that abrogated their overlord status, derived from their privileged position as Muslims within the Turkish Empire.

Treatment of Prisoners

During the course of a February 1993 night, as I stood watch over our position above the Croatian coastal town of Skradin (a town with many Serb monuments as well, including a 14th-century church) and wondered when the real shooting would start, history, ignored by the foreign meddlers in the Yugoslav mess, marked the sky: red tracers from 20-m.m. guns streaked between our position and the Croats', sometimes crisscrossing each other like a giant game of tic-tac-toe.

In 1992, in Serb Cajnice, close to the besieged Muslim town of Gorazde, I lived on military Spam and rationed bread; that was the time when all the world was talking of Serb "concentration camps" where Muslims, as the claim went, were "intentionally starved." On the Bosnian-Serb-Romanian Mountain, that same summer, food was even scarcer than in Cajnice: homemade cheese and army bread were all we ate there (not bad fare, but monotonous); there was no U.N.

"humanitarian aid" for the women and children of the high plateau above the Zepa region, where convoy after convoy of white U.N. trucks traveled. After the trucks, the Muslims of Zepa usually attacked our positions, sneaking by our patrols and guards at night and murdering the very same young and old Serbs, too weak for the rifle, who had smiled at us, confident that we would defend them.

Still, Muslim prisoners of war in the Serb camps were fed the same rations as our troops—Spam they often would not eat, nor anything derived of pork, but we had nothing else to offer them, or ourselves. Not far from us, in Sarajevo, in over a dozen unregistered camps, our imprisoned noncombatants went hungry, week after week, month after month; in the Muslim Croat Bradina camp, near Konjic in Herzegovina, Serb women and children were kept in a railway tunnel and, from time to time, either tortured, raped, or murdered, according to their captors' whim. Mostar, the capital of Herzegovina, which had a prewar population of over 30,000 Serbs, today has only 400 left: taken out night after night, one by one, they disappeared, into that same, Croat darkness.

Propaganda Efforts

At Elie Wiesel's insistence, the Serb camp at Manjaca was emptied at the end of 1992, but many of its Muslims came back to Bosnia several weeks later as armed soldiers of Islam, while the Croats and the Muslims still maintain their clandestine camps, where Elie Wiesel's envoy, journalist Daniel Schieffer, was never allowed to visit. A year before the hysteria about "raped Muslim women" hit the Western media, reports of hundreds of genuine, documented cases of punitive, cold-blooded rapes of Serb women and girls in Croatia were presented to the Yugoslav public, but none of the Serbian-speaking foreign journalists in Belgrade considered them worthy of mention. As for the Serbs' own propaganda effort, their attitude may best be summed up by the reluctance of Herzegovinian Serb peasants to have the media present at the exhumation of the thousands of Serb noncombatants murdered by the Croat Ustashi in World War II. Asked what they had against the airing of these events (the communist government had previously filled in many of the execution pits with concrete, to cement its concept of "Brotherhood and Unity"), the peasants replied that "Serbs do not exploit their dead."

Bosnian Muslims Have the Right to Use Violence

by Muhamed Sacirbey

About the author: *Muhamed Sacirbey is the United Nations ambassador from the Republic of Bosnia and Herzegovina.*

Editor's note: The following speech calls for a United Nations resolution to end an arms embargo against Bosnia-Herzegovina. After the speech, the U.N. Security Council voted against the proposed resolution.

Two questions and two questions only are relevant in evaluating the merit of this draft resolution:

First, has the Security Council compelled the necessary measures to stop the aggression and genocide directed at the Republic and citizens of Bosnia and Herzegovina; and second, if not, what are the new and necessary measures that should be undertaken to stop this never-ending aggression and mayhem, particularly should the arms embargo on the Republic of Bosnia and Herzegovina be declared *de jure* [by law] invalid in accordance with the U.N. charter's guarantee of the right of self-defense.

Some may attempt to confuse the matter by redefining the issues in order to excuse failure, justify inaction and mask a lack of real commitment to deal decisively with the problem.

Consider the Results

Integrity necessitates that we appraise the Council's measures primarily on the basis of results and not grandiose statements made within this chamber.

Fifteen months after the Serbian aggression was initiated; eleven months after we all first saw television pictures of Bosnian victims in Serbian concentration camps; ten months after the heralded London Conference and its many promises; eight months after Lord David Owen and Mr. Cyrus Vance issued their first set of constitutional principles for Bosnia and Herzegovina; three

Muhamed Sacirbey, a speech delivered to the United Nations Security Council, June 29, 1993.

months after we signed the Vance/Owen plan; and after the visits of countless well-meaning or self-serving high-profile individuals, mediators and delegations to Bosnia and Herzegovina, the agony continues and there is no light at the end of the tunnel.

The Illusion of Progress

Only, more conferences and meetings are proposed. New mediators are appointed while others are retired. Ever more diluted sets of principles supposedly insuring Bosnia's sovereignty, territorial integrity and justice are once again restated. More negotiations, without the means or the will to implement them, are endlessly pursued. More delegations come to Bosnia. More Bosnians die in Bosnia because a drunken Serbian soldier satisfies his perversity by indiscriminately firing his artillery piece into a crowd of defiant civilians. Indefinite negotiations, conferences and so-called initiatives do not necessarily advance the cause of peace. But it is clear that some would use the perception of motion to create the illusion of progress.

We, the Bosnians, are dead tired of running on this treadmill of cynicism that exhausts us with bitterness, hopelessness and helplessness while serving the public relations interests of certain political leaders. Clearly,

> *"We, the Bosnians, are dead tired of running on this treadmill of cynicism that exhausts us with bitterness."*

the necessary measures have not been taken to bring peace, and the Bosnians subsequently find themselves no further along the road to peace but utterly drained by the journey.

So we come to the second question: What are the new and necessary measures that should be undertaken to bring peace? Bosnia consists of hundreds of cities and towns and of thousands of villages. Who will defend most of our citizens who happen to live in these non-safe areas when it seems that even the designated safe areas are not safe? Among the member states here today are some who strongly advocated the establishment of safe areas in six Bosnian cities as delineated in Resolution 824, and later committed themselves in Resolution 836, and I quote . . . "to insure full respect for the safe areas referred to in Resolution 824" and reaffirmed in that Resolution the ". . . unacceptability of the acquisition of territory by the use of force and the need to restore the full sovereignty, territorial integrity and political independence of the Republic of Bosnia and Herzegovina."

Silence on Bosnia

Let me inquire of those who were so zealous for the adoption of these measures, the reasons for their deafening silence today. Why was it not enough for you to respond when shells rained upon the safe area of Gorazde? Was it not a clearly observed violation of Sarajevo's safe area status when the Serbians lobbed several shells into a playground killing and maiming tens of children? When will you be prepared to respond if the Secretary General's implementation report on 836 apparently relies upon the conduct of those who still ignore the basic norms of civilized behavior? How can you have an effective deterrent force if you, up to now, lack the will and commitment to confront aggression?

> *"How long can those of us living in the non-safe areas survive . . . unless you allow us the means of self-defense?"*

But the most critical question is— For how long do you expect those of us living in disease-plagued Srebrenica, and the other five so-called safe areas, to suffer the indignity, decay and uncertainty of these new holding pens? How long will you have a commitment to stay? Finally, for how long can those of us living in the non-safe areas survive in our home unless you allow us the means of self-defense? Even assuming effective implementation and enforcement, the "safe areas" Resolution at best can only benefit some of our people temporarily and none of our people permanently.

The latest supposed option to promote peace in Bosnia and Herzegovina comes directly from the unfortunate [Croatian] President Franjo Tudjman and [Serbia's] Slobodan Milosevic, the man who initiated aggression and who has been identified as a war criminal by several NGOs [nongovernmental organizations] and the U.S. State Department. Inconceivably, immediately after declaring his own plan (Vance/Owen) dead, Dr. David Owen embraced Milosevic's plan. A novel approach in healing as well as diplomacy. Adopt the peace plan of the war-maker, subject the victim to the criminals' goodwill and save a pluralistic nation by partitioning it. If Bosnia and Herzegovina wanted to commit suicide, we do not need the assistance of the Dr. Jack Kevorkian of mediation and diplomacy.

Even more incredibly, after having committed themselves and us to the Vance/Owen plan, certain members of the European Community adopted Dr. Owen's view because they were unwilling to confront the Serbians to pressure for adoption and implementation of their initial peace plan of choice.

Dismantling Bosnia

Even though this so-called plan calls for ethnic division, we are assured that this is not a partition plan. Mr. Milosevic's vision clearly portends partition and the eventual disintegration of Bosnia and Herzegovina. I suggest recent history has taught us that it is Mr. Milosevic's view that has the greater commitment behind it. Nonetheless, we are told that even if the new proposals fall far short of stated goals, we must accept the diminished results. We are now being urged to accept the new realities.

Those who in fact have actively endeavored to limit our options now tell us that we have no other options. To his Excellency, the Representative of France, could the French people have been convinced that Vichy France was an acceptable alternative to the majesty of a free and sovereign France?

Is it historically justified to ethnically partition a pluralistic, multi-religious society that already over 500 years ago was a safe haven of tolerance and multiculturalism when Jewish refugees, escaping the bigotry of Western Europe and Spain, came to Bosnia?

To his Excellency, the Representative of the Russian Federation, did the defenders of Stalingrad persevere to allow 50 years later in Europe the fascist siege of Sarajevo?

To his Excellency, the Representative of the United Kingdom and Northern Ireland, Sir David Hannay, when Sir Winston Churchill was being persuaded that he had no option but to capitulate to Hitler, he offered "give us the tools and we will finish the job." If this response is worthy of the British people, then I believe that the British people would agree it is also worthy of the Bosnians.

The Republic of Bosnia and Herzegovina has waited for the most empowered members of the Security Council to fulfill their commitment to confront the Serbians in the peacemaking effort. Only [their] having failed their commitment have we now sought to reassert our right to obtain the means of self-defense. It is not enough to feed us at a subsistence level while we continue to be indiscriminately murdered. It is unethical to tell a hungry people that they must sacrifice self-defense in order to be fed. But, if a choice is to be made between humanitarian relief and self-defense, we have unequivocally told you which option we choose. To ignore the Bosnian people's choice on this matter goes beyond arrogance and seeks to mask the failure to honor responsibility.

> *"The Bosnians must be provided with the leverage . . . to confront the undiminished aggression."*

A Mockery of the United Nations

The permanent members of the Security Council claim an elevated status on the basis of their special commitment to the membership of the United Nations to take the necessary measures to maintain international peace and security. By their permanent membership to this body, and veto power, they are in a position to dictate action or inaction. In the case of the Republic of Bosnia and Herzegovina, the permanent members have failed in their special responsibility, but some of them continue to insist on dictating life and death for Bosnia in a way that makes a mockery not only of the U.N. charter, but of commitments [to protect Bosnian safe areas] made by this body a mere three and a half weeks ago.

The Republic of Bosnia and Herzegovina claims no special status within the family of nations, but we do not agree to be reduced to a lower status so that certain permanent members of the Security Council can carry forward with the illusion of their elevated responsibility. Neither do we appreciate being treated

103

with disdain because we dare to challenge certain permanent members on their unique responsibility and status.

We are persuaded that we should be grateful for the selective humanitarian aid that Bosnia receives, but we understand that this aid is a meager substitute for resolute action. We also understand that while committed and courageous individuals endeavor to save Bosnian lives on the ground, the intended goal is in fact protecting the public image of compromised leaders.

Whether peace is to come to Bosnia and Herzegovina through confrontation or through negotiations with the aggressor, there is only one choice with respect to this Resolution; the Bosnians must be provided with the leverage to undertake fair and promising negotiations or, in the alternative, to confront the undiminished aggression. So far Bosnia had not received this assistance from the most prominent members of this Council. You have no more authority to demand any further concessions from us, but only to free us of the shackles that diminish our self-defense and our capacity to pursue negotiations.

Violence Against Israel Is Justified to Free Palestine

by Ibrahim Ghawshah, interviewed by KEYHAN

About the author: *Ibrahim Ghawshah is a spokesman for Hamas, a militant Palestinian resistance organization that seeks a free Palestine. He was interviewed by a correspondent for KEYHAN, one of the official daily newspapers of the government of Iran.*

KEYHAN: You are the spokesman of a movement that is considered to be an offshoot of the international Muslim Brotherhood organization. How do you assess the current Islamic movement in the aftermath of [the Persian Gulf War]? What changes and divisions have taken place inside this movement?

Ibrahim Ghawshah: Naturally, I am going to speak from the vantage point of Hamas [Islamic Resistance Movement], which is considered part of the movement of the Islamic world and has a unified and cohesive policy. I agree with you that trivial differences exist in the political programs of most of the Islamic movements, which are constantly fluctuating and moving from one country to another. However, as regards the basic and general issues, there is no difference of opinion at all.

Finding an Islamic Solution

In general, the Islamic movement declared the following as its definite stance: The condemnation of the occupation of Kuwait by Iraq and the condemnation of the shaykhdoms' invitation to the American forces and their continued presence in the region. We believe that a solution to this crisis should be found within the framework of the Islamic countries.

This is why the Islamic movement began its activities in mid-September 1990 and convened meetings with the officials of Saudi Arabia, Iraq, and the Islamic Republic of Iran. As a follow up to these efforts, delegations of various Islamic liberation movements visited Iran, Iraq, Syria, Yemen, and Egypt.

Unfortunately, the Egyptians did not allow us to meet with the leaders of that

Excerpted from an interview of Ibrahim Ghawshah by KEYHAN that appeared in the November 27, 1992, issue of the *Foreign Broadcast Information Service Daily Report*. Reprinted with permission.

country and Saudi officials did not allow the delegation to visit Saudi Arabia to carry out our obligations to prevent bloodshed. The Islamic movement warned all parties that international Zionism was the only group that stood to benefit from the crisis, and that American and Western forces are the instruments of Zionism.

KEYHAN: Despite the fact that a peace accord has been reached between the Hamas and the Fatah movements, once again the Palestinian scene is the venue of a bloody war between Palestinian factions. Who is instigating these conflicts? Who stands to gain from them?

Ghawshah: If we accept that there is a power that aims to pit Muslim groups against one another so that their blood may be shed, the name of "international Zionism" should be mentioned. The Gulf crisis, all the crises of the Islamic world, and the differences between the Palestinian branches are all planned and implemented by Zionist agents.

Regarding the clashes: Many people were hoping that there would be [Palestinian] elections for autonomy. Peace and calm were needed for the elections to be carried out, as elections could not be held in conditions of intifadah [civil uprising]. During his address in Madrid in 1991, Yitzhak Rabin called for the intifadah to be suspended as a precondition. We are well aware that the U.S.-Zionist plan will never result in autonomy if the intifadah continues. Therefore, all the clashes were aimed at temporarily halting the intifadah and were part of the enemy's plan to keep these groups so involved in internecine strife that they would not utilize their resources against the Zionist enemy.

> *"Hamas is . . . adamant that the intifadah should not be suspended."*

These clashes were instigated so that Palestinian aspirations and hopes would become undermined and hollow and thus the Palestinians would become so indifferent that they would accept whatever plan or proposal [was] placed before them.

All these plots and plans were aimed at suspending the intifadah and the implementation of the autonomy plan. I wish to stress that the Islamic resistance by Hamas, as the largest Islamic movement in Palestine, will continue with all its might. Hamas is, therefore, adamant that the intifadah should not be suspended.

The Zionist Plot

KEYHAN: You said that the intifadah cannot fight international Zionism by itself, that it needs the assistance of the Arab and Muslim nations. We see that most of the Arab and Islamic countries are seeking to improve their relations with the Zionist enemy. How, then, can the Arab and Muslim people be hopeful and how can the intifadah continue along its course in the hope of victory? Does the Islamic movement have a program to initiate an upheaval?

Ghawshah: This question has many aspects and, God willing, I will try and answer this question as fully as possible.

First, I agree with you that there is a dangerous plot under way that threatens the entire region; that is, the plot to have the Arab, Islamic fold accept the Zionists. If, God forbid, this materializes and Arab-Israeli relations improve, as we mentioned earlier, it would engulf all aspects including the political, cultural and social spheres. In this way Israel would be able to attain its strategic objectives of a Greater Israel without fighting.

> *"The Zionist regime will attack Iran, Pakistan, and all Islamic countries."*

This is an even greater danger than a military one because the economic resources of the Zionists are extremely advanced scientifically and technologically. They have vast material and specialized resources. God forbid, if by means of signing peace accords the Arabs and Israelis reach a compromise and they implement their plan for autonomy, many Arab workers will be absorbed into the Israeli factories. Arab businesses will collapse because they will not be able to compete with the Israelis' modern industries.

Thus, Israel will dominate the region like Japan dominates southeast Asia and the Arabs will all become employees of the Jews.

Zionist Destruction

Second, when the Zionist regime plans its strategies, it does not take into account merely the resources and capabilities of the Palestinian nation and Arab peoples. It plans to destroy all the resources and powers of the Muslim nations. The Zionist regime will attack Iran, Pakistan, and all Islamic countries. It is not too farfetched to say that it will harm the resources of these countries to disrupt their industry and technology. The rulers of Islamic countries should be warned of the discord-generating plans of the Zionist enemy.

The best example of this is the attack by the Zionist regime on the Iraqi nuclear plant in the beginning of the eighties. Now the despots of Jerusalem have become even more advanced and strong as regards missiles and enjoy unlimited U.S. support. The United States announced a massive grant worth $10 billion to Israel and the acceptance of hundreds of thousands of [Russian immigrant] Jews. It is highly probable that in the future, the Zionists may also receive loans from European countries, including Germany.

What is the objective of this assistance? The objective is the economic and social development of the Zionist regime so that it can become predominant in the region.

Strengthening Muslim Power

KEYHAN: What is the objective of your visit to the Islamic Republic of Iran?

Ghawshah: To strengthen relations with the Islamic Republic of Iran, the first Islamic government established in the twentieth century. We believe that whenever an Islamic government is established in the region, the path for the liberation of Jerusalem becomes smooth. We hope that before the end of the twentieth century, we will have another Islamic government established because it would boost the power and capability of the Muslims.

KEYHAN: It appears that this is the first independent visit by Hamas leaders to the Islamic Republic of Iran. Could you tell us how successful it has been?

Ghawshah: This is the second visit by a Hamas delegation to Iran. We were invited by the Islamic Republic of Iran's Foreign Ministry, and we have been welcomed. During our talks we have exchanged views on the Palestinian question, on which there is complete unanimity of views. We visited Iran to follow up earlier meetings and to find more support for the Palestinian intifadah.

KEYHAN: Yasir 'Arafat said that Saddam Hussein has deceived the Palestinians by hurling a few missiles toward Israel. As a Palestinian, what is your assessment of 'Arafat's statement after years of having cordial relations with Saddam?

Ghawshah: I think this question should be put to the relevant persons. However, from the perspective of the Hamas, which moves in line with the general interests of the Muslims and does not concern itself with individuals, I can only say: The Hamas movement declared its clear stance of being part of the world Islamic movement during the war between Iraq and the United States. Even though we do not agree with the despotic regime in Iraq, we supported the people of that country against the U.S. and West's attacks against Iraq.

Supporting Attacks on Israel

On principle we oppose all dictatorial regimes that suppress the freedom of the people and do not permit them to air their opinions. This is our general view. We would have liked for the Iraqi military power, comprised of some 60 military battalions, to have helped liberate Palestine rather than attacking a neighboring Muslim country.

However, we support all actions that work against the Zionist regime and try to deal a blow to it. Our stance was, therefore, very clear on the missiles that fell on the Zionist enemy. We would have wanted this to have continued. We wanted the Iraqi ground forces and other Arab countries to join the fray as well because the enemy was the Zionist enemy. If they had done so, peace, tranquillity, security, and stability would have reigned in the region.

True peace can only be attained by returning the Palestinians to their homeland and returning the Zionist aggressors to the countries from

"We would have liked for the Iraqi military power . . . to have helped liberate Palestine."

where they have come. It is illogical for a nation to say that it has a 4,000-year link to a land but that the nation that was driven out only 40 years ago has no right to return, especially considering that the land is its homeland. Should the world and United Nations forget these people?

KEYHAN: The [post-Gulf War] Middle East peace talks have been encountering consecutive stalemates. Will the next session suffer the same fate or will the negotiators attain tangible results?

Ghawshah: Right from the outset, it was clear that there would be an impasse. Those who claim that the talks got bogged down in Madrid are lying. The Arab and Palestinian delegations went to Madrid through a closed tunnel because the conference agenda did not take into account any of the Arab interests. Most of the Arabs who went to Madrid did not have any other plan in hand (meaning a military proposal in the event of opposition to the peace conference). The balance of power favors the Zionists.

> *"The Zionists would not be willing to part with even an inch of Palestinian land."*

The Palestinian delegation participated at the lowest level (the plan for autonomy). It tried to convince the Palestinian public that by participating in the talks it would have the power to maneuver and to gain the upper hand with its Zionist rivals. Thus, it would be able to extort concessions, which it could not attain by means of holy war or struggle.

We Islamists warned the Palestinian delegation that the Zionists would not be willing to part with even an inch of Palestinian land. The Palestinian delegates accuse the Islamists of lacking political acumen, and of being ignorant of the culture of politics. In any case, the Arab side participating in the talks has admitted that no progress has been made in the talks.

Golan Heights Occupation

KEYHAN: There are rumors that Syria will reach an agreement with Israel. Is this true? How true is this rumor?

Ghawshah: This is not true. First, the Zionists do not seem willing to withdraw entirely from the Golan Heights.

Second, the Syrians insist on a complete Israeli withdrawal from the Golan Heights, the West Bank, and the Gaza Strip.

Third: There is a lot of anxiety in Israeli society regarding the Golan Heights because Israel officially announced their annexation in 1981. Nearly half of the residents are Israeli, who are not prepared to leave.

On the other hand, in view of the strategy of Rabin, who is a militarist, it cannot be foreseen that he will agree to a complete withdrawal. This would be tantamount to permitting the Syrian forces to dominate the northern areas of occupied Palestine and this is the most densely populated area of occupied Palestine.

These reasons indicate that there will be no progress [soon]. We expect certain measures and actions to be taken to divert the public so that the Palestinian nation will not be able to influence the delegations [in] Washington for talks.

KEYHAN: In the event of a peace accord between the PLO [Palestine Liberation Organization] and the Zionist enemy, what will be the position of the Hamas? Will the operations for the holy war continue?

Ghawshah: First of all . . . the Hamas movement and other Islamic and national movements will resist this plot in all its stages and will strive to nip it in the bud. If we cannot do so, we will call on the people to boycott the autonomy elections so that the flimsy bubble-like position of those supporting autonomy will become obvious to the world. If the United States and Zionism succeed, with the help of their lackeys (the Madrid team), in implementing this autonomy plan, the Islamic movement will combat it with all its resources and experience.

I advise them to think carefully and be vigilant; the Islamic movement will not lay down its arms. There are no such terms as compromise and surrender in the Islamic cultural lexicon. The prophet of Islam (peace be upon him) has taught us the meaning of jihad and fortitude. Therefore the obsequious groups should comprehend and know that the continuation of this trend will extract a massive price. Some of them have already realized this and have declared their concurrence with the holding of a referendum within and outside the occupied territories.

Violence by the Irish Republican Army Is Justified

by Anonymous, interviewed by Morgan Strong

About the authors: *The subject of the following interview is an anonymous "provo," or fighter, in the Irish Republican Army (IRA). He was interviewed by Morgan Strong for* Playboy, *a monthly men's magazine. Strong is a contributing editor to* Playboy *and a television network news consultant.*

PLAYBOY: You are a provo, an active soldier of the I.R.A. What made you join the I.R.A. in the first place?

I.R.A. PROVO: I've been involved in the struggle from a very early age, when I was twelve or thirteen. I won't be so naïve as to say I was politically aware at that age, but I did know exactly what I was doing. My involvement in the republican movement was sort of a gut reaction to what was happening around me. To a degree, it was doing what my friends were doing, joining the youth movement of the republicans.

PLAYBOY: It was a rebellion, then?

I.R.A. PROVO: It was a little bit of excitement, adventure. Youthful rebellion, I suppose, is against either the home or the school. Mine was against the state. Once I did get involved, I became more aware. I looked up to the older people in the I.R.A.

No Right of Occupation

PLAYBOY: Was it hero worship?

I.R.A. PROVO: Well, they would talk to me about politics I didn't understand fully. But I knew, in my heart, that what I was doing was right. What I saw in the streets—the British army and the police had no right to be here. They said they were here to protect us. But what I saw was that they were not here for us.

I had members of my own family end up in prison. I had an older brother who was constantly harassed by the British army. He received a number of heavy beatings in the barracks. He ended up being sentenced to a term in prison for being in the I.R.A. That made me want to join, made me want to resist British rule.

PLAYBOY: You knew you weren't joining the boy scouts; but did you know how harsh the I.R.A. life would turn out to be?

I.R.A PROVO: When I found myself in prison, I wasn't too pleased about it. I was just seventeen; it was something I had hoped never to experience. When I was in prison, I was with hundreds of people who were there for the same reason I was. I then began to develop politically.

PLAYBOY: Still, you were among some hard cases. Could you really develop freely?

I.R.A. PROVO: I spent, really, most of my adult life in prison. By the time I was released, I was convinced that what I was doing was right. I had no regrets then and I have none now. I don't regret going to prison. In fact, in some ways, I'm glad I was in prison. Prison, from my experience, brings out the best in people. Of course, it also brings out the worst.

Thoughts About Killing

PLAYBOY: How does it make you feel today to be taking someone's life, whether that of a British soldier or of a Protestant who opposes the I.R.A.?

I.R.A. PROVO: I have now been involved for a number of years with the I.R.A., involved operationally. I've been trained in the use of weapons and explosives—mortars used in Belfast within the past couple of days. I've been in sniper attacks that have taken on British patrols and in operations with the use of booby-trap mines. I've been in operations involving the assassination of police, the U.D.A. [Ulster Defense Association] and members of the British army in and out of uniform.

I mean, I've had exposure to *all* the urban operations in which the I.R.A. engages in an urban environment. And I can say, for myself and for others involved in operations that resulted in the death of enemy, we have never felt good about it. We know it's something we have to do. Soldiers have to take life—usually shooting someone three hundred yards away. But here it's close-up. Nobody feels joy in taking life. It's something that we have to live with.

PLAYBOY: What about the civilians who suffer?

I.R.A. PROVO: I'm not immune to the suffering we've caused. As members of the republican movement, we're all aware that our actions have led to death on the enemy side. But

> *"By the time I was released [from prison], I was convinced that what I was doing was right."*

I've seen death on my side. I've seen the wives and mothers and sons and daughters and brothers of comrades on my side who have given their lives. It's something I have to live with.

PLAYBOY: Let's get to the I.R.A. itself: There are stories that it's funded by extortion, racketeering, gunrunning and drug sales. What do you say?

I.R.A. PROVO: [*Heatedly*] Let's look at my personal situation. I was arrested not long after I left high school. I haven't worked since; I have no trade or qualifications. I have no income, but—

> *"They said they were going to kill me, that they were going to put one in the back of my head."*

PLAYBOY: Can't you collect unemployment from the government?

I.R.A. PROVO: Yes, but to collect, I would have to go at the same time every week to sign for the check. That ties me down to where my movements can be observed. They will know where I'll be on a specific date at a specific time. That, for an active volunteer, is not wise.

PLAYBOY: Then how do you live without an income?

I.R.A. PROVO: I rely on my family—my wife, parents, brothers and sisters. They are the people who feed and clothe me. I stay in different houses, rarely the same house two nights in a row. Sympathetic people provide me with a bed. And the I.R.A. gives me help. They're not going to let me starve or go without a decent pair of shoes. If I were a racketeer, I'd have a nice house, a car, nice clothes, instead of being constantly on the run.

The Underground Life

PLAYBOY: You've been on the run for a long time. What does it do to you not to have had any of the material pleasures in life?

I.R.A. PROVO: I have no desire for those things—the cars and all that. But I'd love to have a house to be with my wife and children, to have a job and earn a wage and provide for my family. There is *nothing* worse for me than to know that I can't help them. When I do see my children, it breaks my heart. I know I can't be with them for long. Christmas is approaching: I'd love to be with them for Christmas, watch them on Christmas morning when they get up to see what's under the Christmas tree. To be with them on their birthdays. To take my wife out for dinner, to spend some time with her. I can't do those things with my family. It places them under immense pressure. I think they suffer more than I do.

PLAYBOY: In what sense?

I.R.A. PROVO: I can get about these areas. I can avoid the police and the British army. There are plenty of people who will let me slip through their house, over their walls. But they *know* where my family is. I have a record and I'm targeted.

PLAYBOY: Targeted, literally?

I.R.A. PROVO: I was stopped recently by an armored car. I was surrounded by five of them. They had rifles and side arms and they slapped me around. Then they said they were going to kill me, that they were going to put one in the back

113

of my head. But that's a fact of life here; that can happen to me any time.

PLAYBOY: You say you were first arrested as a teenager and wound up spending seven years in prison. What was the charge?

I.R.A. PROVO: I was found in possession of explosives and arrested under the Emergency Provisions Act. I was caught red-handed, so they weren't interested in establishing guilt. They wanted to find out where I had gotten the explosives and what they were going to be used for.

PLAYBOY: Were you interrogated at length?

I.R.A. PROVO: No. If I had been arrested after placing the explosives, I would have had a rough time. They would have had to establish proof that I had placed them. As it was, there was no question.

PLAYBOY: Then getting caught red-handed was to your advantage?

I.R.A. PROVO: Yeah. I would have had a more physical sort of interrogation than I actually had. [*Smiles*] But the interrogation lasted for only three days. Then I was charged and sent to Crumlin Road prison. . . .

Family Support

PLAYBOY: During your long stay in prison, how did your family survive?

I.R.A. PROVO: In many ways, I was better off than they were. I knew that no matter how bad the day was, at the end of it, I'd have a meal and a bed. But my family had to provide for me. They were in court when I was there and they were constantly being harassed by the police and the army. My home was raided numerous times while I was in prison *because* I was in prison.

PLAYBOY: Why would they raid your home? They knew where you were.

I.R.A. PROVO: My family was targeted as one that had to be watched. But I was in prison with many people whose families didn't support what they were doing, but they stood by them and became targets for harassment because of that. It's one of the stupid things the British government does and can't see that it does. By themselves, they exposed the myth that they were the peace keepers. People saw for themselves that all they were interested in was putting people down, asserting their position in this country.

PLAYBOY: Have there been more recruits into the I.R.A. as a consequence?

> *"Every time I attend a funeral of one of my comrades who has been killed, it strengthens my resolve."*

I.R.A. PROVO: In many ways, there have been. Before I went to prison, when I heard someone else had been sent to prison, it strengthened my resolve. Every time I attend a funeral of one of my comrades who has been killed, it strengthens my resolve; I'm not going to let that person down! Seeing people sacrifice their lives for me and for our comrades and families—I wasn't going to forget that.

PLAYBOY: You described the I.R.A. and its goals as noble and sacrificing; many people see you as terrorists and criminals.

114

I.R.A. PROVO: Criminals! Criminals are in it for gain! What have I gained? How have we profited? Why would we experience the physical and mental torment we have for self-gain? I could have left the [five-year Long Kesh] prison protest at any time, said, "I've had enough." I would have been allowed to leave. There were some who reached the breaking point. That's understandable. I was just lucky to survive. The best any of us can hope for is torture and death. . . .

Questions of Terrorism

PLAYBOY: How do you feel when you hear yourself referred to as a terrorist?

I.R.A. PROVO: Terrorism—ah, well, was the bombing of German civilians during World War Two terrorism? When Margaret Thatcher and others talk about the I.R.A.'s killing men, women and children, do they forget about their own past? It's easy when you're in power to excuse this. In the Falklands, for instance, there are stories about the capture and torture of Argentinian soldiers by the British—British marines' cutting prisoners' throats! Is that acceptable just because it happened in an international conflict?

"The British government can say what it wants, what we are. . . . Terrorism is a convenient cloak."

PLAYBOY: No, but isn't that just rationalizing your own terrorism?

I.R.A. PROVO: No, it's a central question. If you take a situation such as the bombing of Libya, for example, in which men, women and children were killed, is that an acceptable act of war or is it terrorism? States kill in the most horrific fashion; it just depends on what side of the fence your definition of terrorism is. But we don't have the chance to present our argument because of the media ban against us. And it's not just we who are banned but members of Sinn Fein—a legal political party.

PLAYBOY: Do you argue that if you were allowed a legal forum, you'd be understood and the war might end?

I.R.A. PROVO: The British government can say what it wants, what we are—because our answer will not come across. Terrorism is a convenient cloak.

PLAYBOY: But couldn't politics be a cloak for you—if your real aim were to settle grudges? Or to seek some personal gain?

I.R.A. PROVO: If we're as bad as that, why do we have the support of the community? I and the people I work with could not survive *without the help and support of the people of the community!* For me to move and operate in these areas, I need people who allow me to come into their homes. And they do that at the risk of their own lives.

Would they do that if they were intimidated? If they thought I was in this for personal gain? They do it because they support what we're doing. I can't drive down the street in a car that's going to be used in an operation; I'll be picked up immediately. So civilians who will take that risk drive the cars. They'll drive our arms and explosives to a certain point, drop them off. Then we'll take them, move into position and engage an army patrol. Then we'll withdraw, hide our weapons, and people give us places to dump them.

PLAYBOY: We've heard that you even have your own MASH unit.

I.R.A. PROVO: Yes. If we're wounded, we can't go to hospital, because we'll be immediately arrested. We can treat minor wounds in a sort of mobile van. If we're badly wounded, it's up to the people "on the ground" to send us to hospital.

PLAYBOY: Does the I.R.A. ever discipline its members?

I.R.A. PROVO: The only time the I.R.A. will take action against its own members is when they transgress the rules, disobey orders or when they inform. It's a terrible step for the I.R.A. to decide to execute one of its own members. The I.R.A. has strict laws and a constitution. I know if I break one of those rules what the consequence is.

PLAYBOY: What is it?

I.R.A. PROVO: [*Smiles*] Execution. It's not a decision taken lightly. There is a whole process of investigation. The person accused has to have the allegations presented to him and he or she is given an opportunity to respond. You simply cannot accuse someone. You have to prove the charge, you have to provide evidence.

PLAYBOY: What's an example?

I.R.A. PROVO: Passing on information to British army intelligence. There is a rigid internal procedure, and the I.R.A. Council, which is the governing body, have the final say. And if they're not satisfied, they will refuse to proceed.

Protestant Atrocities

PLAYBOY: Interesting that you have all these rules and legal procedures, when it's such a brutal, chaotic war. Who is more brutal, the I.R.A. or its Protestant counterpart, the U.D.A.?

I.R.A. PROVO: When I was in prison, there were hundreds of U.D.A. members who were serving time for some of the most brutal murders ever committed. The U.D.A. and the Ulster Volunteer Forces were involved in butchering people. They tried to terrorize, instill fear in the nationalist population. They would kidnap people, take them somewhere, torture them. They would gouge out their eyes, cut their throats, cut off their genitals. Their victims were subject to the most horrific forms of murder. And they freely admitted to having committed them.

> *"[Protestant fighters] were involved in butchering people. They tried to terrorize, instill fear."*

PLAYBOY: But they were arrested by the British, weren't they?

I.R.A. PROVO: The only reason they're in prison is that the methods were so terrible, they were an embarrassment. But the leader, Danny Murphy, was released.

PLAYBOY: Murphy, that's an Irish name.

116

I.R.A. PROVO: Yes, he was born a Catholic but married a Protestant and be-came a member of a loyalist organization.

PLAYBOY: How could he have been released from prison after committing murder?

> *"Afterward, I think, I didn't want to [kill]—but it had to be done."*

I.R.A. PROVO: He served time for the *attempted* murder of two Catholic nurses. He was caught with the weapons used.

PLAYBOY: Nurses? Why try to kill two presumably innocent women?

I.R.A. PROVO: Because they were Catholic. He was released, and shortly thereafter, a man by the name of Joseph Donegan was taken from the Falls, in Belfast, and held for four days. He was brutally murdered, his throat was cut, all his teeth had been torn out, his face bashed beyond recognition, cigarette burns all over his body. Danny Murphy carried out that killing.

PLAYBOY: How do you know?

I.R.A. PROVO: We knew. He was then targeted by the I.R.A. and was actu-ally caught in the loyalist stronghold of Shankill. Now, Danny Murphy wasn't brutalized. He was shot dead. There's no nice way to kill a person, to take a life, whether it's done by a bomb or by a bullet or by clubbing someone to death or whatever. But the I.R.A. kept to its standards. There was no brutality. He was shot in the head. It was quick.

A Provo's Ordeal

PLAYBOY: Do you ever get a chance to ask yourself what you're doing as you go off on an "operation"?

I.R.A. PROVO: Well, if I stopped and thought during an operation, I might not go on. But first of all, I think of the danger to myself. I take the gun in my hand. There's a very good chance I'll get killed. If I'm killed, I know the conse-quences for my family: They'll have to live with it the rest of their lives. My children will be without a father. And the reverse is true: If I blow away a British soldier, the same applies to him. But, unfortunately, you can't think of it in those terms.

PLAYBOY: How *do* you think of it?

I.RA. PROVO: Afterward, I think, I didn't want to do that—but it had to be done. You know, at times, it *does* wear you down. At times, you want to stop because it's too much. You have to say to your comrades, "I need to think, to get away from the shooting!" And you go to a friendly house and sit for a week and think.

I believe that if I continued to do what I'm doing and *didn't* have doubts, I'd have a problem. To stop every now and then and think, Now, where is this tak-ing me? What have I achieved? But just to go on, no holds barred, saying, "I am right, I am right"— then it's a problem.

PLAYBOY: Does the danger of the operation itself have an effect on you?

I.R.A. PROVO: Sometimes, before an operation to engage the Brits, I get butterflies in my stomach. I feel sick, I don't want to eat or drink—all I want to do is get the run going. Do what I'm to do, get back. My nerves are racing, my adrenaline is going.

Once I get back to a safe place, I can sit back. I'll be shaking and have to calm myself. Have a cigarette, a cup of tea and talk with the people I've been with, analyze the operation, talk about it, what happened. None of us are supermen. If it were like the movies, it would be so nice.

PLAYBOY: There doesn't appear to be any end in sight. The British have simply become more rigid, enacted more laws to deal with the situation. And you—how long can you keep this up?

I.R.A. PROVO: I believe we're going to win. What the British government are doing is playing their last card. In 1981, Mrs. Thatcher said that the hunger strike was the I.R.A. playing its last card. But since 1981, the I.R.A. has gotten stronger and carried out operations that no one ever imagined they could: the Brighton bomb, for example.

British Desperation

PLAYBOY: That was the bomb that exploded in the hotel in Brighton, nearly killing Thatcher?

I.R.A. PROVO: Yes. [*Smiles ruefully*] We came *so* close to our objective, which was to remove the British war cabinet. There have also been operations the I.R.A. has carried out on the Continent—not against the inhabitants of France or the Netherlands but against British forces stationed there.

The British government is now talking about legislation that will prevent republicans' standing for election. They are trying to introduce legislation that compels the public to take a nonviolent oath. If they don't take the oath, then they can't stand for election. They have already eroded a suspect's right of silence. The British government are now eating away at their own system of justice, at their basic rights.

They may try to introduce legislation that will outlaw Sinn Fein. They may reintroduce internment without trial. *That*'s their last card. They're all acts of desperation. There's a wind of change in the loyalist community, members of the community who have become disenchanted with their own leadership. They now see that they've been led up a path that goes nowhere. The social and economic conditions that were endured by the Catholics for generations, the Protestants are now forced to endure. Unemployment, poor wages, poverty are now endemic to both communities.

> *"We came* **so** *close to our objective, which was to remove the British war cabinet."*

PLAYBOY: You mean the British are abandoning the Protestant community?

I.R.A. PROVO: The Protestants are beginning to see that the British government no longer regards them as equals. They are beginning to see that the only interest the British government has here is economic and strategic. That they don't care about the population, only what can be gained for their own interests.

Restoring Irish Culture

PLAYBOY: If what you fight for should ever come true—if Ireland is ever re-unified—what would you expect to happen?

I.R.A. PROVO: We want to bring back the Irish culture. It's been taken from us, the foreign culture has been imposed on us. The culture now is a rat's nest. The native Irish culture had a different set of values, which said that everyone was entitled to a share of the wealth and production of the country. Everyone was entitled to be treated as equal regardless of religion, color, sex, whatever. And we believe in secularism; that church and state are separate.

PLAYBOY: That wouldn't be greeted with any enthusiasm in the south, where the Catholic church is powerful.

I.R.A. PROVO: The Church has its place, but not in government. Ireland has a right to be governed by its people—not by any other entity or state. We look forward to a society where everyone has a role. It will be up to the people to decide. Once we put the guns away, they're put away for good.

Violence Is Justified to Protect the Purity of the White Race

by David Lane

About the author: *David Lane is an inmate at the Leavenworth federal penitentiary in Leavenworth, Kansas. Lane is serving a forty-year sentence for murder, racketeering, and robbery.*

As it grows ever more evident that there is no peaceful solution if we are to secure the existence of our race, our folk will be forced to abandon the conservative hoax. If their allegiance to our executioners' religious and political institutions is greater than their instinct for racial survival, then they are the enemy. If they obey the first law of nature, the preservation of their own race, then they must become total implacable, fanatic, and ruthless enemies of our executioners' institutions. This we call the revolutionary mentality.

The time has long passed for endless tomes demonstrating intellectual sophistry whether it be in deciphering alleged history (secular or religious) or theories that wrap logic five times around a crooked tree.

Fabled History

These tomes are demonstrably immaterial and irrelevant. Irrelevant because history is a fable. Every power system, religious and secular, for at least 2000 years, has continuously altered, rewritten, backdated, invented, and slanted all previous historical records, which in turn were false to begin with. The propaganda of the victor becomes the history of the vanquished. The issue that concerns us is clearly defined in present day circumstances. A reasonable observation of central Africa in comparison to central Europe is enough to horrify any sane white person who has learned how to think. White males should be equally horrified that the beauty of Aryan women may soon perish from the earth.

Having once competed in the materialistic ZOG [Zionist Occupation Govern-

David Lane, "Wotan Is Coming," *WAR: White Aryan Resistance*, April 1993. Reprinted with permission.

ments] controlled American capitalistic system, I learned to hate the term positive attitude, as it was a staple in the sales seminars, used to inspire materialistic swine toward ever greater greed. Nonetheless, a positive attitude is necessary if it is combined with action. To that end, in the future, we will hopefully focus our words and teachings on what we must do to win. The problems we face have already been delineated countless times. It takes only one paragraph to define the problem and only 14 words to state our goal.

Denying White Separateness

The problem, in one paragraph, particularly the portion underlined, is as follows: America and the Zionist Occupation Governments deny us exclusively white countries and everything necessary for our continued existence as a biological and cultural entity. White people who resist are destroyed socially, economically, and politically. Those who continue to effectively resist the murder of their race are imprisoned or assassinated. We are a small minority on earth. The inevitable result of racial integration is a percentage of interbreeding every year, leading to racial death by miscegenation. Forced integration is therefore deliberate malicious genocide.

It takes only fourteen words to state our goal, our cause, our passion, to wit; "we must secure the existence of our people and a future for white children."

It takes only one sentence to justify our actions, to wit, we obey the first law of nature which is preservation of our own kind.

Wotan: Necessary Violence

So, let's go on to strategy. Resistance to tyranny within an occupied country necessarily forms into certain structures. Most basic is the division between the political or legal arm, and the armed party which I prefer to call Wotan [German for Odin, the supreme god and god of war in Norse mythology] as it is an excellent anagram for the will of the Aryan nation. The political arm is distinctly and rigidly separated from Wotan. The political arm will always be subjected to surveillance, scrutiny, harassment, and attempted infiltration by the system. Therefore the political arm must remain scrupulously legal within the parameters allowed by the occupying power. The function of the political arm is above all else to disseminate propaganda. The nature of effective propaganda is magnificently detailed in [Adolf Hitler's] *Mein Kampf*, and condensed in *88 Precepts*. The political arm is a network and loose confederation of like minded individuals sharing a common goal.

> *"We must secure the existence of our people and a future for white children."*

Wotan draws recruits from those educated by the political arm. When a Wotan "goes active" he severs all apparent or provable ties with the political arm. If he has been so foolish as to obtain "membership" in such an organization, all records of such association must be destroyed or resignation submitted.

The goal of Wotan is clear. He must hasten the demise of the system before it totally destroys our gene pool. Some of his weapons are fire, bombs, guns, terror, disruption, and destruction. Weak points in the infrastructure of an industrialized society are primary targets. Individuals who perform valuable service for the system are primary targets. Special attention

> *"Some . . . weapons are fire, bombs, guns, terror, disruption, and destruction."*

and merciless terror is visited upon those white men who commit race treason. Wotan has a totally revolutionary mentality. He has no loyalty to anyone or anything except his cause. Those who do not share his cause are expendable and those who oppose his cause are targets. Wotan is mature, capable, ruthless, self-motivated, silent, deadly, and able to blend into the masses. Wotan receives no recognition for his labors for if the folk knows his identity then soon the enemy will also. Wotan are small autonomous cells, one man cells if possible. No one, not wife, brother, parent or friend, knows the identity or actions of Wotan.

Death to Traitors

In particular, if you are a white male who commits race treason, the day is coming when you will be visited by Wotan. Your demise will be unpleasant.

Judges, lawyers, bankers, real estate agents, judeo-christian preachers, federal agents, and other assorted treasonous swine take note, Wotan is coming. Your wealth, your homes, your women, and your lives are at risk when you commit treason. Pray that you die quickly. One day Wotan will feed your repulsive carcasses to the vultures and bury your bones under outhouses that our folk may forever pay fitting tribute to your memory. That day is called "Ragnarok" [Norse concept of doomsday].

Serbs Have Committed Heinous War Crimes

by Lawrence S. Eagleburger

About the author: *Lawrence S. Eagleburger served as U.S. deputy secretary of state from 1989 to 1992. That year, he succeeded James Baker as secretary of state, serving until January 1993.*

An important milestone was reached with the convening of the 1992 London International Conference on the former Yugoslavia. Commitments were made both by the parties to the Yugoslav conflict and by the international community itself—commitments to ensure unimpeded delivery of humanitarian aid; to lift the barbaric siege of cities; to halt all military flights over Bosnia-Herzegovina; to group all heavy weapons under UN monitoring, to open up and shut down all detention camps; to tighten sanctions against the aggressor; and to prevent the conflict's spread to neighboring regions and countries.

Some of those commitments have been kept, particularly in the area of sanctions monitoring, and in efforts to prevent a further widening of the war. Most importantly, London established a negotiating mechanism centered in Geneva, which has brought the international community and the various ex-Yugoslav parties together on an ongoing basis, and which, thanks to the efforts of Cyrus Vance and Lord David Owen, remains a viable forum for an eventual settlement of the war.

Serbs' Broken Promises

But let us be clear: Most of the commitments made in London have not been kept, and the situation inside the former Yugoslavia has become increasingly desperate. Thus, we discuss how the international community will respond in order to force compliance with the London agreements, and thereby accelerate an end to the war.

It is clear in reviewing the record since London that the promises broken have been largely Serbian promises broken. It is the Serbs who continue to besiege

Lawrence S. Eagleburger, "The Need to Respond to War Crimes in the Former Yugoslavia," *U.S. Department of State Dispatch*, December 28, 1992.

the cities of Bosnia; Serb heavy weapons which continue to pound the civilian populations in those cities; the Bosnian Serb air forces which continue to fly in defiance of the London agreements; and Serbs who impede the delivery of humanitarian assistance and continue the odious practice of "ethnic cleansing." It is now clear, in short, that Mr. Slobodan Milosevic and Mr. Radovan Karadzic have systematically flouted agreements to which they had solemnly, and yet cynically, given their assent. Today we must, at a minimum, commit ourselves anew to the London agreements by:

> *"The promises broken have been largely Serbian promises broken. It is the Serbs who continue to besiege . . . Bosnia."*

• Redoubling our assistance efforts and continuing to press for the opening of routes for aid convoys, so that widespread starvation can be avoided;

• Strengthening our efforts to prevent the war's spillover, particularly in the Kosovo, which we will not tolerate; and

• Tightening and better enforcing sanctions, the surest means of forcing an early end to the war.

But we must also do more. It is clear that the international community must begin now to think about moving beyond the London agreements and contemplate more aggressive measures. That, for example, is why my government recommended that the UN Security Council authorize enforcement of the no-fly zone in Bosnia, and why we are also willing to have the Council re-examine the arms embargo as it applies to the Government of Bosnia-Herzegovina. Finally, my government also believes it is time for the international community to begin identifying individuals who may have to answer for having committed crimes against humanity. We have, on the one hand, a moral and historical obligation not to stand back a second time in this century while a people faces obliteration. But we have also, I believe, a political obligation to the people of Serbia to signal clearly the risk they currently run of sharing the inevitable fate of those who practice ethnic cleansing in their name.

Knowledge of War Crimes

The fact of the matter is that we know that crimes against humanity have occurred, and we know when and where they occurred. We know, moreover, which forces committed those crimes, and under whose command they operated. And we know, finally, who the political leaders are to whom those military commanders were—and still are—responsible. Let me begin with the crimes themselves, the facts of which are indisputable:

• The siege of Sarajevo, ongoing since April 1992, with scores of innocent civilians killed nearly every day by artillery shelling;

• The continuing blockade of humanitarian assistance, which is producing thousands upon thousands of unseen innocent victims;

124

• The destruction of Vukovar in the fall of 1991, and the forced expulsion of the majority of its population;

• The terrorizing of Banja Luka's 30,000 Muslims, which has included bombings, beatings, and killings;

• The forcible imprisonment, inhumane mistreatment, and willful killing of civilians at detention camps, including Banja Luka/Manjaca, Brcko/Luka, Krajina/Prnjavor, Omarska, Prijedor/Keraterm, and Trnopolje/Kozarac;

• The August 21, 1992, massacre of more than 200 Muslim men and boys by Bosnian Serb police in the Vlasica Mountains near Varjanta;

• The May-June 1992 murders of between 2,000 and 3,000 Muslim men, women, and children by Serb irregular forces at a brick factory and a pig farm near Brcko;

• The June 1992 mass execution of about 100 Muslim men at Brod; and

• The May 18, 1992, mass killing of at least 56 Muslim family members by Serb militiamen in Grbavci, near Zvornik.

Identifying Those Responsible

We know that Bosnian Serbs have not alone been responsible for the massacres and crimes against humanity which have taken place. For example, in late October 1992 Croatian fighters killed or wounded up to 300 Muslims in Prozor, and between September 24-26, 1992, Muslims from Kamenica killed more than 60 Serb civilians and soldiers.

We can do more than enumerate crimes; we can also identify individuals who committed them. For example:

• Borislay Herak is a Bosnian Serb who has confessed to killing over 230 civilians; and

• "Adil and Arif" are two members of a Croatian paramilitary force which in August attacked a convoy of buses carrying more than 100 Serbian women and children, killing over half of them.

We also know the names of leaders who directly supervised persons accused of war crimes, and who may have ordered those crimes. These include:

• Zeljko Raznjatovic, whose paramilitary forces, the "tigers," have been linked to brutal ethnic cleansing in Zvornik, Srebrenica, Bratunac, and Grobnica; and who were also linked to the mass murders of up to 3,000 civilians near Brcko;

> *"Borislay Herak is a Bosnian Serb who has confessed to killing over 230 civilians."*

• Vollslay Seselj, whose "White Eagles" force has been linked to atrocities in a number of Bosnian cities, including the infamous incident at Brcko;

• Drago Prcac, commander of the [Serbian] Omarska Detention Camp, where mass murder and torture occurred; and

• Adem Delic, the camp commander at [Bosnian] Celebici where at least 15

Serbs were beaten to death in August 1992.

I want to make it clear that, in naming names, I am presenting the views of my government alone. The information I have cited has been provided to the UN War Crimes Commission, whose decision it will be to prosecute or not. Second, I am not prejudging any trial proceedings that may occur; they must be impartial and conducted in accordance with due process. Third, the above listing of names is tentative and will be expanded as we compile further information.

Serbs Must Explain Actions

Finally, there is another category of fact which is beyond dispute—namely, the fact of political and command responsibility for the crimes against humanity which I have described. Leaders such as Slobodan Milosevic, the President of Serbia, Radovan Karadzic, the self-declared President of the Serbian Bosnian Republic, and General Ratho Mladic, commander of Bosnian Serb military forces, must eventually explain whether and how they sought to ensure, as they must under international law, that their forces complied with international law. They ought, if charged, to have the opportunity of defending themselves by demonstrating whether and how they took responsible action to prevent and punish the atrocities I have described which were undertaken by their subordinates.

> *"[Serb leaders] have somehow convinced themselves that the international community will not stand up to them."*

I have taken the step today of identifying individuals suspected of war crimes and crimes against humanity for the same reason that my government has decided to seek UN authorization for enforcing the no-fly zone in Bosnia and why we are now willing to examine the question of lifting the arms embargo as it applies to Bosnia-Herzegovina. It is because we have concluded that the deliberate flaunting of Security Council resolutions and the London agreements by Serb authorities is not only producing an intolerable and deteriorating situation inside the former Yugoslavia, it is also beginning to threaten the framework of stability in the new Europe.

It is clear that the reckless leaders of Serbia, and of the Serbs inside Bosnia, have somehow convinced themselves that the international community will not stand up to them now, and will be forced eventually to recognize the fruits of their aggression and the results of ethnic cleansing. Tragically, it also appears that they have convinced the people of Serbia to follow them to the front lines of what they proclaim to be an historic struggle against Islam on behalf of the Christian West.

It is time to disabuse them of these most dangerous illusions. The solidarity of the civilized and democratic nations of the West lies with the innocent and brutalized Muslim people of Bosnia. Thus, we must make it unmistakably clear that we will settle for nothing less than the restoration of the independent state of Bosnia-Herzegovina with its territory undivided and intact, the return of all refugees to their homes and villages, and, indeed, a day of reckoning for those found guilty of crimes against humanity.

It will undoubtedly take some time before all these goals are realized, but then there is time, too, though not much, for the people of Serbia to step back from the edge of the abyss. There is time, still, to release all prisoners; to lift the siege of cities; to permit humanitarian aid to reach the needy; and to negotiate for peace and for a settlement guaranteeing the rights of all minorities in the independent states of the former Yugoslavia.

But in waiting for the people of Serbia, if not their leaders, to come to their senses, we must make them understand that their country will remain alone, friendless, and condemned to economic ruin and exclusion from the family of civilized nations for as long as they pursue the suicidal dream of a Greater Serbia. They need, especially, to understand that a second Nuremberg awaits the practitioners of ethnic cleansing, and that the judgment, and opprobrium, of history awaits the people in whose name their crimes were committed.

Mass Rapes Committed by Serbs Are War Crimes

by Manuela Dobos

About the author: *Manuela Dobos teaches Russian and East European history at the College of Staten Island, City University of New York.*

In July 1992 the American, British, and French media accounts of the detention centers in Bosnia-Herzegovina evoked a public outcry in Western Europe and the U.S. Serbian and Bosnian Serb armed forces were holding the mostly Bosnian Muslim civilians in camps where they were being starved, tortured, and killed in order to drive the survivors from conquered territory, to carry out "ethnic cleansing."

Rape Accounts Emerge

And disclosures of new horrors were yet to come. As the International Committee for the Red Cross and foreign journalists gained entry to some of the camps and Serb authorities released some prisoners, the story of mass rape of women detainees emerged in August 1992. In September, the Women's Commission for Refugee Women and Children, connected with the International Rescue Committee, sent a delegation to Croatia, where there were already some 450,000 primarily women, children, and elderly refugees from Bosnia-Herzegovina. The delegation found that many of the mostly Muslim, but also Croatian women refugees told of repeated and brutal gang-rape over a period of months, often followed by murder. In some instances their Serb captors deliberately held them if they became pregnant so they would have to give birth to Serb babies.

Both the stages of pregnancy upon release and the refugees' accounts indicated that sexual abuse began with the first attacks by the Yugoslav National Army in March 1992 against the Muslim-led, constitutionally multi-ethnic government of Bosnia-Herzegovina. The abuse was continued by the Bosnian Serb units that eventually took over from the Army. Feminists in Croatia conducted

Manuela Dobos, "Rape: War Crime Against Women and a Nation," *Peace and Democracy News*, Summer 1993. Reprinted with permission.

interviews that confirmed that there had been a massive and deliberate assault on women victims. In September they issued appeals for international intervention against rape and for its perpetrators to be prosecuted as war criminals. In these appeals the feminists warned that "rape in this war is the tactic of the Yugoslav Army, i.e., the Serb and Montenegrin armies, to invade and occupy territory. . . . [It is] a developed war technology," a "gender-specific onslaught that is systematic." One of the most diligent reporters of these experiences, Croatian writer Slavenka Drakulic, has described rape "as a method of ethnocide." The interviewers concluded that untold thousands of women and children were still being held as a part of the Serbian forces' ethnic cleansing campaign.

Foot-Dragging on Rapes

It was only with the second report of the United Nations Rapporteur on Human Rights in former Yugoslavia, presented in November 1992, that the UN and other international observers recognized mass rape in detention as a major part of ethnic cleansing in the Bosnian-Herzegovinian phase of the war in former Yugoslavia. Indeed, foot-dragging has characterized the response to this abuse of women's human rights: the U.S. State Department collected its own information in November 1992 but did not release it for a month. And though rape clearly falls under the war crimes definitions of the Geneva Conventions, it has virtually never been prosecuted, which indicates a tendency not to take it seriously.

U.S. and Western women's organizations also reacted late, mistrustful of media sensationalism and unwilling to take sides, or to submit to manipulation to do so. There were notable exceptions to this hesitation. Besides the Women's Commission for Refugee Women and Children mentioned previously, the New York-based Center for Reproductive Law and Policy responded promptly. The Center helped organize European doctors to perform late abortions on as many of the pregnant victims as could be escorted out, in order to avoid potential legal obstacles in Croatia. (In its subsequent work assessing the needs of the rape victims, the Center established that in fact no such legal obstacles existed and that there was no crisis of babies being born there and being abandoned.) It was the Women's Commission of the American Jewish Congress which in early December 1992 first organized protests against Serbia's perpetration of rape and genocide in front of the "Yugoslav" Mission to the UN in New York. The Commission also began lobbying in Congress for U.S. support to the Bosnians.

> *"Many . . . women refugees told of repeated and brutal gang-rape over a period of months, often followed by murder."*

The hesitation of Western feminist, peace, and human rights groups in responding quickly to the accounts of mass rape of Bosnian Muslim women was understandable, if unfortunate. In the first place, rape has been reported on all sides of the conflict. Beginning in the Croatian phase of the war, from July to

December 1992, rape of both Croatian and Serbian women occurred. As Susan Brownmiller, a historian of rape, pointed out in reviewing the situation in former Yugoslavia, "there is nothing unprecedented about mass rape in war. . . . Sexual trespass on the enemy's women is one of the satisfactions of conquest. . . . Balkan women, whatever their ethnic and religious background . . . are victims of rape in war."

Indeed, the investigations by the European Council, Amnesty International, and Helsinki Watch conducted between November 1992 and February 1993 included reports of abduction, rape, and forced prostitution of Serbian as well as Croatian and Muslim women. For instance, according to an account in the August 17, 1992, *Guardian* (London), Croatian paramilitaries calling themselves "The Fiery Horses" abducted, beat, and raped three Serbian women. The opposition Belgrade newspaper *Borba* ran a series on war rapes, which included the testimony of a captured Bosnian government soldier who admitted raping both Serbian and Muslim women.

War undeniably brings out male violence that may otherwise lie dormant. The SOS Hotline in Belgrade for Women and Children Victims of Violence has registered an increase in all types of male domestic violence

> *"Balkan women, whatever their ethnic and religious background . . . are victims of rape in war."*

since the beginning of the war, and its pronounced increase every day after the evening war news on TV. There has also been a drastic rise in the persecution of and violence against homosexuals.

Propaganda Aims

Another motivation for the hesitation of Western feminists is the suspicion of exaggerated claims. Indeed, governments of countries that are targets of Serbian aggression may be tempted to inflate the numbers of rape victims. It is in the interest of the Croatian and Bosnian governments to give out high figures on Serbian rapists and none on their own soldiers in order to garner the political and possibly military support that the European Community and the United States have been so far unwilling to give. Moreover, Franjo Tudjman's Croatian government has seized upon high figures to place sole blame on the Serbs for the sexual abuse its own soldiers have not been discouraged from perpetrating. This is in order to mobilize all Croats against all Serbs, regardless of gender. Some women's groups in Croatia are supporting the government in this aim: it is reported that they denied participation to Serbian feminist and peace groups in an international conference on war crimes against women organized in Zagreb in 1992 for West European parliamentary women.

Croatian feminists unwilling to lend themselves to the propaganda aims of their government and openly opposed to acts of rape by Croatian soldiers have been pilloried, witch-hunt style, in the government-controlled press: they have been publicly attacked for "raping Croatia." Partly in response to these attacks some, though not all, Croatian and Serbian women's and peace groups have moved away from fixing—or denying—blame, and, for now, are limiting themselves to working together to help the victims. In addition, many U.S. peace and feminist activists have been loath to take sides in the conflict. Thus, a January 1993 demonstration called in front of the UN in New York by the

> *"Some . . . women's and peace groups have moved away from fixing—or denying—blame."*

Women's Action Coalition to protest war-time rape refused to allow anti-Serb Bosnian Muslims to join them. They were concerned that Bosnian Muslim participation would make the demonstration appear "partisan" and pro-war. The same evenhandedness toward all sides in the conflict informed presentation of the global abuse of women's human rights at an April 1993 public meeting sponsored by the group MADRE in New York. Spokeswomen from Bosnia, Croatia, and Serbia were the main feature of the meeting, but so little was explained that the impression was given that all sides were equally guilty of rape and equally responsible for the war.

Serb Abuses Continue

Protesting rape in general and aiding the victims have not stopped the victimization of Muslim women by Serbian ethnic cleansing. Though one has to oppose propagandistic use of women's suffering, it must be recognized that the abuse of women in Bosnia-Herzegovina continues and is overwhelmingly and undeniably the result of the aggressive and genocidal project of the Serbian Republic under Slobodan Milosevic. One must "take sides" in this war, while vigorously taking action against rape and gross human rights violations on all sides.

Of course, it has been very difficult to ascertain definitively the actual number of women raped, in large measure because of the reluctance to report the assaults. Particularly, although not exclusively, among Muslim women, the fear of not being accepted back into their community, as well as the profound self-loathing this trauma entails, makes women want to repress the memories and remain silent.

The numbers of rape victims put forward have varied from a few thousand to ten times that, and all are estimates. Authenticated cases run in the hundreds: Dr. Shana Swiss of the Women's Commission of Physicians for Human Rights, who followed up the UN Rapporteur's investigation, found 119 cases of pregnant rape victims in six hospitals in Croatia, Serbia, and Bosnia. Nevertheless, Dr. Swiss is sure that this is a very small percentage of the actual number, and says that while there are cases of Serbian women raped by Croats or Muslims, "the great majority of the victims are Muslim women raped by Serb irregular soldiers."

Indeed, inquiries conducted by the European Council [EC] in December 1992, and Amnesty International in January 1993, as well as Helsinki Watch and others, all come to the same conclusion. In addition, these groups find that the gross asymmetry in numbers of Serb and Bosnian Muslim victims of sexual abuse is directly connected to its use in Serbian ethnic cleansing.

The EC's Investigative Mission into the Treatment of Muslim Women in the former Yugoslavia, led by Dame Anne Warburton and Simone Weil, sought specifically to "arrive at a view [as to] . . . whether or not the rape of Muslim women could be properly described as 'systematic.'" They found that a "repeated feature of Serbian attacks on Muslim towns and villages was the use of rape or the threat of rape as a weapon of war to force the population to leave their homes. . . . The delegation saw examples of statements and documents from Serbian sources which very clearly put such actions in the context of an expansionist strategy. . . . Viewed in this way, rape cannot be seen as incidental to the main purposes of the aggression but as serving a strategic purpose in itself. While the delegation was in no doubt that the conflict provides a cloak for criminality of all sorts, it felt that the type and scale of rapes being reported point towards a deliberate pattern."

Systematic Abuse

As in the EC findings, the Amnesty report emphasizes the need for more information to confirm the allegations, but "believes that the rape and sexual abuse of women, the great majority of them Muslims, by Serbian forces has occurred in many places in Bosnia-Herzegovina and in some cases has been carried out in an organized or systematic way, with the deliberate detention of women for the purpose of rape and sexual abuse. Such incidents would seem to fit into the wider pattern of warfare, involving intimidation and abuses against Muslims and Croats that have led thousands to flee or to be compliant when expelled from their home areas out of fear of further violations." The Amnesty document also brings together some of the many reports on detention for the purpose of rape perpetrated by the forces of Serbian paramilitary groups such as the "White Eagles," or the followers of Arkan, the *nom-de-guerre* of an internationally wanted criminal and former secret police agent, or the openly fascist Serbian Radical Party leader, Vojislav Seselj. These are the already well-known shock troops of Serbian ethnic cleansing.

> *"The great majority of the victims are Muslim women raped by Serb irregular soldiers."*

Rape and femicide in the war in former Yugoslavia are, then, primarily a part of genocide and ethnocide, and will therefore stop only when Milosevic and his henchmen are stopped. Since every single step taken by the great powers as an alternative to stopping the Serbs militarily—or to allowing the Bosnians to arm themselves for defense—has only resulted in further escalation of Serbian armed aggression and ethnic cleansing, the dilemma for peace and human rights groups has been great: how do we avoid violence and still save the Bosnian Muslim people? Thus far women's organizations have not, for the most part, addressed this dilemma though their response continues and is growing. The following is a sample of what is taking place in New York City.

"Rape and femicide ... in former Yugoslavia are, then, primarily a part of genocide and ethnocide."

The Ad Hoc Women's Coalition Against War Crimes in the former Yugoslavia encompasses many organizations, each of which is leading an action program for the women of former Yugoslavia. One such program originating with the Center for Global Women's Leadership at Rutgers University included issues related to war crimes against women on the agenda of the June 1993 UN World Conference on Human Rights held in Vienna. The Coalition is demanding that the UN establish a permanent war crimes tribunal with women represented to give special attention to gender-specific violations of the Geneva Conventions. Further, members of the Coalition are working to have all governments commit to a policy of making war criminals triable in national courts. As part of this effort the New York-based Center for Constitutional Rights and the war crimes unit of the City University of New York Law School have filed a multimillion dollar civil suit in New York against Bosnian Serb warlord Radovan Karadzic on behalf of two Bosnian women victims of rape.

Many have long urged such action. In September 1992, for example, the above-mentioned European Council Investigative Mission into the Treatment of Muslim Women called for support of those bodies within the former Yugoslavia collecting documentation for future trials. Reports indicate that among the hordes of men with guns as well as their leaders there is a pervasive feeling of unaccountability. Forcefully pursuing the identification, apprehension, and prosecution of all connected with the atrocities committed on women will stop many in their tracks. However, there is an immediate danger that needs to be specifically addressed: an unknown number of Bosnian women and children are still in Serb captivity, and as Muslim enclaves fall to the Serb forces, there will be more. Fear of the threat of witnesses to war crimes surviving to testify about what has happened to them may prompt their captors simply to murder them. People who want to protect these women will need to confront the issue of how to do so. To engage the problem seriously they first and foremost should call for an end to the UN arms embargo, which has served only to prevent the Bosnian government from defending its people while their extermination is pursued by the fifth largest army in Europe.

Protecting the Vulnerable

Moreover, the current mandate of the UN forces also has to be challenged. While it has not yet taken up the issue of lifting the arms embargo, the Ad Hoc

Coalition does call for the expansion of the mandate of UN peacekeeping forces to include protection of vulnerable populations such as women and children and to close the detention camps, as the Security Council already has demanded. Concurrently, U.S. and European women are working ever more closely with women's groups in the former Yugoslavia, where a feminist movement has existed for many years. The Network of East-West Women and the Women's Action Coalition keep a vigil each Wednesday at 5 p.m. at the United Nations in solidarity with the Women in Black, a women's organization that has been demonstrating in Belgrade amid great difficulties, at the same hour of the day, since the war began. The Women in Black, vilified by other Serbs, are specifically protesting the war with its atrocities and rapes as carried on by their own Serbian government.

The Center for Reproductive Law and Policy has continued its involvement with the rape victims by assembling a highly informed report on the needs of the refugee victims in Croatia. It is raising money for payments to go to the largely volunteer staff from women's groups and professions, which is quite knowledgeable but without resources for dealing with the mammoth medical and psychological problems of the rape victims. The Center and other groups are trying to implement the delivery of culturally and psychologically sensitive services for what is still an unknown number of victims of wartime sexual abuse and ethnic cleansing.

> *"The Women in Black, vilified by other Serbs, are specifically protesting the war with its atrocities and rapes."*

Women are initiating more and more actions, both here and in Europe, to come to the aid of women in former Yugoslavia. These actions only bring hope, however, if simultaneously directed at saving the Muslims of Bosnia-Herzegovina from continuing expulsion by Serb forces using rape, murder, starvation, and bombardment to accomplish their goals. Britain, France, the United States, and the UN have cynically used "evenhandedness" to cover up for doing nothing, thereby giving the Greater Serbia forces deadly advantage. The result has been that more than one half of Bosnia's two million Muslims are refugees and 100,000 are dead or missing.

Violence in the Arab World Is Unjustified Cruelty

by Kanan Makiya

About the author: *Kanan Makiya is the author of* Cruelty and Silence: War, Tyranny, Uprising, and the Arab World, *from which this viewpoint is excerpted. Makiya, a graduate of the London School of Economics, is also the author of* Republic of Fear: The Politics of Modern Iraq, *written under the pseudonym Samir al-Khalil.*

The Gulf Crisis [Iraq's invasion of Kuwait, the Persian Gulf War, and the 1991 Iraqi uprising against Saddam Husain] was never simply a matter of foreign manipulation or of the evil man playing the demagogue; it was at bottom an Arab moral failure of historic proportions, for which everyone who cares for the future of this part of the world must feel personally responsible. Something, somewhere along the line, has gone profoundly wrong in the Arab world; Saddam Husain merely typified it and acted it out. In [my] book, I do not claim to have fully explained what went wrong; my purpose is to acknowledge and describe it. Amidst the tempest of emotions released by the Gulf war, *Cruelty and Silence* was conceived with this in mind.

Cruelty Is Never Justified

While cruelty and violence overlap, they are not the same. Violence can be justified according to the ends that it pursues (for instance, as an act of self-defense). There can be violence between equals. Cruelty, on the other hand, can never be justified because it is the intentional infliction of physical pain on individuals who are in a position of weakness. For there to be cruelty, there has to be subjugation and powerlessness in some form. Psychological or social cruelty is beyond the scope of [my] book, but to a large extent both follow from—and feed into—physical cruelty. The violation of the human body by force or with an instrument of some kind has a visceral, irrational, and irrevocable quality about it. It is the bedrock under all the layers of horrible things that human beings do to one another.

The cruelty that I am concerned with has nothing to do with "genes" or "pre-historic causes"; it is political in cause and universal in effect. Its mere occurrence is an affront to everyone's humanity and this makes it cut across national and religious boundaries and sensibilities. Cruelty of such a universal kind has grown in many parts of the world in recent years, at faster or slower rates (one has only to think of the break-up of Yugoslavia and the daily death toll in Sarajevo). One of the key questions is: Has cruelty grown in the Arab world in the last two or so decades? And if so, what forms has it taken?

Certainly it grew in Iraq during the decade of the 1980s. The latest cycle of invasion, occupation, war, and uprising that Saddam Husain unleashed on the region ended cataclysmically with the Ba'thi regime still in place. In the course of the [opposition] uprising, Iraqi hopes were raised and then dashed. Yet nothing could ever be the same again. One of the most closed countries in the world had been opened up, and virtually every Arab, for a brief moment, had something urgent to say on the subject. Most importantly, the victims of cruelty were beginning to speak, and to tell stories, as they had never done before. . . .

Arab Silence

If cruelty is individual, then silence is collective. It arises from the actions of many individuals working, consciously or unconsciously, as a group. Breaking with silence as a way of dealing with the legacy of cruelty is thus itself necessarily a collective act. While the cruelties that are talked about in [my book] were going on, the Arab intellectuals who could have made a difference if they had put their minds to it were silent.

Like cruelty, the silence of Arab intellectuals is not immutable. Many sensitive Arab minds are profoundly aware of how deep the intellectual and cultural malaise inside the Arab world became during the 1980s. The main point is that the collective Arab silence toward the cruelties that are so often perpetrated in the name of all Arabs originates from many years of thinking in a certain way; it is, therefore, not an essentialist or an unchangeable condition; it is *a politics of silence*. During the Gulf crisis, the form that this politics of silence took was the myth of Saddam as some kind of saviour, and its mirror image, the idea that the crisis and ensuing war grew out of the machinations of Western racism or imperialism. . . .

"The cruelty . . . is political in cause and universal in effect. Its mere occurrence is an affront."

We will never stop debating what is truth, but no one should ever have to be in any doubt over what is cruelty. [My] book is a polemic in favor of calling things by their rightful names; of recognizing failure and of taking responsibility for it. Unlike the satisfaction I felt in telling the stories of [interviewees] Khalil, Abu Haydar, Omar, Mustafa, and Taimour, I found no pleasure in dissecting the words of Arab intellectuals.

But it had to be done. Things have gone too far now and there is no turning back from the road that Saddam Husain himself first opened up when he entered Kuwait on August 2, 1990. The stakes are very high because in the end this is a fight over the kind of future the Arab world wants, a struggle over that persistent Middle Eastern question: "Who is an Arab?" In this fight, I seek to be fair, but I do not claim to be impartial. My purpose is not personal, but my style is. I want to tap at the roots. I want to reach into the emotional heart of things instead of staring uselessly at intellectual mirrors. In the meantime, the graves of the dead are still open in the Arab world. . . .

> *"The collective Arab silence toward the cruelties . . . is a* **politics of silence."**

The Kurdish Massacres

I already knew the extermination campaign [by Iraq's government against Iraqi Kurds] had a name: *al-Anfal*. From my reading of secret Iraqi government documents seized by the Kurds in March of 1991—when, in the wake of the Gulf war, the *peshmerga* [Kurdish guerrillas] fought their way into all the major Kurdish cities in the north, taking brief control of government buildings and military installations—I also knew the essential tools of the campaign, tools refined in this century by the likes of Adolf Hitler and Pol Pot: demolished villages, transfer points, poison gas, firing squads, mass graves. Among the countless official documents seized by the Kurds—Kurdish leaders talk of tons, truckloads—are detailed, mostly handwritten lists of "eliminated villages" whose inhabitants were rounded up and have disappeared. The Kurds have also carefully compiled their own lists of those, mostly but not exclusively men and boys from rural villages, who were taken away and are presumed dead. Two weeks before arriving at the Fort of Qoratu, I'd visited a fort outside the town of Dohuk where, eyewitnesses told me, eight thousand Kurdish men and boys were brought in 1988 and then vanished. It is not possible to say precisely how many Kurdish lives were taken during the period the *Anfal* campaign was waged, but evidence from the highest levels of the regime itself suggests that the number of those killed is not less than 100,000. Kurdish leaders estimate the number is greater than 180,000. . . .

[The following is an account of a young survivor of the Kurdish massacres.]

As far as anyone knows, Taimour 'Abdallah, from the village of Qulatcho, is the only human being to have experienced firsthand the darkest innermost workings of the *Anfal* campaign and lived to tell of it. This much I already knew in London, although I did not really know what the *Anfal* campaign was about, or if the [fifteen-year-old] boy's account could be believed; it had been such a wooden and stilted interview. The *Anfal* was at that point just a name for me, one that kept on cropping up in the copies of the secret police documents which I had been given and which maybe had something to do with large num-

137

bers of Kurds disappearing in 1988. Many survivors like [chemical attack survivor] 'Abdallah al-'Askari had witnessed the attacks on their villages or other rounding-up operations inside northern Iraq. But only one person "disappeared" and then by a miracle "reappeared" to tell us what had happened to him. . . .

> Did they take you away from Topzawa [prison] in army lorries like those that had taken your father away?
>
> No, they were white vehicles that were locked.

(This is a puzzling answer for which I have no explanation. Unfortunately, I didn't pursue the line of questioning. Henceforth Taimour and I will both be referring to these vehicles as lorries.)

> Did you know who the men in charge were?
>
> No.
>
> How many people were there in each lorry from Topzawa to the place where the shooting happened?
>
> I think it was about one hundred people in each lorry.
>
> Were they all women and children?
>
> Yes. . . . Just before reaching the place of the shooting, they first let us off the lorries and blindfolded us and gave us a sip of water. Then they made us go back inside. When we arrived, they opened the door, and I managed to slip aside my blindfold. I could see this pit in the ground surrounded by soldiers.
>
> Were your hands tied?
>
> No.
>
> When they opened the door of the lorry, what was the first thing you saw?
>
> The first thing I saw was the pits, dug and ready.

Taimour explained to me on a separate occasion that he had pushed the blindfold slightly aside so that he could see without the soldiers realizing it. Hands were obviously needed to clamber off the lorries and into the pits efficiently. The blindfold is a classic technique for isolating victims psychologically

> *"Kurdish leaders estimate the number [of Kurds killed] is greater than 180,000."*

from one another, thus reducing the chances of a collective effort to rush the guards and make a run for it. Taimour saw the pits the instant the doors of his lorry were opened. He was still on the elevated platform at this point.

> How many pits did you see?
>
> It was night, but around us there were many.
>
> Four or five holes?
>
> No, no, it was more.
>
> More than five, six, seven holes?
>
> Yes, yes.
>
> Describe your pit.
>
> The pit was like a tank dugout. They put us in that kind of a hole.
>
> They pushed you directly off the truck into the pit?
>
> Yes.
>
> How high was it? One meter? Two meters? Could you stand up inside?

It was high.

How high?

Up to the sash of a man.

How many people were put inside?

One pit to every truck.

And how many people were in a truck?

About one hundred people.

Was it just a massive hole?

It was rectangular.

Was it cut very precisely by a machine?

By bulldozers as you would make a pit for a tank. . . .

I imagine an extraordinary state of collective numbness had gripped everyone inside the pit. It is reminiscent of the reaction of Jews being herded into the gas chambers as described in accounts of the Holocaust. No one protested because they were totally resigned to the fact that they were going to die. Then the shots started coming from two directions; apparently only two men doing the firing. A bullet hit Taimour in the left shoulder, a flesh wound. He looked up and saw that he'd been shot by the soldier standing directly before him, whom he began running toward.

Did you actually reach the soldier?

Yes.

Did you grab onto him?

I grabbed his hand, then . . .

His hand or his foot?

His hand.

But you were in the pit?

No, I came out and I ran.

You ran out of the pit and grabbed the soldier. That is what happened.

Yes.

Did you say anything to him?

I said nothing. I took his hand. Then the other soldier shouted at the one I
was holding and told him to throw me back in the pit.

Taimour rushed out of the pit in the direction of the incline, which would have been used by the bulldozer to make the hole. A ring of soldiers were on that bund, including one of the two doing the shooting. The other soldier had to have been on the opposite side, shooting into the hole along the line of the incline. Reaching the top of the hole by a miracle, Taimour

> *"The pit was like a tank dugout. They put us in that kind of a hole."*

wouldn't have just taken his executioner's hand; he would have had to grab at it, begging with his face, and maybe even his voice. There is no evidence, however, of this extraordinary emotional moment in Taimour's choice of words.

Did you look into the soldier's face?

Yes.

Did you see his eyes?

Yes.

What did you see? What could you read in his eyes, in the expression on his face?

He was about to cry, but the other one shouted at him and told him to throw me back in the pit. He was obliged to throw me back.

He cried! He was about to cry.

How far away was the officer who shouted?

He was close to him.

The soldier who pushed you back into the hole, was he the one who shot you the second time?

Yes. This soldier shot me again after he received the order from the officer who was standing beside the pit. When he shot me the second time I was wounded here [he points].

A second bullet was fired as he was being pushed into the hole, and entered Taimour's lower back. Both appear to have been light flesh wounds, although by the end of his ordeal the boy would have lost a lot of blood.

The same one who almost cried shot you a second time!

Yes, he was forced to, the other one had told him to shoot.

You fell back into the hole?

Yes.

Were the bullets coming in a continuous stream or just sporadically?

They were stopping and starting shooting again and again.

What was happening to the people around you while the shooting was going on? Did any of them call out, shout, scream, say something that you remember?

People were not shouting.

No one said anything?

No. . . .

What happened after the shooting stopped?

The soldiers went away and were talking with each other. It was nighttime.

They were milling about behind the bund of earth waiting for the bulldozers to come and level out the pit, covering up the crumpled bodies. A few minutes passed like this with Taimour cowering among the bodies, pretending to be dead. Then he says he clambered out and took one last look inside.

"The other soldier shouted . . . and told him to throw me back in the pit."

I came out of the pit and looked inside. I saw something moving. It was a girl. I said to her, "Get up, let's go," and she said, "I'm afraid of the soldiers, I can't come."

Tell me more about her.

We were sitting in the pit. She was beside me and she had been hit by a bullet in her hand.

She was smaller than you?

She was a very little child.
What was she wearing?
Kurdish clothes.
She got hit in the hand. . . . Did she say anything else?
No.
What about the rest of the people, were they all dead?
They didn't make noises.

When Taimour spoke to the little girl, a few minutes had passed since the end of the shooting. In that last look back into the pit, Taimour saw his mother Sarah, and three sisters, Gaylas, Leyla, and Serwa. He also saw three of his aunts, including Hafsa who didn't have any children, and Ma'souma who had eight. Then, when the soldiers weren't looking, he sprinted off to a nearby empty pit and jumped inside. With a piece of metal, he dug a hole in the sand and curled up in it under the cover of darkness. There he stayed for a while, watching as the bulldozers came and covered up the hole. Vehicles were driving around between the pits. At some point they left and he either fainted or fell asleep. After regaining consciousness, and making sure everyone had gone, Taimour got out of the pit and started walking out into the desert. . . .

Is there something you want out of life very much?
Yes.
What?
To be a known person.
A known person?
Yes.
Known for what?
The *Anfal*.
Do you want to be known more for the *Anfal* or for being a *peshmerga*?
For *Anfal*.
What do you mean "known for *Anfal*"?
I want the world to know what happened to me.

141

Terrorism by the Irish Republican Army Is Not Justified

by Herb Greer

About the author: *Herb Greer is an American writer living in England. Greer is a contributing editor to* The World & I, *a monthly magazine of culture, politics, and science.*

Fascism is becoming ominously fashionable again in Europe. On the continent it is manifested principally as violent xenophobia. But a more classic version has operated for more than twenty years in the United Kingdom. It is a cabal dedicated not only to the brutal hatred of foreigners, but to the exploitation of Jacobin rhetoric about human rights while consistently violating those rights; to the aim of a dictatorial one-party state; to the use of murder and mutilation of dissenters from its vicious brand of politics; to the dehumanization of its opponents; to a callous indifference to ordinary civilian life, expressed in random bombings; and to the ascent to power through illegal violence; and to an irredentism, based on mendacious history, that recalls the 1930s campaign of Adolf Hitler to recover the Sudetenland.

The Irish Myth

This is, of course, a description of Ulster's Provisional IRA/Sinn Fein, which exist together as two arms on one body. The most remarkable aspect of this murderous conspiracy is that it thrives on generous emotional and moral support from the United States—specifically from a blockheaded, ignorant, and vicious section of the Irish American community, which organizes and propagandizes along the same irredentist lines (and sometimes in almost the same words) as the 1930s pro-Hitler German-American Bund.

Relatively few Americans (or, in fact, Britons) know or care much about the troubles in Ulster. This general ignorance and indifference has guaranteed a transatlantic success for IRA propaganda, both at a popular level and in the media, which tend to reflect the IRA version of Anglo-Irish history. It goes something like this: In the twelfth century a brutal English or Saxon invading force attacked and occupied a United Celtic Irish Nation, which has ever since been fighting to free itself from British domination. After World War I a partial victory was obtained with the eventual establishment of an Irish Republic. But Ulster remained, and still does, under the Saxon heel, preventing the reuniting of Ireland into a nation once again. The Provisional IRA is the latest band of freedom fighters in this eight-hundred-year struggle.

> *"This murderous conspiracy . . . thrives on generous emotional and moral support from the United States."*

The eight-hundred-year-struggle myth was actually invented in the nineteenth century by Irish nationalists, and almost every single aspect of it is a lie. Americans who speak of the ancient Irish nation are uninformed. Nationalism in Ireland, as in the rest of Europe, was primarily a nineteenth-century phenomenon. Seven centuries ago, the island was a kaleidoscopic pattern of tribal kingdoms with a common Celtic language and culture, but no unifying loyalty or consciousness of the sort that is implied by the word *nation*. Loyalty in that age was to the person of the local tribal chief. The so-called high king had no general authority over the tribes and no administrative structure to rule them. In short, the ancient Irish nation never existed. . . .

The Present Troubles

The present spate of troubles began with a series of demonstrations at the end of the 1960s, when a civil-rights movement surfaced in Ulster with the objective of securing civil rights for the Catholic minority under British rule. The Irish nationalist goal of a unified Ireland played no part in it at first. But the movement was infiltrated by Republican extremists, who manipulated demonstrators into illegal provocations against the Protestant police. A police riot against civilians at Burntollet Bridge between Ulster and Londonderry was a brilliant success for the extremists. Bloody riots followed in Londonderry and Belfast, with plenty of police brutality, much of it displayed on television. The Stormont Parliament was dissolved and Ulster began its present period of direct rule from Westminster.

The old official IRA was supposed to protect Catholics during sectarian riots. This time they could not match the onslaught of Protestant goon squads and police brutality and fell out of favor with the Catholic community. With political encouragement and laundered financial support from the Irish government in Dublin, a younger and more vicious faction in the Republican movement organized itself as the Provisional IRA, which rejected the democratic line evolved by the official IRA and enthusiastically revived the fascist tactics of random bombing and killing that continue two decades later.

Even as the Provos began their long career of terrorism, the Protestant ascendancy was cracking for quite different reasons. Media exposure, political and economic pressure from the United States, and closer British attention to injustice against Catholics had begun to destroy the old scheme of things in Ulster. Paradoxically, the criminal atrocities of the Provos have had only one real political consequence in Ulster: to preserve the emotional skeleton of the old order, intensifying old hatreds, increasing Protestant wariness, and deepening emotional support for reactionary Protestant terrorism.

The IRA's Tactics

Since the 1960s many of the old IRA tactics have been tried: A hunger strike by convicted terrorists attracted press and media coverage, but was broken by the determination of Margaret Thatcher's government. Provocations in the form of bombings and murder have been intense, but the British, unlike the Provos, were able to learn from history. There was one early public relations disaster for the security forces—"Bloody Sunday" in 1972, when IRA terrorists fired at British troops through a screen of civilians, drawing return fire that killed seven civilians and six terrorists, whose weapons were removed by their colleagues. The media projected the incident as a gratuitous attack on innocent civilians. Over time the British army has generally got its act together, weeding out those who have allowed themselves to be provoked, and acquiring a formidable discipline in combatting IRA terrorism; soldiers who have broken the strict rules of engagement have been prosecuted as have been Ulster police mavericks who collaborated with Protestant terrorists.

> *"A younger and more vicious faction . . . enthusiastically revived the fascist tactics of random bombing and killing."*

Gradually it has become clear that the IRA tactics [of provoking retaliation] are not going to work in Ulster. Indeed, the Provos are now effectively marginalized both in the north and the south of Ireland. What little electoral support Sinn Fein enjoyed in the Irish Republic was wiped out by an official media ban on the cabal's spokesmen, much like that imposed on the *Front de Liberation Quebecois* by Pierre Trudeau in 1970, with the same result. The British have actually treated Sinn Fein and the Provos more *liberally* than the Irish government. A media ban exists in Britain, but only on the actual voices of terrorists and their political cabal. This ban is regularly circumvented by the simple gambit of dubbing actors' Irish-accented voices onto the television images of terrorist spokesmen.

The viciousness of the Provos has shrunk their support even in Ulster to a tiny minority in the Catholic community, most of whom despise the terrorists now. One reason for this is the ruthless oppression of Catholic dissenters by the

144

Provos, who mutilate or murder any civilian who dares to oppose them openly. There are other, more sinister causes. Inexorably a change in the terrorist organization has begun to take place. Their campaigns of bombing and murder, which only serve to attract media attention, have become a routine matter even in mainland Britain. With the goal of Irish unity further away than ever (the south, with severe economic problems, no longer wants the danger to public order and hideous expense that Ulster represents) and with the Protestant majority now held on a short leash by the British government, the Provos prima facie rationale has been a nullity for some time.

Money from Crime

Like the Sicilian Mafia, the Provos sprang up as a response to what the Catholic community saw as oppressive government by foreigners. As the Provos have grown politically more irrelevant, there has been an increasing and deepening involvement in purely (i.e., nonpolitical) criminal activity, disguised as fund-raising for the cause. Protection rackets, corruption, social welfare scamming, building-industry rakeoffs, simple robbery (both in Ulster and the Republic of Ireland, where the favorite targets are banks), and drugs are the principal local means of IRA fund-raising. The vicarious terrorists in America who support the Provos have taken great care to play down another vital source of money and arms. Most of the present IRA arsenal of weapons and explosives, especially the Czech-made Semtex used for bombing, was contributed by Col. Muammar Qaddafi, who hails the Provos as fellow revolutionaries and freedom fighters. American fans of the IRA have been remarkably silent on this close relationship.

Genuine backing for IRA terrorists is thinner on the ground in Ireland—both Ulster and the Republic—than for the Mafia in Sicily. Though the modus operandi of both organizations are similar, like much of the localized tolerance for *Cosa Nostra* compliance with the IRA is extorted from Catholics by a threat (often carried out) of mutilation and murder, both used to enforce a rule of silence akin to the Mafia's *omertà*. This close Irish-Sicilian family resemblance also remains unremarked in the United States, even among political officials who ought to be better informed. During the American election campaign candidate Bill Clinton wrote a fawning letter to an IRA supporter in Connecticut parroting IRA assertions of excessive British violence and human rights infractions in Ulster (the IRA's onslaught on human rights was not

> "The viciousness of the Provos has shrunk their support even in Ulster to a tiny minority."

mentioned) and promised to send an American representative to meddle in the negotiations between Ulster, Dublin, and Westminster. Congressman Joseph Kennedy and his uncle Teddy have both made statements that throw a veil of justification over IRA terrorism.

The bland (and occasionally willful) ignorance of American politicians is matched by the treatment of Ulster terrorism in the media, who continue to treat the violent fascist Republican cabal as a side equivalent to the British government in its claim to legitimacy. The sincerity of the terrorists has attracted approval even among respectable American journalists who prefer not to remember that Adolf Hitler was one of the most sincere men of the century. I myself have seen a private statement by an editor of *The Atlantic* expounding the IRA's propaganda view that they are "fighting for freedom as they see it," adding that the magazine itself is committed to a "God-like" view, staying "above" the conflict. This repellent determination to avoid moral commitment on a clear issue of terrorism is lamentably typical of a certain strain in American journalism and represents a surrender to that species of fascism by default.

The simple view of solving the Ulster troubles by restoring lost territory so that Ireland can be "a nation once again" has neither historical nor political merit. As an Irish nationalist writer pointed out as long ago as 1905, not even the cultural argument will hold water. The Irish are now essentially an English-speaking people, west British in culture. The nineteenth-century Celtic revival (which actually began in England) was and is purely ceremonial and artificial and bears no organic relationship to contemporary life in Ireland. The only living cultural token of separation between the two peoples is religious—the Catholic-Protestant divide. Even that is becoming less significant in an increasingly secularized society. The present furious debate in Ireland on abortion is a symptom of this change.

> *"Compliance with the IRA is extorted from Catholics by a threat . . . of mutilation and murder."*

A Bloody Family Feud

The violence in Ulster is less a national liberation struggle than a bloody family feud in the British Isles. It is no longer even a plausible quest for justice, but an emetic game of tit-for-tat slaughter. On the British mainland in March 1993 the IRA bombed to death two children—one small boy of three and a twelve year old. This was closely followed by the Ulster Volunteer Force's cold-blooded sectarian murder of three Catholic building site workers in Londonderry. The British government has responded to events in the past two decades as the violent Republicans have not, with a flexibility of social policy—including antidiscrimination measures—and an imposition of discipline and law on the security forces that has often hampered the efforts to contain IRA activities. Many of the leading terrorists are well enough known to the security forces to be recognized and even spoken to in the street; but the due process of British law, rigorously applied, will not permit their arrest and trial without solid admissible evidence.

The unemployment and economic stringencies of the present time are shared not only by Catholics and Protestants alike in Ulster but by the whole of the United Kingdom. Foreign investment in Ulster does nevertheless continue, despite the best efforts of the Irish-American "Bund" and the brothers Kennedy to stop or slow it, with the British government making real progress in sharing the benefits of that investment with both religious groups.

American Support Sustains Violence

Nonetheless, the Provos persist with their obstinate, anachronistic, and pointless resort to bombing and other, less easily farded, crime. With all its political rationale rotted away by history and current events, it continues to evolve slowly but surely into a purely criminal conspiracy whose eventual aim looks more and more like plain profits from what the Mafia families call "business." For all of its existence the Provisional IRA has expected and received the greatest part of its moral, political, and financial support not from the Ireland whose interests it falsely claims to represent, but from the gullible, the ill-informed, and sometimes the malicious among the Irish-American community and those who trawl them for votes. For as long as these Americans (whose number exceeds the population of the Irish Republic) and their mouthpieces in Congress and the media continue to swallow and regurgitate the historical and contemporary myths purveyed by Sinn Fein/IRA, for just that long will these terrorists continue their self-interested butchery of human beings. Until now Noraid, the Irish-American Caucus, the Irish-American Labour Coalition, and other proterrorist clones have worn the blood on their hands as a badge of pride. Just so did the 1930s German-American Bund glory in the persecution and murder of European Jews. It remains to be seen how long the enthusiastic support for Ulster's fascist terrorists will remain an open and suppurating chancre on the face of 1990s America.

> *"The Provos persist with their obstinate, anachronistic, and pointless resort to bombing."*

147

German Neo-Nazi Assaults Against Immigrants Must End

by Revolutionary Communist Party, USA

About the author: *The Revolutionary Communist Party, USA, is a political party based in Chicago.*

It was just after midnight, early Saturday morning, May 29, 1993, in Solingen, Germany. Twenty people slept inside the three-story house of the Gencs, a working class family of Turkish immigrants. A Nazi gasoline bomb came flying in—no warning, little time to escape. Five people died.

Three sisters were burned to death: Hatice Genc, 18, Hulya Genc, 9, and Sayime Genc, 4—all born in Solingen. A friend, 13-year-old Gulictan Yuksel, died with them. A relative, Gulsun Ince, 27, jumped from the upper windows to her death. Three other children were hospitalized.

Witnesses heard a shout of "Heil Hitler" and saw four Nazi skinheads running away as the fire started. Freshly painted swastikas were found on nearby buildings.

Daily Assaults

To immigrant workers in Germany, this brutal murder was nothing new. Nazi gangs have been attacking immigrants all over Germany, day after day. Fire-bombings, beatings, street harassment, sometimes mass attacks on refugee centers. Authorities estimate Nazis carried out 17 murders and more than 2,200 racist attacks during 1992. In Solingen itself, two mosques and a Turkish supermarket were firebombed that same month.

But this time was different. After the Solingen firebombing, the immigrants rose up—angry, fierce, unafraid. For years, the German ruling class has tried to isolate the immigrant proletarians and tried to make them feel like temporary "guests" in a land they helped rebuild from rubble after World War 2.

After Solingen's fire, the streets raged day after day. Turkish and Kurdish

Revolutionary Communist Party, USA, "Street Fighting in Germany Answers Nazi Attacks," *Revolutionary Worker*, June 13, 1993. Reprinted with permission of the *Revolutionary Worker*, the weekly newspaper of the Revolutionary Communist Party, USA. *Subheadings have been added and the original title changed by Greenhaven Press.*

youth, plus many Germans, fought the police through the streets of Solingen. They put the *stamp of the proletariat* on the political landscape. It marks an important change for Germany.

Public Outrage

A bourgeois reporter asked an uncle of the Genc family if the firebombing would cause him to leave Germany. The worker answered, "Why should we go because of a couple of pigs? I'm not going to be a coward and run."

As news of the firebombing spread, thousands of people converged on the burned-out house on Solingen's Werner Street—sorrowful and angry. Banners, flags and spray-painting soon covered the charred building. Children left dozens of toys in honor of the murdered girls. Turkish youth burned swastika flags. A Serbian neighbor described how he helped one woman escape the flames, hearing the cries of children inside. One German neighbor cried: "We've known this family for 15 years. Our children go to school together. What is the sense of this?"

The German national government headed by Helmut Kohl sent its interior minister to the burned house—he was booed. The crowd was in no mood for phony tears from a government that fans anti-immigrant hatred.

Through Saturday night, hundreds gathered around bonfires outside the house. Then, on Sunday, they moved into the streets of Solingen. According to bourgeois press reports, there were at least two marches—one apparently led by Islamic forces and the other by leftist and revolutionary forces. (There are sharp political divisions inside the Turkish immigrant community, including between the fascist "Gray Wolves" movement and the powerful revolutionary currents.)

Some forces demanded that the German government ban the various Nazi parties. Meanwhile other voices brought out the truth: that the German state itself is backing the Nazi street thugs in many ways, and that the struggle against such attacks requires the self-organization of the people. Protesters chanted: "We want Nazi blood." One speaker reportedly told the crowd, "We have one answer to this violence—which is to answer violence with violence." CNN broadcast news footage of bright red banners that waved over the heads of marchers. One giant red flag carried the face of Mao Tsetung.

Banners denounced the Turkish government's reactionary war on Kurdish people. Others rejected the German parliament's moves to keep refugees out of the country. Some people chanted, "Allah is Great."

> *"The German state itself is backing the Nazi street thugs in many ways."*

Radical German youth joined in the protest, wearing khaffias and bandannas over their faces. Police fired warning shots over the crowds.

Protests spread to other German cities. Sunday night, street fighting started in Solingen. Barricades of tires and old furniture burned on the main streets. Police attacked, confrontations spread.

Monday, street demonstrations of thousands started again. *The Times* of London wrote: "About 150 Turkish protesters also blocked access to Bonn airport for several hours, stationing their cars on a road leading to the airport." Superhighways were blocked in Cologne and Solingen. Solidarity marches sparked off in Frankfurt, Berlin and Hamburg.

> *"The major ruling class parties spout the same ugly anti-immigrant nationalism as the Nazis."*

Then, at night, gathering around bonfires of tires and mattresses, several thousand young Turkish and Kurdish streetfighters attacked the business district. Over a thousand riot police were mobilized in Solingen, and repeatedly the people outmaneuvered them in fluid street fighting. Some reports said 50 Turkish immigrants were arrested. There was similar fighting in Bonn, Augsburg and Bremen.

Demonstrations by day, street fighting by night—the pattern continued all week. Street fighting broke out again after the funeral in a Cologne mosque. In Hamburg, thousands of German and Turkish streetfighters faced police water cannon.

Germany's Coverup

The German ruling class solemnly denounced the Nazi attack in Solingen. But they didn't wear that mask long. Chancellor Kohl pointedly refused to go to Solingen, saying he does not believe in "grief tourism." Meanwhile, authorities started denouncing the rebellion of the masses—calling the people "criminals" on "a looting spree" and blaming the revolutionary organizations of Turks, Kurds and Germans. The chauvinist media complained that "foreigners" were bringing chaos into an otherwise orderly Fatherland. The national government threatened that those arrested in the Solingen rebellion and unnamed "ringleaders" would be considered for deportation. This will be familiar to our readers, who know the U.S. government went after Latino immigrants after the 1992 Los Angeles rebellion.

Meanwhile, the authorities claimed that one lone 16-year-old without organized Nazi ties had firebombed the Solingen home. This is being denounced by the people as a coverup: Eyewitnesses saw *four* Nazis run from the house, and everyone knows Nazis were waging an organized harassment campaign in Solingen. Under pressure, the authorities backed off their position and arrested three more skinheads. But they still tried to claim that the firebombing resulted from a drunken "boys will be boys" prank—not from an organized Nazi campaign.

This tactic is typical: Authorities officially condemn the Nazis' violence while covering up Nazi crimes, and the major ruling class parties spout the same ugly anti-immigrant nationalism as the Nazis. In June 1993 the lower house of parliament, including the Social Democrats, cut back on the rights of refugees to seek asylum. And two days later, in yet another Nazi-like move, the parliament greatly restricted abortion rights for women—taking away the choice that had existed for decades in eastern Germany. A sign in front of the burned Solingen house read: "First fruit of the asylum law—Murder in Solingen."

German Imperialism

The rise of violent Nazism fits in with the interests and plans of German imperialism. It poisons a section of German youth, especially unemployed working class youth, blinding them to their real internationalist and revolutionary class interests. "Foreigners" are blamed for "taking German jobs, apartments and benefits," just as Jews were targeted by Nazis in the 1920s and '30s. The hated old Hitlerite slogan *"Juden Raus!"* (Jews out!) has been adapted by today's skinheads who chant *"Ausländer Raus!"* (Foreigners out!).

At the same time, Germany's ruling class doesn't want to *openly* wave their old Hitlerite banners. German imperialism has expansionist ambitions throughout neighboring countries—where people remember *only too well* the oppression German imperialism under Hitler brought at gunpoint! An aide for Kohl expressed the growing ambitions of the German imperialists: "Perhaps in time, the United States will take care of places like Central America, and we will handle Eastern Europe" (*Newsweek*, February 26, 1990).

The growing wave of Nazi attacks is only the most violent attempt to intimidate and isolate a powerful, restless section of the proletariat in Germany—the millions of immigrant workers. The German state, and the chauvinist nationalism of many German people, caused many immigrant workers to feel isolated and powerless. They were treated like they are unwelcome "guests" without even a right to *speak out* about their oppression in Germany.

There have been massive peaceful demonstrations of Germans protesting Nazi murders and some street fighting in the past—especially in Berlin's Kreuzberg District, where German radicals and immigrant youth trashed Nazis together. But in Solingen, it felt like the whole community of immigrant workers—with allies among other sections of people in Germany—rose up to defy the Nazis, the ugly climate of German nationalism and the heavy hand of German law-and-order. The U.S. imperialist newspaper *New York Times* wrote: "Such outbursts had been all but unheard of in Germany."

> *"In Solingen, it felt like the whole community of immigrant workers . . . rose up to defy the Nazis."*

An important section of the proletariat has raised its fist in the heart of Europe, and the ripples this set off are reaching far and wide.

Hindu Violence Against Muslims Is Barbaric

by Vibhuti Patel

About the author: *Vibhuti Patel lives in New York City and is a writer for* India Today, *a newsmagazine published in New Delhi, India.*

I grew up in the Bombay that Salman Rushdie immortalized in his novel "Midnight's Children." He and I, a Muslim in hiding and a Hindu in America, share an abiding love for the city of our childhood. It was an oasis of peace, charm and gracious living, where mothers had afternoon tea with children and where politics and violence were kept at bay by a population that prided itself on being cosmopolitan and secular.

Bombay's Multiculturalism

Our city's multiculturalism was evident everywhere—in our schools, neighborhoods, bazaars and workplaces. As a teen-ager, then as a working woman, later as a mother returning from New York with young daughters, I felt safe in Bombay, even on deserted streets late at night. My Bombay visits invariably recharged my batteries, and each time I returned refreshed and ready to take on the streets of New York once again.

Over the past 20 years, I noticed our city changing in small ways. But my family's home was still the same.

Perched on a hill with a view that stretches over distant suburbs to the horizon, it is an old apartment building (my friends had dubbed it "the aerie"), secluded from the hustle and bustle of the metropolis, on a shady, tree-lined road where one can still hear wild parrots at dawn. The large walled compound offered endless opportunities for unrestricted play, adventure and friendships for my daughters on vacation.

Hindu Demagogues

Now all that has changed drastically as demagogic Hindu nationalist politicians, charging that the Government has turned its back on India's 730 million Hindus while pandering to its 100 million Muslims, are trying to force it out of power. So far, their effort to mount a massive protest rally in New Delhi has failed.

Religion in India is taken seriously but, periodic eruptions aside, it has been a private affair. Most of us came of age in post-independence India. Our parents subscribed to the secular ideals of Mahatma Gandhi and Jawaharlal Nehru. Our secularism has not been a denial of religion but a respect for differences. And Bombay, India's most modern city, enshrined this tradition of tolerance.

> *"Hindu nationalists . . . have a program of violence and intimidation intended to expel Muslims."*

That pluralism is being torn asunder now, not by "fundamentalist Hindus" (an oxymoron—there is no official Hindu dogma, no "fundamentals" that Hindus agree on) but by self-servingly callous politicians across India. These opportunists of every party divide and rule, exploiting the economically disadvantaged of all religions by fanning their fears.

Bombay's heterogeneous society has thus been sectarianized by a chauvinistic party, the Shiv Sena, whose 40,000 activists have built a power base in the city, the capital of Maharashtra state. In past years, this party, campaigning along linguistic lines on a Maharashtra for Maharashtrians platform, had sought to expel south Indians and other "outsiders" who flock to Bombay in search of jobs.

In a bid for political supremacy in the state, the Shiv Sena has leaped on the countrywide bandwagon of Hindu nationalists, who want India to be a Hindu nation, not a secular state, and who have a program of violence and intimidation intended to expel Muslims.

The Bombay Riots

During the January 1993 Bombay riots, the feuding politicians of the state's ruling Congress Party were paralyzed by ineptness and intraparty rivalry, and the police force was immobilized by the Shiv Sena's infiltration of its lower ranks. Thus, the violence could neither be prevented nor stopped.

"Bombay is burning! I can see the fires from the windows," gasped my sister-in-law when I telephoned on my return to New York. Everything had been peaceful as usual over the holidays that I had just spent there. Now, I was told, there were Hindu-Muslim riots all over the city. A couple of miles away, a slum was singled out for destruction by the Shiv Sena. The entire area was blockaded by angry Hindus. Muslim families were cornered and had to climb the arid hill behind their huts that leads steeply to the foot of our compound.

I was stunned. The only living creatures ever to come up that hill and over our wall were the occasional wild peacocks during the monsoon. Now came these families from below the hill—toddlers in tow, infants in arms, small suitcases holding their belongings—about 100 Muslims, clambering over the short wall onto the lawn. They sped across the compound and left through the front gate as miserably as they came, making their way to the railway station and out of the city. Gone, perhaps forever.

My brother was shaken up. He knew that hill first-hand. As a young boy, on a dare, he had tried to go down it but had to come back up, unable to negotiate a firm foothold on that rough terrain. With small children of his own now, he could empathize with these families.

No sooner had these unfortunates left than the Hindu mob followed. Armed with sharp swords, kitchen knives, monkey wrenches, the crowd was as unlikely as Birnam Wood coming to Dunsinane. The police, in collusion with the hooligans, told my brother they would not respond "until three or four are dead."

Stopping the Mob

Strings were pulled at the highest levels and a police battalion arrived just as the first of the threatening mob approached the wall. After repeated warnings, the officers fired into the mob, killing one and injuring two. The bodies rolled down the hill as the residents and the children of our building gaped in shock.

The mob scattered but its leader returned later to kidnap the compound's chief security guard "for questioning." Two days later, he was released, badly beaten. The hoodlums, seeking revenge, wanted to know who had called the police and who had given refuge to a resident's Muslim employee and his family. I was worried for my brother's safety.

Since then we have learned of the pogrom in which more than 600 were butchered. The property of Muslims was systematically burned and hundreds of thousands of Muslim families fled Bombay in panic.

Here in New York I am continually asked about "ethnic cleansing." I try to explain there is nothing ethnic about this barbarism. Muslims in India are not racially different from the Hindus; we are all the same. Yes, the religion is different but that never prevented enduring friendships and harmonious co-existence.

> *"There is nothing ethnic about this barbarism. Muslims in India are not racially different from the Hindus."*

My grandmother's oldest friend was her Muslim physician, who doled out free medicines to his poor patients, Hindus and Muslims alike. My father's mentor was a cultured Muslim patriarch, with whose vast family my father spent his happiest formative years. My own best friend since high school is a Muslim who is closer to me than a sister. And these are not exceptions. The lives of Hindus and Muslims have been so entwined over the centuries that it is not easy to disentangle them.

Pleas for Sanity

Even at this distance, I hear the cris de coeur of ordinary Bombayites—Hindus, Muslims, Christians, Jews and Parsis—pleading publicly for a return to

154

sanity. For now, though, one cannot tell whether life there will ever be as before. Our beloved city has been devastated; we have been violated.

Our home no longer feels safe. I used to see continuity in my little niece's living in that eyrie and playing in that garden as I had done, decades before her. Now I am not sure. The police are still standing guard in my brother's compound. Anything could erupt anytime.

What I have lost is my home—that quality of life, that degree of security, that easy camaraderie that cut across religious lines. That loss is irreparable.

Chapter 3

What Are the Causes of Ethnic Conflict?

CURRENT CONTROVERSIES

Ethnic Conflict: An Overview

by Robin Wright

About the author: *Robin Wright is a staff writer for the* Los Angeles Times *daily newspaper.*

In Georgia, little Abkhazia and South Ossetia both seek secession, while Kurds want to carve a state out of Turkey. French Quebec edges toward separation from Canada, as deaths in Kashmir's Muslim insurgency against Hindu-dominated India pass the 6,000-mark. Kazakhstan's tongue-twisting face-off pits ethnic Kazakhs against Russian Cossacks, while Scots in Britain, Tutsis in Rwanda, Basques and Catalans in Spain and Tuaregs in Mali and Niger all seek varying degrees of self-rule or statehood.

Tribal Hatreds

The world's now dizzying array of ethnic hot spots—at least four dozen at last count—starkly illustrates how, of all the features of the post-Cold War world, the most consistently troubling are turning out to be the tribal hatreds that divide humankind by race, faith and nationality.

"The explosion of communal violence is the paramount issue facing the human rights movement today. And containing the abuses committed in the name of ethnic or religious groups will be our foremost challenge for years to come," said Kenneth Ross, acting executive director of Human Rights Watch, a global monitoring group based in New York.

Indeed, xenophobia, religious rivalry and general intolerance of anything different are often now more anguishing and cruel—not to mention costly in human lives and material destruction—than the ideological differences that until recently divided the world.

The reversion to some of the oldest organizational principles of humankind reflects an attraction seemingly more potent than the prevalent 20th-Century principle of assimilation either by choice or by force—concepts such as the

U.S. "melting pot" or communism's "dictatorship of the proletariat."

Why is ethnicity so powerful? And why now, at the end of the 20th Century, in defiance of so much that the period has stood for?

Since Communist doctrine began unraveling in 1989, conventional wisdom has linked the psychology and politics of hatred to the end of totalitarian rule that repressed ancient rivalries.

History Catches Up

Today's clashes between Serbs and Bosnian Muslims, for example, date back centuries to political and cultural hostility between the Ottoman and Austro-Hungarian empires. In Sudan, Africa's largest state, the war pitting Christian and animist black Africans in the south against the Arab Muslim north has roots in the 19th Century—even before the birth of the modern state.

"To a large extent, history is catching up with us. Most ethnic conflicts have a background of domination, injustice or oppression by one ethnic group or another," explained John Garang the U.S.-educated chairman and guerrilla commander of the Sudan People's Liberation Movement in the south.

"In our case in the Sudan, it goes back centuries to the slave trade. The northern Sudanese were the slave traders selling people from the south," he said in an interview.

Yet the proliferation of hatreds is not simply history's legacy to the Post-Modern Era, a cruel trick that has made old differences seemingly emerge out of thin air after disappearing for decades. History provides only the context.

"Ethnicity is not enduring and unstinting; it's shaped and given form. And what we take to be historic and ancient is often modern and recent," said Augustus Richard Norton, a political scientist at the U.S. Military Academy at West Point.

The passions have instead been produced by a confluence of diverse factors ranging from modernization and migration to democratization and limited resources, according to specialists. They flourish on fear and uncertainty.

The most basic cause stems from the Modern Era, which opened the way for cultural standardization and mass migration, the latter capped in the 20th Century by the largest movement of humankind in history.

On the eve of the 21st Century, fewer than 10% of the world's 191 nations are still ethnically or racially homogeneous.

"Xenophobia, religious rivalry and general intolerance of anything different are often . . . anguishing and cruel."

The impact of global migrations and intermixing is reflected in a stark fact: Depending on definition, there are now between 7,000 and 8,000 linguistic, ethnic or religious minorities in the world, according to Alan Phillips, director of Minority Rights Group, a human rights monitoring organization based in London. In fact, virtually every ethnic

158

group has a minority branch living somewhere outside its own borders.

The sheer magnitude of migrations in an ever more crowded world makes clashes and conflict virtually unavoidable.

The amalgamation of the world's peoples has already resulted in a host of otherwise unlikely skirmishes—between descendants of Africans and Koreans in white-dominated Los Angeles, or between Asian Indians and blacks in a South Africa ruled by descendants of Dutch and British settlers.

Concerns of Cultural Decline

Ethnic and religious tensions have also risen due to anxieties that minority cultures will be eliminated—a not unjustified fear. In the 19th Century, South America boasted 1,000 Indian languages; in the late 20th, there are fewer than 200, according to the U.N. [United Nations] Development Program's 1993 Human Development Report.

Courtesy of communications and technology, modernization is also standardizing everything from dress to music, while industrialization and Westernization have challenged traditional skills and arts, especially in developing countries.

Even in Communist Tashkent, Islamic Tehran and island-nations like Taiwan, oral folklore is increasingly being replaced by Arnold Schwarzenegger videos, ethnic music by Madonna and Metallica tapes.

> *"There are now between 7,000 and 8,000 linguistic, ethnic or religious minorities in the world."*

"The forces of modernization have given many people a sense that they don't belong anywhere, or that there's nothing permanent or stable in their lives," explained Allen Kassof, director of the Project on Ethnic Relations in Princeton, N.J.

"It's quite understandable that they then seek something that seems eternal and can't be taken away from them. One is membership in a group. Another is a belief system or religion."

Some cultures are already minorities in their own lands: Native Fijians are outnumbered by descendants of indentured Indian workers. Kazakhs are only 40% of Kazakhstan, about equal to descendants of Russian settlers in the large former Soviet republic. And throughout North and South America, Indian populations have dwindled to small percentages of the total.

"Cultures need to be respected and constantly asserted or they die. Hence the determination of many groups, particularly indigenous peoples, to participate actively to preserve and reassert their identity," the U.N. Development Program report added.

The proliferation of minorities in the 20th Century—and the consciousness accompanying it—has effectively created a new set of incentives for conflict. "The conflicts of the future are likely to be between people rather than states over issues related to culture, ethnicity or religion," Mahbub ul Haq, a special

U.N. Development Program adviser and former Pakistani minister of finance and planning, said in an interview.

Power Quest

The second factor is the deliberate manipulation of longstanding fears and passions by contemporary governments.

"[The year] 1992 has made clear that the roots of most of these conflicts lie less in eternal antagonisms than in particular governmental abuses that exacerbate communal tensions," according to Human Rights Watch's 1993 World Report.

In a variation of the old divide-and-rule tactic, a growing number of regimes have recently tried to build followings by exploiting ethnic, religious and other differences.

President Samuel K. Doe's heavy-handedness against all Liberian tribes except his own Krahn people and President Mohamed Siad Barre's manipulation of Somalia's diverse clans sparked two of Africa's nastiest civil wars. Both nations have since imploded.

In Sri Lanka, an estimated 20,000 have been killed and more than 1.5 million displaced since 1990 in a contemporary conflict sparked by age-old discrimination by predominantly Buddhist Sinhalese against minority Hindu Tamils.

Other governments claim that ethnic separatist or independence movements have forced responses that violate human rights.

On the grounds of fighting secessionists, the Indian government justifies torture, abductions and murder of Kashmiri Muslims and Punjabi Sikhs, and the Turkish government excuses abuses in handling minority Kurds, reports Human Rights Watch.

At the core of both tactics is a new breed of ethno-politicians "who see their future power base as lying in leading ethnic communities. They appeal to the basest human instinct by portraying a group as threatened from outside," Kassof said.

Among the most blatant examples have been former Communist leaders in Eastern Europe and the former Soviet republics—such as Serbian President Slobodan Milosevic and Uzbekistan President Islam Karimov—who are both trying to sustain their own careers by making fear and hate primary tools of politics.

"The proliferation of minorities . . . has effectively created a new set of incentives for conflict."

In Sudan, Garang charged that civil war erupted largely because Hassan Turabi, the power behind Khartoum's government, wanted to impose Sharia, or Islamic law throughout Sudan.

"Contemporary leaders use the accumulated historical animosity for their own political and economic gains. Turabi uses it to promote his Islamic agenda, which we consider a threat to our way of life and a violation of our human rights," he said. "And when those conditions reach a level of intolerance, then people go to war."

The rising ethnic tension over minority Hungarians in Romania, Slovakia and the rump Yugoslav nation—mostly remnants of the old Austro-Hungarian empire—is also less linked to the demise of communism than to post-Communist leaders who are exploiting the issue.

> *"Contemporary leaders use the accumulated historical animosity for their own political and economic gains."*

"The hatred is new, but it's built around traditional differences that, but for nationalist appeals of opportunistic leaders would not have been transformed into hostility or warfare," explained Ross.

Democratization and Insecurity

The third major factor is related to ideology—both the current wave of democratization worldwide and the lack of alternatives.

Transitions to democracy, for example, can create uncertainty that fuels ethnic and religious passions, and eventually rivalries. "The problem is not democracy *per se*, but the turbulent transition to democracy," said Jack Snyder, a Columbia University political scientist.

As the former East Germans and Russians, South Africans and Jordanians have learned painfully, even political shock therapy does not produce overhauls overnight. Along the way, reforming governments have faced increasing unemployment, inflation, crime waves, public disillusionment and even resistance.

In South Africa, much of the black-on-black violence, now bloodier than black-white clashes during decades of apartheid, is a product of changing times. Zulus particularly have been reluctant to surrender their legendary identity, and the tacit power that went with it, in a new multiracial state.

"The tremendous psychological pressure on human populations from political change creates a sense of anxiety that frequently makes people seek refuge in belief systems that involve definitions of membership and belonging," Kassof said.

Ironically, the absence of an alternative to democracy also encourages ethnic and religious passions.

"Inter-communal strife is a product of the discrediting of alternative ideologies. The idea of Western democracy, while appealing to many, lacks an antithesis to those who do not want to adopt it as a way of life," Ross added. "So people fall back on their primordial identities, like religion and ethnicity, when there is no alternative available."

The most visible case is the explosion of political Islam in places like Algeria and Egypt. But as Islamists redefine identities and agendas, Algeria's ethnic Berbers and Egypt's Coptic Christians sense new threats—and are acting accordingly.

The final factor relates to resources and economics. At the simplest level, the struggle to survive can spawn or deepen ethnic or religious hatreds.

"The more limited the resources the greater the danger of ethnic strife," said Garang. In Sudan, the multilayered hostility between northerners and southerners, Arabs and Africans, Muslims and Christians has been exacerbated by a hostile desert environment and the chronic recent cycle of drought and famine.

For a range of reasons not necessarily bad or intentionally divisive, ethnic groups are also often positioned differently in an economy. Again, change can accentuate differences, triggering hostility or drastic action.

Czechoslovakia was a prime example. Czechs were better positioned, due to their skills and economic activities in their republic, for radical market reforms. But the same plan hurt the Slovaks, because their economy centered on once-profitable but now outdated military and heavy industries difficult to adapt to free market conditions or the new European Community markets.

"This created very different incentives for the two republics and contributed significantly to Czechoslovakia's breakup," Snyder said.

For all the dangers unleashed by ethnicity, however, scholars and analysts all counsel against condemning or trying to block ethnic expression. "It's misguided to attack the politics of ethnicity as opposed to the intolerance of many ethnic politicians," Snyder warned.

"Ironically, the absence of an alternative to democracy also encourages ethnic and religious passions."

"It's perfectly appropriate, for example, for black leaders to organize politically or to define their interests collectively along black lines, because neither suggests an intolerance of alternative ways of life or other races. It's their right."

Many also contend that there is no way to stop or reverse ethnicity. "Our tendencies toward separatism and tribalism seem to reflect something very deep in the human condition, which scholarship confirms," Kassof said.

Yet some hold out eventual hope that ethnicity will be less divisive. "At the end of the day, we will eventually have one human community," said Garang. "But that is still a long time away."

Nationalism Causes Ethnic Conflict

by Jay Stuller

About the author: *Jay Stuller is a free-lance writer in San Francisco. His articles have appeared in several magazines, including* Audubon *and* Smithsonian.

Fueled by intense blood-feud passions that few Americans have experienced, or can even fully understand, ethnic animosities once again are burning throughout the world. This tribal revival is rapidly becoming the international epidemic of the 1990s. Today, we see it as the ethnic violence that is destroying Yugoslavia and may yet fracture India. But it also may make headlines as hypernationalism—when a single ethnic group dominating one country, say Germany or Japan, feels threatened by a changing world. It was ethnic conflicts, after all, that helped start both world wars. Ironically, the breakup of the Soviet Union has catalyzed much of this tribal revival. If left unchecked tribalism may become more dangerous than any U.S.-USSR showdown, many experts believe.

After all, superpower beefs, tempered by fear of massive mutual destruction, are one thing. Blood feuds are another. Ethnic conflicts are the most savage among the human species.

Tribal Clashes

Today, ethnic groups—or people with common ties of ancestry, language, culture, nationality, race, religion or some combination of several elements— are binding tighter and tighter, and seeking control over their destinies. These tribes include people without countries, minorities and even majorities in lands controlled by others.

For much of this century, nationalism integrated diverse faiths and cultures into unified countries. Now many countries are breaking apart, or threatened because of these tribal clashes:

• *Serbs vs. Croats.* Since the end of World War II, authoritarian communist governments kept a lid on the historically contentious Balkans. Today, 50 years

Jay Stuller, "Tribal Wars," *The American Legion Magazine*, January 1993. Reprinted by permission, *The American Legion Magazine*, copyright 1993.

of suppressed hatreds are flaring as Orthodox Christian Serbs, Catholic Croats, Muslim Slavs and Albanians seek control over their lives.

The violence literally has torn apart the fabric of what was once the ethnic crazy quilt of Yugoslavia. And similar situations are shredding order within several former Soviet states.

• *Hindus vs. Muslims.* The world's largest democracy, India, is being threatened with disintegration as Sikhs, Hindus, Muslims and Tamils strive—wherever they live in great numbers—for independence or self-determination. Much of the violence is selective, with nationalist assassins targeting leaders of other groups. But the potential for a larger conflict looms at any given moment.

In 1992, for example, in the north Indian market town of Hapur, a seemingly bizarre dispute between Hindus and Muslims—over a religious "miracle" of a snake in a tree—led to riots and deaths. In fact, the fight was really about land ownership, economic and social power, a microcosm of entire nations.

• *Scotland vs. United Kingdom.* A recent poll revealed that half of Scotland wants independence after nearly three centuries as a part of the United Kingdom. As James Kellas of Glasgow University told *U.S. News & World Report:* "If Slovenia and Croatia can be accepted as independent states, why not Scotland?"

• *Quebec vs. Canada.* English-speaking Canada is considering what was once unthinkable. Weary of the "distinct society" demands and threats of secession by French-speaking Quebec, the rest of Canada now seems ready to let the province go.

> *"Ethnic conflicts are the most savage among the human species."*

• *Germany vs. Europe.* And perhaps most disturbing, a reunified Germany is surging with nationalism and exerting its weight in the European Community. Combining that with ethnic fervor—and the concept of Aryan superiority isn't exactly new to German thinking—is a recipe for aggressive hypernationalism. Says James Rollo of the Royal Institute of International Affairs in London, "What we see—some among us, with a shudder—is Germany taking the helm in Europe."

A Threat to America

Are the outbreaks of ethnic violence, separatism and such merely local troubles? Or will they endanger America and its interests?

The latter is entirely possible, according to John Mearsheimer, chairman of the University of Chicago's political science department. If any one European state attempts to become a "hegemony" or dominant power on the Continent, says Mearsheimer, the United States and Great Britain have historically responded with force.

Neither Germany, France, the old Soviet Union nor any other state appears to have such designs—right now. What's worrisome is that a number of the new and reformulated European nations have access to, or the capability of building, nuclear weapons. If, say, the Ukrainians and Russians come into nuclear conflict, adds Mearsheimer, "we've all got a big problem." But how likely is that?

"A number of the new and reformulated European nations have access to . . . nuclear weapons."

Well, blood feuds can simmer for centuries. A number of Balkan ethnic groups still seethe at the Turks and the 500-year rule of the Ottoman Empire, which ended with World War I. Hatreds between the Serbs and Albanians date to an incident in 1389. The Medieval Crusades still shape Middle Eastern views toward Europe and the West.

"It's difficult for Americans to relate to this depth of passion because we're a fairly young nation," says Stephen Worchel, a professor of psychology at Texas A&M University. "Sure, we feel patriotic, or have ties to Irish, African and other heritages. But where ethnic groups have lived for centuries and even thousands of years, there are much stronger feelings for the land itself."

Ethnic groups express and celebrate their differences in what Benjamin Barber, a Rutgers University political science professor, calls a "Jihad," or holy war. Those waging the battles, he writes, "are cultures, not countries; parts, not wholes; sects, not religions; rebellious factions and dissenting minorities at war, not just with globalism but with the traditional nation-state."

In some cases, there develops what Ervin Staub, a professor of psychology at the University of Massachusetts, calls a "continuum of destruction" that leads to genocide against the out-group. This is what happened to the Jews in Europe during World War II, or the Kurds in Iraq after the Gulf War.

For more than four decades, the United States and the Soviet Union anchored the world's bipolar power structure. Peace in the critical buffer zone of Eastern Europe served both powers. In retrospect, the order enforced by communist authoritarians seems almost like a blessing.

Up for Grabs

The borders and power in the former Soviet Union and Eastern Europe are now up for grabs, a sure-fire trigger for ethnic fighting.

For example, bitter territorial disputes between the Armenian minority and the more numerous Azeris in Azerbaijan, a member of the Commonwealth of Independent States, have taken more than 1,500 lives.

The same thing [brewed] in Czechoslovakia, where the have-not Slovaks display[ed] a growing resentment of the haves, the Czechs who control[led] the economy.

Hungary and Romania have long glared at each other over Romania's treatment of the 2 million ethnic Hungarians who live in Transylvania, which was once Hungarian territory.

However, the greatest threat stems from groups with loyalties that can be manipulated by charismatic leaders. In a Jihad, writes Barber of Rutgers University, "solidarity is secured through war with outsiders. And solidarity often means obedience to a hierarchy in governance . . . fanaticism in beliefs."

Deference to leaders and intolerance of outsiders sets the stage for the rise of a dictator. This also leads to the specter of hypernationalism, where nation-states composed mostly of people from a single ethnic group feel threatened by other states or minority scapegoats, and then lash out.

Hypernationalism is tribalism in its full fury. It motivated the Germanic and Japanese tribes in the 1930s. The result was Hitler's grab of lands populated by ethnic Germans, the Holocaust and more. It also drove Japanese expansionism. And it could happen again in Europe, says University of Chicago political scientist Mearsheimer, if the powers on the Continent do not remain balanced.

The United States probably has neither the interests nor the ability to intervene in most of these situations. We can look on with sadness and despair at the killing in Yugoslavia. While American troops tried to protect the Kurds from Iraqi genocide, the effort was more moral than strategic.

However, since it was ethnic turmoil in the Balkans that sparked World War I, the United Nation's peacekeeping forces in Yugoslavia may help to slow or stop the ethnic war there.

> *"Deference to leaders and intolerance of outsiders sets the stage for the rise of a dictator."*

It is most critical to the United States to thwart or keep in check a potential hegemony in Europe, says Mearsheimer. At the moment, no European nation seems to have hegemonic designs, so there's a growing sentiment for the United States to withdraw from NATO.

History, however, is all too often forgotten, as is the dark side of ethnic passion.

For example, Germany has tried on a new, reunified nationalist pride, and likes it. But its immigration problems are stirring up a terrorizing, neo-Nazi fringe. And ultra-right wingers are winning a few local elections. In further echoes of the 1930s, Germany also seems to be developing border disputes with Poland. Such tribal muscle-flexing suggests the initial symptoms of hypernationalism.

So, what can and should the United States do about the tribal revival, particularly in Europe? Among other experts, Mearsheimer argues that the United States must continue its efforts to discourage the proliferation of nuclear weapons to keep them out of the hands of hot-headed countries.

Spreading Democracy

Likewise, the United States, Great Britain and the Continental powers should work together to limit any potential hegemony, an argument for America's continued presence in Europe. Hypernationalism in any European nation, says Mearsheimer, "will be a force for trouble unless curbed."

As for the growing fragmentation of the nation-states, the United States can do little. Probably the best policy for America is to continue to churn out and spread its global culture of democracy and the free market—from free elections to McDonald's—and keep the tribes talking to each other.

We aren't completely hopeless as a species, argues University of Massachusetts professor Staub.

"The way to overcome the barriers and perceptions of threat is through socialization, which means frequent contact," he explains. "Global communications is part of it, but so is international contact that puts everyone on equal footing. Working on projects together goes a long way toward overcoming the urge to devalue and hate another group."

Granted, the world has no shortage of projects. Cleaning the environment, especially in Eastern Europe and the former Soviet Union, will demand global cooperation. Still, the kind of situations found throughout Europe, and wherever political power threatens to change, is a formula for violence.

Ethnic passions helped start both world wars. It can happen again, unless the tribes of the world learn to live together.

Religious Radicalism Causes Ethnic Conflict

by Mark Juergensmeyer

About the author: *Mark Juergensmeyer is dean of the School of Hawaiian, Asian, and Pacific Studies and a professor of religion and political science at the University of Hawaii in Honolulu. Juergensmeyer is the author of* The New Cold War? Religious Nationalism Confronts the Secular State, *from which this viewpoint is excerpted.*

"There is a desperate need for religion in public life," the dean of Egypt's premier school of Islamic theology told me. He meant, he went on to say, that there should be not only a high standard of morality in public offices but also a fusion of the religious and political identities of the Egyptian people. From his point of view, the Islamic religion is "a culturally liberating force," which Egypt as a nation urgently needs in order to free itself from the last vestiges of its colonial past. "Western colonialism has gone," the dean explained, "but we still have not completed our independence. We will not be free until Egypt becomes a Muslim state."

A New Cold War

In interviews I conducted in half a dozen troubled countries during the late 1980s and early 1990s, I found that his point of view is not idiosyncratic. The longing for an indigenous form of religious politics free from the taint of Western culture has been expressed by many in countries that have become independent in this century: not only by Egyptians, but by Central Asians and other Muslims from Algeria to Indonesia, and by Ukrainians, Sri Lankans, Indians, Israelis, Mongolians, and intensely religious persons of a variety of faiths throughout the globe. In fact, what appeared to be an anomaly when the Islamic revolution in Iran challenged the supremacy of Western culture and its secular politics in 1979 has become a major theme in international politics in the 1990s. The new world order that is replacing the bipolar powers of the old Cold

War is characterized not only by the rise of new economic forces, a crumbling of old empires, and the discrediting of communism, but also by the resurgence of parochial identities based on ethnic and religious allegiances. Although Francis Fukuyama, among others, has asserted that the ending of the old Cold War has led to an "end of history" and a worldwide ideological consensus in favor of secular liberal democracy, the rise of new religious and ethnic nationalism belies that assertion. Moreover, proponents of the new nationalisms hold the potential of making common cause against the secular West, in what might evolve into a new Cold War. . . .

Why Religious Confrontations Are Violent

A disturbing feature of the new movements for religious nationalism is the ease with which some of their leaders resort to violence. The Sikh leader Sant Jarnail Singh Bhindranwale praised his young lieutenants for hijacking an airplane and called for full concessions to his demands from India's political leaders "or their heads." Iran's Ayatollah Sayyed Khomeini said he knew of no command "more binding to the Muslim than the command to sacrifice life and property to defend and bolster Islam." A right-wing Jewish leader in Israel told me in passing, "Of course we have no problem with using force to win our religious goals." Not only have a number of political leaders fallen at the hands of religious assassins in recent years, but so have thousands of defenders of both the secular states and the religious revolutions.

Revolutionaries of all kinds are violent, and it is not surprising that religious revolutionaries are as well. Yet the ferocity of some religious nationalists is jarring: they seem to be even more violent than necessary, and they cloak their violence in religious rhetoric. The question is whether there is a special relationship between religion and violence that makes this ferocity possible and gives an added impetus to the violent behavior of religious revolutionaries.

Even ordinary religion contains a strand of violence. Some of the world's most significant religious symbols are stained with blood. The savage martyrdom of Husain in Shi'ite Islam, the crucifixion of Jesus in Christianity, the sacrifice of Guru Tegh Bahadur in Sikhism, the bloody conquests detailed in the Hebrew Bible, the terrible battles celebrated in the Hindu epics, and the religious wars described in the Sinhalese Buddhist Pali Chronicles—all these events indicate that in virtually every religious tradition images of violence occupy a central place. For

> *"The ferocity of some religious nationalists is jarring: they seem to be even more violent than necessary."*

that reason, any attempt to understand the violence of religious nationalism must begin with an understanding of the violent nature of religion in general.

A spate of studies attests to the fact that the seeming ubiquity of these symbols of religious violence is not coincidental. The authors of these studies, including René Girard, Walter Burkert, and Eli Sagan, give social and psychological reasons for the virtual universality of violence in religion. According to Girard's thesis—probably the most articulate and most widely discussed explanation—violent religious symbols and sacrificial rituals evoke, and thereby vent, violent impulses in general. Girard is here following the lead of Sigmund Freud, but unlike Freud Girard pinpoints as the root cause of violence "mimetic desire"—the desire to

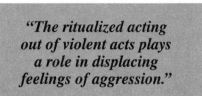

"The ritualized acting out of violent acts plays a role in displacing feelings of aggression."

imitate a rival—rather than sexuality and aggression. Girard thinks ritualized violence performs a positive role: by allowing members of societies to release their feelings of hostility toward members of their own communities, it enables groups to achieve increased social cohesion. "The function of ritual," claims Girard, "is to 'purify' violence; that is, to 'trick' violence into spending itself on victims whose death will provoke no reprisals." Those who participate in ritual are not consciously aware of the social and psychological significance of their acts, for Girard claims that "religion tries to account for its own operation metaphorically."

Symbolic Violence

Much of what Girard says about the function of symbolic violence in religion is persuasive. Even if one questions, as I do, Girard's idea that mimetic desire is the driving force behind symbols of religious violence, one can still agree with him that, in most religions, sacrifice occupies a central place and that the ritualized acting out of violent acts plays a role in displacing feelings of aggression, thereby allowing the world to be a more peaceful place in which to live.

But what about real acts of religious violence? The death squads of Sikh and Sinhalese revolutionaries, the terrorists among militant Lebanese and Egyptian Muslims, and the religious soldiers pledged to Jewish and Christian causes are all engaged in violence in a direct and nonsymbolic way. At first glance their actions do not appear to fit Girard's theories, nor do they result in the peaceful displacement of violence that ritualized forms of religious violence are supposed to produce.

On closer inspection, however, some of these real cases of violence do seem to fit the pattern after all because the violence is committed in an almost symbolic way. The acts themselves—such as the hijacking of American planes by Muslim terrorists and the murder of a busload of Hindu pilgrims in the Himalayan foothills by a band of radical Sikh youth—are performed dramatically. They are illegal, abnormal, and shocking acts, carried out with the intention of vividly displaying the destructive power of violence. All acts of killing are violent, but these are even more violent than death inflicted during warfare or through capital punishment, in part because they have a symbolic impact. They are deliberately designed to elicit feelings of revulsion and anger in those who witness them. In some cases the killing takes the form of religious sacrifice. Martin Kramer has demonstrated that when the Lebanese Hizbollah group of terrorists chose one of their own to be a martyr/victim to lead a suicide attack against Americans and Israelis, their choice had all the characteristics of a sacrificial victim in traditional religious rites.

Still, most real acts of religious violence do not easily fit the Girardian scheme. The reason, I believe, is that most acts of religious violence are less like sacrifice than they are like war. One can think of religious warfare as a blend of sacrifice and martyrdom: sacrificing members of the enemy's side and offering up martyrs on one's own. But behind the gruesome litany is an idea that encompasses both sacrifice and martyrdom and much more: the dichotomy between the sacred and profane. This great encounter between cosmic forces—an ultimate good and evil, a divine truth and falsehood—is a war that worldly struggles only mimic. . . .

Religious Sanction for the Use of Violence

The language of cosmic struggle is easily exploited by political activists who want to give sacred legitimacy to worldly causes. Sometimes they do so only for the sake of public relations. In other instances it is for a much more important purpose: empowerment. Because religion has the ability to give moral sanction to violence, and violence is the most potent force that a nonlegal entity can possess, religion can be a potent political tool.

The Sikh case is an interesting example of religious legitimization. Among the Sikh concerns are a number that most people in India would regard as perfectly legitimate—the inadequacy of Sikh political representation and the inequity of agricultural prices. These issues did not need the additional moral weight of religion to give them respectability. In fact, the Sikh businessmen and political leaders who were primarily concerned about such issues were seldom supporters of Bhindranwale and his militant followers, at least early on. Even when they were later drawn into his campaign, their relation to him and his strident religious language remained ambivalent.

"Most acts of religious violence are less like sacrifice than they are like war."

One political demand, however, was not widely supported at the outset, and it desperately needed all the legitimization that it could get, including the legitimacy it could garner from religion. This was the demand for Khalistan, a separate Sikh nation. Although it was seen initially as a political solution to the Sikhs' desire for a separate identity, it soon became a religious crusade. Separatist leaders such as Jagjit Singh Chauhan appealed to Bhindranwale for support and were greatly buoyed when he said, "I have always expressed myself in favor of mobilising the entire Sikh world under one

171

flag." They cheered when he stated further that he would fight for a separate identity for the Sikhs, "even if it demands sacrifice."

Despite these fighting words, Bhindranwale never explicitly supported Khalistan. "We are not in favor of Khalistan nor are we against it," he said, adding that "we wish to live in India" but would settle for a separate state if the Sikhs did not receive what he regarded as just respect.

> *"Virtually all religions . . . sanction violence that gives them political power."*

Whatever his own reservations about the Khalistan issue, his appeal to sacrifice made his rhetoric attractive to the separatists. It also suggested another, potentially more powerful result of the sacralization of political demands: the prospect that religion could give moral sanction to violence.

Violence in a Just War

Even though virtually all religions preach the virtues of nonviolence, it is their ability to sanction violence that gives them political power. The Sikh tradition, for instance, ordinarily applauds nonviolence and proscribes the taking of human life. Even Bhindranwale acknowledged that "for a Sikh it is a great sin to keep weapons and kill anyone." But he then went on to justify the occasional violent act in extraordinary circumstances and said that "it is an even greater sin to have weapons and not to seek justice." Many other religious leaders, be they Christian or Muslim or Native American, agree. They believe that the rule against killing may be abrogated in unusual circumstances when social or spiritual justice is at stake.

Killing is often justified during a "just war"—a conflict that is deemed appropriate because the end merits it and the means to achieve it may in fact moderate the violence that existed before the conflict. First stated by Cicero, the theory of just war was developed by [Saints] Ambrose and Augustine into a Christian doctrine that was later refined by Thomas Aquinas. It has analogues in Jewish, Islamic, and many other traditions as well. Christians supporting the liberation struggle in Latin America have speculated that there can be a "just revolution" as well as a "just war."

A similar question was raised by Meir Kahane regarding his own movement for establishing a religious state in Israel and the West Bank. According to him, Jewish law allows for two kinds of just war: obligatory and permissible. An obligatory war is required for defense, while a permissible war is allowed when it seems prudent. The determination of when conditions exist for a just war is to be made by the Sanhedrin or a prophet (in the case of permissible war) or a Halakhic [Talmudic legal] state (in the case of obligatory war). None of these religious entities exists in the present day. In the absence of such authorities, the existence of the necessary conditions is to be determined by any authoritative interpreter of Halakha, such as a rabbi. Kahane was himself a rabbi and perhaps for that reason felt free to pass judgment on the morality of his own movement's actions.

National Pride

Kahane called on the people of Israel to rise up and reclaim the West Bank in a just war. He argued that defense was not the only religious basis for warfare: national pride was also a legitimate reason. He reminded the Jews that their claim to the West Bank came from a 2,000-year-old vision that originated when the Jews came "out of the fear and shame of exile." And now, he asked them, "What about our national pride?" He pointed out that Jews were afraid to go to the Mount of Olives, much less to Judea and Samaria. He urged them to fight to retain their self-esteem and pride.

Kahane also justified acts of violence as expressions of the war that is already raging but that is seldom seen—the battle for the reestablishment of a Jewish state, the enemies of which are both Arabs and secular Jews. "Every Jew who is killed has two killers," Kahane explained: "the Arab who killed him and the government who let it happen." This logic exonerated Kahane's use of force not only against Arabs but against his own people.

In using violence against cosmic foes, the lives of individuals targeted for attack are not important. "We believe in collective justice," a right-wing Jewish leader explained. By that he meant that any individual who was part of a group deemed to be the enemy might justifiably become the object of a violent assault, even if he or she were an innocent bystander. In a cosmic war there is no such thing; all are potentially soldiers. "War is war," Kahane explained. One of the purposes of violence against civilian Arabs is to "scare them" and not let them assume that they can live in Israel peacefully or normally.

Some of Kahane's Arab opponents made precisely the same argument in justifying their struggle against the Israelis. The Palestinian leader Sheik Ahmed Yassin, in defending the *intifada* [uprising], explained that it is necessary in order to show the Israelis that the Palestinian situation is intolerable and should not be treated as ordinary. "There is a war going on," the sheik explained, implying that the *intifada* is simply an expression of a larger, hidden struggle.

Sheik Yassin justified his people's use of violence through the Islamic sanction for violence in the case of self-defense. He expanded the notion, however, to include the defense of one's dignity and pride as well as one's physical self. One of Yassin's

> *"An obligatory war is required for defense, while a permissible war is allowed when it seems prudent."*

colleagues, Sheik 'Abd al-Aziz 'Odeh, explained that the Islamic *intifada* is different from the *intifada* waged by secular supporters of the PLO [Palestine Liberation Organization] in that the Islamic struggle is a moral struggle as well as a political one and comes from religious commitment. It is also part of a tradition of Islamic protest against injustice. The *intifada* is a "sign from God," the sheik proclaimed, indicating that "the people need Islam as a center."

The *intifada* is sometimes described as a holy war but not always. The concept of jihad, although important, is not central to the thought of all Islamic nationalists. Defense of the faith—including the traditional mores of the faith—is a sufficient basis for political action. In Egypt, in part because of the influence of the writings

> *"In using violence against cosmic foes, the lives of individuals targeted for attack are not important."*

of Abd Al-Salam Faraj, the "neglected duty" of jihad has increasingly been applied to political and paramilitary struggle as well as to military combat. Even in a political context, however, Muslim activists stress that jihad has a wider meaning than violent encounters with an enemy. At Cairo University, Professor Ibrahim Dasuqi Shitta explained that the "neglected duty" is a call for a general engagement against the forces of evil in the world, a battle that can be waged through economic policies and social service as well as through political and revolutionary action.

Violence Begets Violence

Most religious nationalists are able to find within their religious traditions an existing justification for violence that they then apply to their own revolutionary situations. Buddhist activists find themselves in an interesting position in this regard because their tradition proscribes any sort of violence, including the killing of animals. One might think that the doctrinal commitment to *ahimsa* [nonviolence] would prevent both monks and the laity in Buddhist societies from accepting the idea that violence could be morally approved or justified as an act of sacred war.

Yet in Sri Lanka some *bhikkhus* [monks] have explained the violence of Sinhalese activists in religious terms. Some monks told me that they actively participated in violence because there was no way to avoid violence "in a time of *dukkha* [suffering]." In such times, they said, violence naturally begets violence. Politicians who are violent and are seen as an enemy of religion might expect violence in return as a sort of karmic revenge. During such times evil rulers are always overthrown. "We believe in the law of karma," one of the bhikkhus added. "Those who live by the sword die by the sword."

The killing of Sri Lanka's prime minister by a Buddhist monk in 1959 underscores the seriousness of the monks' involvement and the degree to which they, like their clerical counterparts in every other religious tradition, are able to justify violence on moral—or rather, supramoral—grounds. Like violent actors in Sikhism, Islam, and Christianity, Buddhist militants have identified their political targets as enemies of religion and have thus been given sanction to take their lives. Those who want their use of violence to be morally sanctioned but who do not have the approval of an officially recognized government find it helpful to have access to a higher source: the metamorality that religion provides. By elevating a temporal struggle to the level of the cosmic, they can bypass the usual moral restrictions on killing. If their struggle is part of an enormous battle of the spirit, then it is not ordinary morality but the rules of war that apply. . . .

Claiming Power Wins Respect

Violence is empowering. The power that comes from the barrel of a gun is direct; the indirect, psychological dimension of this power may be even more effective. As Frantz Fanon argued in the context of Algeria's war of independence some years ago, even a small display of violence can have immense symbolic power by jolting the masses into an awareness of their own potency. In this sense there are in the Punjab, as in Sri Lanka and elsewhere in the world, aspects of social revolution embedded in violence that at first glance seems to be only religiously inspired.

It can be debated whether Bhindranwale succeeded in jolting the masses in the Punjab into an awareness of their own capabilities, but the violent actions of the militants among them have certainly made the masses more appreciative than they were of the militants' power. Militants are treated as if they possessed an authority rivaling that of the police and other government officials. One of the problems in the Punjab is that villagers in the so-called terrorist zones around Batala and Tarn Taran are unwilling to report terrorist activities to officials. The radical youth have even set up their own courts and governmental offices.

By being dangerous, these young religious radicals have gained a certain notoriety, and by clothing their actions in the moral garb of religion they have given those actions legitimacy. Because their activities are sanctioned by religion, they are not just random acts of terror but are strategic political actions: they break the state's monopoly on morally sanctioned killing. By putting the right to kill in their own hands, the perpetrators of religious violence are making a daring claim to power on behalf of those who previously had been impotent and ignored by those in power.

For these reasons it is not surprising that many radical movements for religious nationalism have been accompanied by violence. What is surprising is how many of them have not turned in a violent direction—even those that are as committed to their ideals and are as revolutionary in their goals as the violent ones. Although religious revolutionaries of all persuasions see a cosmic struggle emerging between the old order they wish to bury and the new religious nations they are pledged to create, a sizable number of them subscribe so deeply to democratic procedures and human rights that the violent potential of their struggle is tempered.

> *"Most religious nationalists are able to find . . . an existing justification for violence."*

Economic Prejudice Causes Ethnic Conflict

by Thomas Sowell

About the author: *Thomas Sowell is a syndicated columnist and a senior fellow at the Hoover Institution, a conservative think tank at Stanford University in Stanford, California.*

Hostility toward racial, religious, linguistic, and other minorities has been an all too common feature of human communities around the world for thousands of years. Some minorities seem to be disliked more than others, however, and some particular types of minorities seem to evoke the most seething hatred of all. While former slaves and conquered indigenes, for example, may be held in contempt and treated with cavalier disregard, those who have provoked the most bitterly intense animosities have often been middleman minorities. Middlemen play various roles as intermediaries between producers and consumers. They may be retailers, ranging from peddlers to shopkeepers to international traders, or they may be people who lend money, whether in the petty amounts of a pawnbroker or the vast sums of an international banker. Often the two functions are combined, as when retailers sell on credit and charge interest as part of the price of the goods sold.

Middleman Minorities

The largest of the racially or ethnically distinct groups who have played the role of middleman minority, at some stage of their history, are the 26 million "overseas Chinese" concentrated in various Southeast Asian countries, but also playing similar roles in parts of the Caribbean and North America. The most famous group in the role of middleman minority has of course been the Jews, the group to whom others have been analogized—the Chinese as "the Jews of Southeast Asia," the Lebanese as "the Jews of West Africa," and West Indians as "the black Jews of Harlem." Other groups who have been middleman minorities include the Armenians in the Ottoman Empire, Indians and Pakistanis scat-

From Thomas Sowell, "Middleman Minorities," *The American Enterprise*, May/June 1993. Reprinted with the author's permission.

tered through various countries along the east coast of Africa, Tamils in Sri Lanka, Japanese in Peru, Ibos in Nigeria, and Koreans in various inner cities of the United States.

While many kinds of minorities in many countries have faced hostility and even violence, truly historic levels of lethal violence have been directed at various middleman minori-

> *"Truly historic levels of lethal violence have been directed at various middleman minorities."*

ties. On more than one occasion in the history of Southeast Asia, the number of overseas Chinese massacred within a week has exceeded all the blacks lynched in the entire history of the United States. In the twentieth century, the scale of slaughter against the Armenians in the Ottoman Empire, and then against the Jews in Nazi-occupied Europe, required a new word—genocide.

Numbers alone, staggering as they have been, do not tell the whole story. When a Sinhalese mob in Sri Lanka dragged a Tamil woman, selected at random, from a bus and then burned her alive in the street—clapping their hands and dancing for joy as she died in agony—they showed a depth of hatred and venom seldom seen, except when directed against middleman minorities. Unfortunately, this ghastly scene has not been rare at all in Sri Lanka during the past generation. Historically, it recalls not only the pogroms against the Jews but also the Nazi Holocaust, where even mass murder was not sufficient to vent all the pent-up hatred, but was supplemented by gratuitous humiliations and tortures.

The spirit of the pogrom has been unleashed against other middleman minorities in various countries in recent times. Pogroms against the Chinese in Indonesia, or against the Ibos in northern Nigeria, have occurred long after the original pogroms in Europe were history. Back in the days of the Ottoman Empire, pogroms against Christian minorities who dominated commerce and finance were not uncommon. Jews in the Ottoman Empire were much less prominent in commerce and finance than were such Christian minorities as Greeks and Armenians—and often Jews were spared in the murderous mob attacks directed at the Christians. It is the role, rather than the people or their religion, which seems to be crucial. Prewar Japanese immigrants encountered far more hostility in Peru, where they were often middlemen, than in Brazil, where they deliberately settled in agricultural communities, in part to avoid the middleman stigma.

The Source of Animosities

While the United States has been spared such intergroup slaughters on the catastrophic scale that has afflicted other countries, nevertheless the attitudes behind such inhuman brutalities are all too evident, on a smaller scale, in the reckless demagoguery and spiteful actions unleashed in our times against Korean or Vietnamese small businessmen operating in various inner-city ghettoes across the country. The special targeting of Korean businesses during the 1992

Los Angeles riots was part of a much larger, nationwide phenomenon, indeed an international and historic phenomenon.

What is there about middleman minorities that brings out such intense animosities, over and above the usual frictions between other racial, ethnic, religious, or linguistic groups? It cannot be simple envy, for wealthier ethnic groups or social classes are seldom hated as much. It cannot be resentment of privileges, for not only are royalty and nobility more popular, middleman minorities often have not even had equality before the law, much less privileges. Certainly the Jews did not have equality before the law during the many centuries of their persecution in Europe, nor have the Chinese in Southeast Asia, the Indians or Pakistanis in either colonial or postindependence Africa, nor the Christians in the Ottoman Empire. All were explicitly second-class in the eyes of the law.

Mass expulsions, as well as pogroms, have been a fate common to middleman minorities. The mass expulsions of Indians from prewar Burma and postwar Uganda, or of the Chinese from various countries of Southeast Asia at various times in history, are all too reminiscent of the fate of the Jews expelled from many European countries in centuries past.

> *"It is the role, rather than the people or their religion, which seems to be crucial."*

When looking at any given middleman minority in isolation, it may seem plausible to attribute the animosity they face to factors peculiar to that group, to the surrounding society, or to a particular period of history. Thus many have tried to explain the persecutions of the Jews in Europe as arising from circumstances unique to the Jewish role in Christian society or Christian history. But when strikingly similar patterns are found in the history of the Chinese in Southeast Asia, the Ibos in Nigeria, and other groups around the world who have played economic roles analogous to those of the Jews, then the question must be faced whether these roles themselves are not a major part of the reason for such unbridled and lethal hatreds.

The Middleman Role

The economic functions performed by middlemen—retailing and money-lending—have long been disdained, misunderstood, and condemned, not only by the unlettered masses but also by the leading intellects of countries scattered over large areas of the globe and long spans of time. Confucian ethics, Islam, and early Christianity have all condemned either one or both of these middleman roles, independently of who performs them.

The biblical condemnation of traders who make a profit from selling a commodity "whole and unchanged" for more money than they paid for it was softened somewhat by St. Thomas Aquinas, who allowed exceptions for risk, transportation costs, and the like. Still, trading was seen as an occupation that required justifications, in a way in which farming or manufacturing did not. Nor is this view peculiar to the Western world. As a Kenyan writer put it:

"If the Asians in Kenya produced things instead of squatting in their *dukas* [shops] to sell at what look like disproportionately high prices, if they scratched the soil themselves to produce, if they worked to produce instead of juggling with merchandise and exploiting opportunities in the consumer market, they would be much more acceptable. . . . If the Asians were just farmers, doctors, teachers, lawyers, skilled technicians, craftsmen, and other 'productive' workers, African attitudes towards them would change."

> *"The economic functions performed by middlemen . . . have long been disdained, misunderstood, and condemned."*

Within the Jewish community, various reformers have wanted to get their fellow Jews out of middleman occupations and into more "productive" occupations. Intellectuals of the Jewish Enlightenment (*haskalah*) sought the "productivization" of their coreligionists, and Jewish philanthropist Baron Maurice de Hirsch was one of many who tried to get Jews into agriculture—in his case, putting tens of millions of dollars of his own money into the effort, which was only transiently successful.

Outsiders have of course been even more severe in their criticisms of the economic roles of middleman minorities. The idea that middlemen are mere "parasites" or "bloodsuckers," rather than people engaged in a "productive" occupation like farming, manufacturing, and the like, has been a common theme in many societies, whether or not the middleman function was performed by a racially or ethnically distinct group. The perennial desire to "eliminate the middleman"—a desire perennially frustrated by economic reality—is another symptom of the notion that middlemen are not "really" doing anything useful.

The Case of POWs

In a famous essay, a British economist who was a prisoner of war during World War II observed both the functions of the middleman and the reactions to those functions in an informal market that developed among his fellow POWs. Much of the economic activity of the prison camp consisted in the trading of various items contained in the Red Cross packages issued each month to each prisoner.

Although the POWs all received the same Red Cross packages, some went through their ration of chocolate or cigarettes before the month was over and borrowed from others who had saved theirs. Lenders might lend three cigarettes near the end of the month, in exchange for repayment of four cigarettes when the next month's packages arrived. In addition to lending at interest in this way, the middleman POWs also circulated around among their fellow prisoners to discover who had food rations or other personal belongings that they were willing to trade for other things they might prefer to have. These POWs became in effect intermediaries bringing about trades between other prisoners who had not gotten together on their own. The economist in the camp noted not only the economic benefits from a variety of middleman activities, but also the social response:

"Taken as a whole, public opinion was hostile to the middleman. His function, and his hard work in bringing buyer and seller together, were ignored; profits were not regarded as a reward for labour, but as the result of sharp practices. Despite the fact that his very existence was proof to the contrary, the middleman was held to be redundant. . . ."

As a result of such public opinion, there developed official policies curtailing middleman activities. These policies brought many inconveniences to the POWs, but apparently no greater economic sophistication. That such prejudices could develop within a relatively short period of time, against individuals not racially or ethnically distinct from those around them, suggests something of the power of sheer economic misconception of the role of distribution.

Even in larger societies in normal times, the importance of distribution is usually appreciated only sporadically, when the distributive system breaks down. It is all too common in famine-stricken countries for food to be rotting on the docks in the port cities while people are dying of hunger in the interior—dying from a lack of distribution of food, rather than lack of food per se. But even such catastrophes as these seldom teach a lasting lesson about the vital role of distribution. Middlemen continue to be seen by many as useless and scheming people who intercept goods on their way from producer to consumer, raking off unearned profits in the process.

> *"The idea that middlemen are mere 'parasites' or 'bloodsuckers' . . . has been a common theme."*

Mistaken Perceptions

When Ugandan dictator Idi Amin accused the Asian middlemen in his country of both "overpricing" to the consumers and "undercutting" competitors, he was voicing one of many self-contradictory complaints about middleman minorities. Economic misunderstandings may be simple, or even simple-minded, but the social ramifications can be complex and deadly. Where economic prejudices combine with racial prejudices, the mixture becomes explosive. Nor is it necessary that all, or most, of the members of a given minority actually engage in middleman occupations in order for the whole group's image to be seen within that framework. Most of the Armenians in the Ottoman Empire, for example, were not businessmen—but a disproportionate share of all the businessmen were Armenians. Moreover, the Turks were much more likely to come into direct contact with Armenians in a middleman role than with Armenians who were peasant farmers. Most Tamils in Sri Lanka are not middlemen, but a disproportionate share of the country's middlemen have been Tamils.

Even among groups who have worked predominantly in commercial occupations during a particular period of history, often they evolve over time into such professional roles as doctors, lawyers, and intellectuals. That has certainly been the history of the Jews in a number of countries, including the United States. Nevertheless, the attitudes of the surrounding society have often been shaped—and set in concrete—by the era when they were middlemen. Moreover, many of the work habits and much of the discipline necessary for success as middlemen have made middleman minorities formidable competitors in intellectual, scientific, and professional occupations as well, creating new resentments among new classes of competitors.

Sudden Prejudice

Misunderstandings and resentments do not, by themselves, lead automatically to persecution or violence, much less to genocide. Often middleman minorities have lived peacefully for years, or even generations, among people who then suddenly turned savagely against them after their economic and racial prejudices have been skillfully exploited by demagogues. For example, there was not a single race riot between the Sinhalese majority and the Tamil minority in Sri Lanka during the first half of the twentieth century, though there have been many ghastly outbreaks of murderous intergroup violence since politicized polarization began to be promoted during the 1956 elections there. Jews were not only economically prosperous, but also widely accepted socially—including high intermarriage rates—in Germany on the eve of the rise to power of Hitler and the Nazis. In short, the potential for tragedy is not tragedy itself, until other factors come into play. Nevertheless, it is useful to examine more specifically what creates this tragic potential more often, or more powerfully, in the case of middleman minorities. . . .

It can hardly be surprising that quite modest success by middleman minorities can provoke major resentments and hostility. Thus arises the anomaly that middleman minorities are most hated where they are most needed—that is, where poor local populations most lack alternative suppliers of the same services—and find their greatest acceptance where more prosperous populations are less dependent on them. Thus anti-Semitism in prewar Poland was strongest in the less developed eastern part of the country, where nearly 90 percent of all commerce was conducted by Jews, who conducted less than 10 percent of the commerce in the more advanced western part of the country. Similar patterns existed in other Eastern Europe countries during the same era. The relatively small numbers of truly wealthy Jews were more likely to be found in the great commercial and

> *"Where economic prejudices combine with racial prejudices, the mixture becomes explosive."*

industrial centers, where they were seldom a majority of the commercial and industrial entrepreneurs, while the masses of struggling Jewish peddlers and small shopkeepers provoked far more resentment in the backward regions.

> *"Quite modest success by middleman minorities can provoke major resentments and hostility."*

Internationally as well, Jews have encountered far less hostility in prosperous societies like Australia, Britain, and the United States than in poorer and less developed parts of Eastern Europe or the Middle East. While Jewish contributions to prosperous nations have been substantial, they have seldom been as statistically dominant in the commerce and industry of such nations as they have been in poorer parts of the world. Jewish firms have in fact been rare in American heavy industry. Nor are Jews unique in being most hated where they are most needed.

Nowhere is resentment and animosity toward the "overseas Chinese" greater than in Southeast Asia, where they created whole industries and whole sectors of the economy and continue to own an absolute majority of the firms in many fields. The success of most of these Chinese businesses is quite modest, but it is a success that is a blow to the egos of the indigenous populations of the region, who have done little to establish such businesses on their own. In the United States, hostility to Korean small businessmen is far greater in poor inner-city neighborhoods, where few others establish stores and shops to serve the local population, than in more middle-class neighborhoods, where many other businesses supply similar services. . . .

The mobilization of the larger community against middleman minorities has often been the work of those losing out to them in open competition, whether in the economy or in educational institutions. Thus the rise of a fledgling business class in the surrounding community, or the beginnings of a new educated class there, is often the impetus for orchestrated campaigns against middleman minorities. Such groups spearheaded the campaigns against the Jews in Europe between the two world wars, against Asians in East Africa, against the Chinese in Southeast Asia, and against first Jews and then Koreans in inner-city ghettoes in the United States. Frustration and wounded egos explain much of this pattern, as well as the perverse pattern of assailing middleman minorities where they are most needed and accepting them where alternatives exist.

When professors in prewar Poland told violently anti-Semitic Polish students that they could "understand" these students' "patriotic fervor," they were precursors of those who today "understand" the "rage" of inner-city rioters and looters who attack Korean stores.

Dispelling Ignorance

Misconceptions and scapegoating do not need this kind of understanding. Economic ignorance needs to be dispelled, not flattered. Those who cry out that their advancement must be achieved "by all means necessary" need to be told that these means must include the kind of unromantic drudgery, in the economy and in the academy, that have advanced other groups from poverty to prosperity. They need to be told that bogeyman theories are a blind alley, even though such theories are promoted by demagogues at all levels, including the Ph.D. level.

There are wider implications to the history of middleman minorities. While racial hostility strikes many groups, it seems most virulent against groups who make others feel inferior, rather than groups to whom they feel superior. Even beyond a racial or ethnic context, there are grim implications to the widespread tendency to resent productivity, and to attack those who create it, even as the benefits of that productivity are welcomed and more of those benefits are sought.

The Political Exploitation of Ethnicity Causes Conflict

by Sonia Shah

About the author: *Sonia Shah is an editor and publisher at South End Press in Boston.*

From Yugoslavia to Northern Ireland, from Sri Lanka to Spain, and from the former Soviet Union to the Occupied Territories, people are raising the banner of ethnicity to cry foul to their neighbors. Even in countries where ethnic conflicts have not exploded into full-scale armed violence—in Canada, France, and the United States, for example—more and more people are uniting as ethnic groups and bringing their grievances into the political sphere.

Cultural Clashes

Ethnicity—the language, values, and histories shared by a group of people—has been evolving and generating itself for most, if not all, of the human age. Ancient history is full of ethnic conflicts, but industrialization, the age of rationalism, and Karl Marx all led us to believe that the day of inevitable cultural collision was over. Yet in the past few years, we have witnessed: the spectacular failure of the broad "Soviet" identity to override ethnic divisions in the former Soviet Union; the bloody rise of ethnic conflict and separatism in Eastern Europe; the growing realization that the glorified American "melting pot" is a dream; and the increasing intensity of long-standing ethnic conflicts around the globe. Our paradigms about the roots of ethnic conflict demand reassessment. The goal of finding truly common ground is much more complex and difficult, ethnic identifications far more tenacious, and class not nearly as cohesive, as was once assumed.

We live in a world of sudden changes, massive cultural collisions, profound multiethnicity, and plethoras of possible group identities—racial, sexual, famil-

Sonia Shah, "The Roots of Ethnic Conflict," *Nuclear Times*, Spring 1992. Reprinted with the author's permission.

ial, economic, ideological, spiritual, etc. Yet people have continued to identify ethnically, and more and more will use that identification politically. For many, perhaps, ethnicity is simply a personal matter, something to describe oneself to friends with, or to plan a wedding around. But somehow, in many parts of the world, that set of meanings that sociologists define as ethnicity has become a political identification, and a basis for political action. Not

> *"Ethnicity has become a political identification, and a basis for political action."*

that the politicization of ethnicity necessarily entails conflict, just as the formation of ideological parties does not necessarily entail conflict—but that ethnic conflict, when it does occur, rests firmly on a basis of ethnic politicization.

Ethnicity has possibly become the predominant grassroots political unit in the world today. In the postcolonial, post-Cold War world, ethnic conflicts threaten to become increasingly intense and frequent, and may present the ultimate challenge to peacemakers in the decades to come. Peacemakers must therefore begin considering the nature of ethnicity—how, when, where, and why it binds people together—and secondly, how it becomes politicized.

The Character of Ethnicity

Most sociologists agree that almost every country in the world is multiethnic. They point out that this may not be immediately apparent, however, because ethnic divisions may look superficially like religious, ideological, or some other kind of cleavage.

Ethnic divisions in North America, Asia, Africa, and South America are perhaps readily apparent to most Westerners. Recent events in the former Soviet Union and Eastern Europe have alerted us to the very real ethnic divisions in that region of the world. Even the western European countries, popularly thought of as relatively homogenous nation-states, are more accurately described as countries where large majorities share space with smaller ethnic minorities. Political scientist Arend Lijphart, of the University of California, San Diego, points out the South Tyroleans in Italy, the Frisians in the Netherlands, the Danish-speaking minority in Germany, and the Lapps in Sweden. By some counts, there are 5,000 distinct ethnic groups in the world today. Possibly, of the 170-or-so sovereign states in the world, only Iceland, Portugal, and Norway are ethnically homogenous.

Although ethnic divisions within states may be nearly ubiquitous, they are not necessarily hard and fast. The character of ethnic identifications is fluid and mutable, to varying degrees, given processes of change. Over time, smaller ethnic groups may submerge the cultural differences that mark them from larger ones. Ethnic divisions may narrow, as cultural exchanges between different ethnic groups blur the lines. There are countless examples of cultural assimilation, accommodation, and adaptation; where once ethnic belonging might mean sharing a language, it later could mean sharing an enemy, or a history.

Some European descendants in America have erased ethnic divisions that were once more salient, between English and German for example, under the somewhat more inclusive "Americanism." Another example could be India, where caste divisions that were once clear and bold—evidenced by language, custom, and appearance—have now become fine and subtle, more a matter of genealogy than identity. As the grounds for belonging change, ethnicities can become wider and more inclusive, breaking down finer ethnic distinctions. There are a few cases of complete cultural assimilation, to the extent that an ethnic distinction blurs until it no longer exists. One sociologist has estimated that the full assimilation of different ethnic groups takes between 300 and 700 years.

Ethnic Solidarity

Wherever there is a case of ethnic accommodation, however, there is a case of ethnic resiliency. The Chinese in America, Tamils in Sri Lanka, and the French in Canada—ethnic groups long in multiethnic states—are just a few examples of groups that have retained a high level of ethnic solidarity. Groups nurture their ethnic solidarity for a spectrum of reasons, from political or economic choice to emotional or social necessity. And each individual may profess different motivations for maintaining ethnic solidarity. One Chinese-American may feel compelled to nurture her Chinese identity to garner meaning and emotional security in a basically hostile American world. Another may do so to rally unity to promote political or economic rights.

Sociologists reckon, however, that in developed countries ethnic identification is generally more of a utilitarian choice than in less developed countries, except for those ethnic groups in developed countries purposefully excluded from cultural accommodation (like African-Americans in the United States, for instance). For those excluded groups in developed countries, and for other groups in less mobile, less developed multiethnic states, the maintenance of ethnicity is an emotionally and socially compelled phenomenon. If an African-American, a Russian Jew, or a lower-caste Hindu tried to submerge their ethnic identities into the larger "American," "Russian," or "Hindu" categories, they would simply not be socially recognized. The extent to which they "choose" to maintain their ethnic identity is thus tempered by the fact that their ethnic identities are continually conferred upon them by the larger society. Czechs in Britain, on the other hand,

> *"Where once ethnic belonging might mean sharing a language, it later could mean sharing an enemy."*

can choose, to some extent, whether they identify as Czechs or Britons, depending on their political, economic, and social goals. Either choice would be socially acceptable; the individual must decide what works for her or him.

The probability of ethnic identification depends, however, not only on the individual's chances of successfully donning a different or more inclusive identity, but also on the individual's mobility—in Czechoslovakia, the Czech may be more likely to identify as Czech as opposed to Slovak; in Britain, as Eastern European; in America, as European; in Africa, as white.

> *"Ethnic groups are undercut by national boundaries, class, race, gender, lifestyle, and ideology."*

Ultimately, the most important gauge of the probability of ethnic identification rests with the individual, and the depth of meaning the ethnic identification confers upon him or her. The nature of human populations today is that ethnic groups are undercut by national boundaries, class, race, gender, lifestyle, and ideology. There are a myriad of ways in which an individual can find a group identity, and a locus for political involvement. In such a world, the overwhelming frequency of people's ethnic identifications, both socially and politically, is the truest testimony of its ability to offer a sense of place and meaning.

Why Ethnicity Has Become Politicized

The circumstances under which one chooses to identify with a certain ethnicity and then bring that ethnicity into the political realm are unique to each circumstance. Still, there are some generalizations about the process of ethnic politicization that can be tentatively raised.

Since people tend to expect greater chances of being understood by others of their ethnic group, it is common for us to migrate with others of our ethnic group. There are many reasons for mass migrations—political expansion, natural disasters, asylum from discrimination, and, in the modern world, filling mass labor shortages, to name a few. Of course, ethnic migrations are nothing new—but presumably, in the past they happened over many generations. Now, mass ethnic migrations happen much more suddenly, and therefore there is less time for the cultural absorption and accommodation necessary for peaceful co-existence. "North Africa presumably absorbed the Vandals," writes sociologist Nathan Glazer, "but presumably they came over generations. The nineteenth-century French came suddenly and were never absorbed. In the end they were expelled after a bloody ethnic civil war."

The decolonization of the Third World also triggered ethnic politicization. Ethnic identifications were one way of unifying against the outside colonizers. After decolonization, ethnic identity could still be used politically as a symbol of anti-imperialist pride. Colonizers in many cases may have nurtured this process by divide-and-conquer strategies, which identified and pitted ethnic groups against each other. In some cases, colonizers divided regions in such a way as to intensify ethnic conflicts, as in Africa, where European colonizers chose to group different tribes into single states. And now, in the postcolonial world, many governments may reinforce ethnic divisions in the political realm, for they are easy to manipulate. As Glazer writes: "A British prime minister who does 'something for the workers' probably doesn't do much and almost certainly does even less for his party. Doing something for the Scots, however, becomes an increasingly attractive and real option for Westminster."

Attempts at Inclusion

The age of nationalism, and the concurrent assumption that people could be cajoled, persuaded, or coerced into subsuming ethnic divisions into a more inclusive ideological identity, on a broad scale, didn't work. The "melting pot" and Sovietism are just two examples. But as sociologist Daniel Bell points out, there are still strong drives to create more inclusive identities—in Africa, the attempt to overcome tribalism; in the Middle East, the attempt to form political and economic federalism; in Europe, the attempt to achieve complete economic integration; and on a grander scale, the international effort to promote the United Nations. Historically, he notes, these tendencies toward the creation of wider political ties have only worked "where there has been a powerful military force to impose an allegiance, or where there has been a 'civil theology' to provide a locus for identification." He points out the examples of the City of God of Augustine, national monarchs, or "Americanism" as a civil theology, as examples where ethnic divisions were submerged beneath a broader banner more-or-less peacefully.

The problem now is that although there is a push for more inclusive identifications, those efforts are not accompanied by concomitant nurturing of meaningful cultural frameworks. We can see this dynamic on a small scale in American politics. The broad groupings that are most politically expedient for disenfranchised groups, like "women" or "people of color," aren't emotionally meaningful enough to cement the group together despite their differences. A Native American working-class mother, for instance, has to give up too much cultural and emotional meaning to identify herself as, simply, a woman in America, or a person of color. Broad, politically expedient identities frequently fail to provide meaning for individuals, who will therefore cling to their ethnic identifications—but possibly without the political structures to accommodate ethnic differences. Thus, ethnicity becomes a political issue, which is easily fanned into conflict.

Change, in general, is much more sudden and profound than it was in the preindustrial era. Many cultures, Bell points out, are still adapting to the accelerated rates of change. While in transition, "large masses of persons find inherited ways and old creeds 'outdated' and new modes and creeds of uncertain validity...the sense of uprootedness spreads throughout entire societies." Unless other identifications are available to take the place of cultural and ethnic ones, the sense of psychological uprootedness will result in

> *"Ethnic identifications were one way of unifying against the outside colonizers."*

an increased attempt to strengthen ethnic ties—one way of doing that is in opposition to other ethnicities. Strands of Islamic culture, some would argue, show signs of efforts to strengthen cultural ties by opposing Zionism, in times when traditional Islam doesn't seem to be answering new, difficult life questions. Identities that rest on opposition, of course, are prime breeding grounds for conflict.

Another reason ethnicity has been used more and more in the political realm is that in today's world, most people must work in groups to promote their political interests, and there is a "strategic efficacy of ethnicity in making legitimate claims on the resources of the modern state," writes Glazer. Class, as Marx defined it, hasn't worked as a cohesive group capable of promoting political and economic interests. Class may be too diffuse, and as ethnic groups frequently work also as class groups (although not vice versa), ethnic claims combine both bald economic interest with a historical, emotionally real tie.

Also, class is necessarily hierarchical; for every class save the highest, class identification entails a sense of inferiority, which would, psychologically, reduce its ability to retain group unity. Ethnicity, as opposed to class, is about difference rather than hierarchy, and since the growing industrialization around the globe has increased people's expectations of the quality of their lives, the need for pride is tantamount. Identifying ethnically thus holds much more resonance than identifying with one's class.

> *"There are still strong drives to create more inclusive identities."*

On a theoretical level, the national borders drawn by colonizers, which ignore ethnic divisions, combined with the deeply entrenched concept of a "nation-state" (where one unified group settles a geographically discrete and politically sovereign territory), has made the issue of ethnicity politically explosive. Ethnic groups in the world today are grossly divided by political boundaries—there is an Arab nation but 21 Arab states, a Jewish state but with less than a quarter of the Jewish nation, and a Kurdish nation divided by four political borders. Yet the concept of a nation-state and "self-determination," where a territorial area is settled by one ethnic group and has its own political borders, is widely looked upon as *the* premiere situation of stability and freedom.

How to Approach Ethnic Conflict Resolution

In many cases, activists must investigate to what extent conflicts defined as "ethnic" really are about ethnicity. How is ethnicity being used—as a banner unifying people across ideological or class differences, as a call to unite against a common enemy, as a front for conflict with a third party, as a push for repressed ethnic pride, as an effort to promote economic interests, or as an attempt to protect cultural markers, like language, religion, or ethics?

Activists must also beware the Marxist paradigm that suggests that greater modernization eases tribal and ethnic affiliations. The theory was that with greater industrialization, people would drop cultural ties to unite along class lines, and with the downfall of capitalism and the institutionalization of socialism, all ties not based on the state would subside, and there would be true state unity. It is possible that if standards of living were basically equal, there would be less reason for conflict. "But the argument that if economic conditions expand ethnic conflict will ease . . . is not automatic. Resources are likely to be unevenly distributed," says sociologist Lou Kriesberg, who is director of the Program on Analysis and Resolution of Conflicts at Syracuse University.

> *"Class . . . hasn't worked as a cohesive group capable of promoting political and economic interests."*

Given the likelihood of unequal resource distribution, some argue that expanding economies actually exacerbate ethnic and other conflicts, because they heighten everyone's expectations of their standards of living, without necessarily increasing everyone's standards. Activists can safely argue that economic justice is a key prerequisite to peace—but must keep in mind the example of industrialized countries of the modern era, where generally and over the last few decades, standards of living have increased without easing ethnic tensions.

The point is that people will unite ethnically for reasons other than economic disenfranchisement—a sense of political disenfranchisement, a shared history of oppression, or, given the pure strength of ethnic ties alone, for cultural autonomy, for example. The Quebec nationalist movement is one example of an ethnic political movement where its upsurges do not bear a direct relationship with the state economy. . . .

Finding Common Ground

On the analysis side, we can begin to find, discuss, or create new notions of sovereignty: we need to find new theoretical ways of approaching the entrenched idea that people can only trust their own, and can be free only if they have their own government. We need more fluid boundaries, and a way of making those more fluid boundaries still meaningful to people with strong ethnic identifications. On a practical level, we must begin to build more concepts of political power-sharing, and to study how different models of power-sharing can work in different societies. And most immediately, we can find, study, and publicize images of peaceful multiethnic societies, both past and present, to inspire and sustain us in these timely and urgent ventures.

Political Crises Intensify Ethnic Conflict

by Stephen Ryan

About the author: *Stephen Ryan is a lecturer in peace studies at Magee College of the University of Ulster in Coleraine, Northern Ireland, and author of* Ethnic Conflict and International Relations, *from which the following is excerpted.*

In [a] general atmosphere of anxiety minorities will be more feared and distrusted than might otherwise be the case. Ethnic groups may be seen as a threat to state security; a Trojan horse serving the interests of outside powers. As a result dominant groups will be less tolerant to ethnic minorities, for in the words of Georg Simmel "groups in any sort of war situation are not tolerant. They cannot afford individual deviation from the unity of the coordinating principle beyond a definitely limited degree." In modern states, of course, nationalism is often the major "coordinating principle."

Dissension Weakens the State

In addition to this, states fear internal dissension because a divided state will be weaker than a united rival. Richard W. Sterling has made this point, arguing that "just as soon as separatist discontent surfaces an affected state becomes relatively weaker than surrounding states whose internal unity is intact. In all cases and in all stages separation affects state power." One might want to take issue with Sterling's absolute tone. It could be suggested that a state might become stronger by allowing an ethnic movement a right to cultural expression or even to accept secession from the state so as to create a less conflict-ridden entity more able to compete with its rivals. Realism could therefore lead to an acceptance of separation rather than a resistance to it. However, it cannot be denied that when ethnic groups are regarded as a source of internal weakness they are often more likely to be persecuted than accommodated. Even the founding fathers of English liberalism, John Locke and John Milton, were suspicious of the toleration of Catholics because they were seen as possible agents of Rome.

Many examples can be provided to show how the view that an ethnic minority is a threat will lead to increased oppression of these groups. The stab-in-the-back theory applied to Jews in Nazi Germany is a good example of this. The Israeli fear of the Palestinians in the West Bank and Gaza is another. The British suppression of the 1916 Easter rising in Dublin involved similar feelings. Other cases would include the Vietnamese treatment of their Chinese minority; the Khmer Rouge persecution of the Vietnamese minority in Kampuchea; the Sandinistas' treatment of the Meskito Indians in Nicaragua; and the Yugoslav treatment of the Albanians in Kossova after Albania had joined the Soviet-led Cominform campaign against Josip Broz Tito in the late 1940s.

World Wars and Ethnic Conflict

Another example is the American treatment of its Japanese population following Pearl Harbor. What is interesting here is that the United States was not only one of the most liberal states of the period, but was also one of the most invulnerable. Yet it still decided in a wave of anti-Japanese hysteria in early 1942 to transport about 80% of Japanese-Americans to internment camps in desolate areas of the country. Furthermore, Frank P. Zeidler has reminded us that this is an event unique in American history only because of the severity of the measures taken and because it linked into a long history of American racist attitudes to Orientals. He points out that during World War I there was at least one lynching of a German-American and many cases of less serious assault. German books were burned and Richard Wagner's and Felix Mendelssohn's marches were removed from wedding ceremonies.

Conflict between the Walloons and the Flemish in Belgium has also been exacerbated by the experiences of two world wars. This is because of the collaboration of many Flemings with Germany in both of these wars. In the First World War, in particular, Germany presented itself as the ally of Flemish nationalism in Belgium, and indeed, in 1917, partly as a result of such encouragement Raad van Vlaanderen proclaimed an independent Flemish state. After the Second World War thousands of Flemings were put on trial for collaboration with the Germans.

This pattern of often exaggerated distrust of ethnic minorities is so common that Donald L. Horowitz is surely correct to point out that such fear cannot be dismissed simply as aberrant psychology, because in the existing state system such worries are based on an ever present possibility. It is also a point made by Martin Ceadel, who writes that "political cultures and

> *"Ethnic groups . . . are often more likely to be persecuted than accommodated."*

strategic situations tend to be found in predictable combinations: the degree of liberalism normally correlates with the degree of security."

Of course it would be a gross exaggeration to claim that ruling elites at all times have this exaggerated fear of ethnic minorities. Attitudes will tend to fluctuate from mild suspicion to outright hostility depending on both the internal and external situations. The attitude of the Grand Vizir of Sultan Hamid, Kibrili Kamil Pasha, to minorities in the Ottoman empire is therefore the exception rather than the rule. He wrote in 1877, against the background of presumed Armenian support for a Russian invasion, that "in Asia Minor . . . it is incumbent upon us as a state to wipe out any subject race which is suspect. For our future security, we should exterminate therefore the Armenian nation so that no trace and memory is left of her." This turned out to be an horrific prediction of what the attitude of some Turkish nationalists to the Armenians was to be in the Great War.

For wartime situations not only increase insecurity, they also provide ample opportunities to link the outside threat with an "internal menace." But being the victim of outright invasion during wartime is only one way in which an often exaggerated fear of an ethnic minority might develop. Feelings of insecurity will also be especially strong in "double minority" situations, where one group may be the majority within a particular state but is the minority group in the region as a whole. Such is the case of the Israelis in the Middle East, the Loyalists in Ireland, the Greek Cypriots in the Eastern Mediterranean and the Sinhalese in the Indian Subcontinent. Ethiopia, ruled by Christians, sees itself surrounded by Moslems and viewed its civil war with Eritrea in this context.

There is an extra twist to some of these double minority situations. For there are some places—such as Northern Ireland—where the minority may become the majority and the dominant group will then be a minority both within the area it traditionally dominates and within the region as well. Fear of this is a major reason why Israel has not annexed the West Bank and Gaza, for it would then have to include within the Israeli state many more Palestinians. The Christians in Lebanon have already reached this situation. For although at the time of the founding of the state they were the largest group, their relative population has declined when compared with the Moslems, and they now feel more insecure than ever about their destiny. . . .

Several writers have expressed dissatisfaction with the existing interstate system and the way it appears to be unable to respond to ethnic conflicts so as to ensure international peace and security whilst paying proper regard for the legitimate claims of the warring communities. The alternatives proposed tend to fall into two categories. The first is the suggestion that an effective system of minority protection should be created based not on states but an international organization. Such a regime would do two things. It would guarantee the rights of ethnic groups and also remove the grievances that might give rise to violent conflicts. The second suggestion is that more thought should be given to improving the techniques of conflict resolution so that a more constructive response can be made to violent ethnic conflicts when they occur.

Chapter 4

Should Nations Intervene in Ethnic Conflicts?

Case Study: The Balkans

Intervention in the Balkans: An Overview

by Friends Committee on National Legislation

About the author: *The Friends Committee on National Legislation (FCNL) comprises appointed members of the Religious Society of Friends, or Quakers. The committee is concerned with many political and social issues, including human rights and American foreign policy, and the views of politicians and government officials toward such issues.*

Editor's note: Ethnic warfare in the Balkans presented this dilemma to European and other nations: whether to intervene militarily and risk the lives of their soldiers and possible escalation of the war, or to withhold forces and risk continued ethnic fighting over territory and more bloodshed. Since many experts predict that future conflicts and wars around the world will similarly erupt from ethnic feuding, nations are likely to face this dilemma again. Thus, the debates and policy decisions regarding military intervention in the Balkans could serve as a useful model for nations in the future. The following overview and viewpoints are therefore included as both specific instance and general paradigm to aid the reader's understanding of the issues raised by such conflicts.

Armed conflicts ravage the former Yugoslavia. Masses of civilians face hunger, malnutrition, and starvation, as well as violent death. Children and the elderly are the most vulnerable. The senseless killing and suffering follow the terrible logic of ethnic bigotry, nationalist pride, religious intolerance, and avenging of historical injustices. In these complex situations, good and evil abide on all sides of the conflict. We cannot categorize those involved in the conflict into victims and executioners or judge them as good or evil. Taking sides will not make things better. We are challenged to remember that every

Excerpted from "Conflict in the Former Yugoslavia," *FCNL Washington Newsletter*, December 1992. Reprinted with permission.

person is a holy place.

At the same time, brutal acts of violence and their tragic human consequences are real. We cannot ignore them; we should not stand aside. How to respond to the conflict in a timely and helpful way perplexes us all, but especially governments and international authorities. Good intentions are not sufficient. Quick action can aid, or it can do additional harm. The moral imperative to do something is clear; the moral and effective course of action is not. FCNL has no ready solutions at hand, and we are humbled by the challenge these conflicts present to those in authority.

> *"Military action in the former Yugoslavia may be seen by many people as necessary."*

We offer these queries for policy makers considering what actions to take in the former Yugoslavia:

• Enemy images: Does the problem definition on which you base your policy action avoid enemy images and seek justice and protection of non-combatant civilians on all sides of the conflict?

• De-escalate the conflict: Does your action create conditions to de-escalate the armed conflict?

• Taking sides: Can the UN or any particular nation be a peacemaker if it becomes a party to the military conflict? Is the action to be taken consistent with the role of peacemaker?

• Conflict resolution: Does your plan of action raise up and use intensive diplomatic and political contact with all parties to the conflict? Is dialogue kept alive?

• Humanitarian aid: Have humanitarian actions been kept separate from political and military agendas? Have humanitarian needs been addressed, no matter what side the civilians are on?

• Options of last resort: Military action in the former Yugoslavia may be seen by many people as necessary, but can this option of last resort deliver on the promise of saving civilians from violence and ending the conflict?

• Refugee assistance: Are international laws for the protection of refugees and displaced persons being upheld? Does your action include assistance for those displaced by the conflict?

• Profits of war: Armed conflict, especially with heavy weapons, is expensive and requires resupply of munitions and parts. Is your action helping to stop the flow of heavy weapons and munitions? Have war profiteers been curbed? Would military enforcement of UN economic and munitions sanctions and UN observers on crossing points from Serbia to Bosnia be helpful?

• Seeking wisdom: Is the action guided by political expediency or by truth? . . .

The International Response

A UN-imposed arms embargo against Yugoslavia (Resolution 713) went into effect in September 1991. Due to continuing Serbian-led violence, the Security

Council approved sanctions against Serbia and Montenegro in May 1992. Medicine and humanitarian relief are exempt from the embargo. On June 18, 1992, the UN Security Council passed resolutions to extend sanctions to all commodities and products. At the urging of the United States, the Security Council approved an exemption to the embargo to allow delivery of television equipment to an independent station in Belgrade, Serbia. The intention is to encourage groups that disagree with [Serbian President] Slobodan Milosevic to voice their opposition. Currently, Milosevic controls all access to Serbian television, making it impossible for dissenting views to be heard.

Sniper Attacks

In February 1992, the Security Council approved a 14,000-member peacekeeping force for Yugoslavia. These forces were deployed in Croatia and Bosnia by May 1992. Concerned about the human suffering in Bosnia, UN negotiators reopened the Sarajevo airport for the delivery of humanitarian aid. One thousand additional peacekeepers were deployed at the airport. The UN relief efforts consistently met with sniper fire as peacekeeping forces attempted to move the aid into the city. By September 1992, sixteen UN peacekeepers had been killed in Yugoslavia.

Alarmed by these tragedies, UN Secretary General Boutros Boutros-Ghali called for an increase of UN peacekeeping troops. The UN Security Council voted in favor of his proposal, approving an additional 5,000 troops for UN peacekeeping efforts in Bosnia-Herzegovina. These troops are provided by NATO members (excluding the U.S.), and operate under UN peacekeeping guidelines—assisting in humanitarian relief efforts and with civilians released from detention camps.

Increased Monitoring

By early November 1992 there were at least 15,000 soldiers, police officers, and civilian administrators deployed by the UN. This number is expected to increase [it reached 24,000 by May 1993], creating one of the largest UN forces in recent history. On November 19, 1992, peacekeeping forces in Bosanska Krupa exchanged gunfire with Serbian forces while bringing food and medical supplies to the small town outside of Sarajevo. This was the first UN relief mission to reach a Bosnian town outside of Sarajevo.

"Use of force has led some to question the role of UN peacekeeping in the post cold war world."

This exchange of gunfire marked a major development in the role of peacekeeping forces authorized in September 1992, when use of force in Bosnia-Herzegovina was approved by the Security Council if necessary to protect relief convoys. UN officials consider it a test case on the continued presence of peacekeeping forces. This use of force has led some to question the role of UN peacekeeping in the post cold war world.

The UN Security Council also agreed to impose elements of a U.S. proposal for a "no fly zone" over Bosnia. The intention of this policy is both to halt Serbian air support for Serb ground forces and to protect humanitarian relief efforts. Observers, placed in airports throughout the region, would monitor Serbian aircraft. Originally the U.S. proposal included calls for "direct enforcement"; however, other Security Council members feared Serbian retaliation against UN troops. U.S. Ambassador Edward Perkins stated that if Serbia violates the "no fly zone" resolution, the United States will seek a "resolution mandating force." On November 23, 1992, the UN released a statement that violations of the "no fly zone" have occurred—that is, that monitors had sighted several Serbian military and non-military aircraft over Bosnia. . . .

> *"The United States is*
> *not going to inject itself*
> *into every single crisis . . .*
> *around the world."*

The European Community (EC) has played a mediator role in the Yugoslavian crisis. In September 1991, the EC held a conference on Yugoslavia at The Hague; little resulted and fighting continued. The EC maintained monitors in Bosnia-Herzegovina until members of the team came under fire and had to be removed. It has supported the sanctions against Serbia and the use of UN military force for the delivery of humanitarian aid.

The United States Reacts

Before the collapse of the Soviet Union, the United States perceived Yugoslavia to be of great importance due to its independence from the Soviet Union. However, when the Soviet Union and its reign over Eastern Europe diminished, so did U.S. interest in the region. The lack of perceived "U.S. interests" in Yugoslavia resulted in caution by the Bush administration in its response to the crisis.

The Bush administration supported EC and UN peace efforts. In December 1991, the U.S. imposed economic sanctions—excepting food and medicine—against the new Federal Republic of Yugoslavia (Serbia and Montenegro). The U.S. has recognized the independence of several former Yugoslavian republics and has assisted in the delivery of humanitarian aid to these republics and in the airlifts to Sarajevo.

Planning for Intervention

In response to calls for U.S. involvement, President Bush said, "The United States is not going to inject itself into every single crisis, no matter how heart-rending, around the world." U.S. Defense Secretary Dick Cheney stated that if the U.S. were to participate in multilateral intervention in the former Yugoslavia, the U.S. role would be "limited to naval and air support."

In June 1992, the Senate passed a resolution, calling on the President to make the UN Security Council "plan and budget for such intervention as may be necessary" in Yugoslavia. Legislation passed that September to revoke the Most Favored Nation (MFN) trade status for Serbia and Montenegro.

On August 11, 1992, both the Senate and House passed non-binding resolutions on Yugoslavia. These resolutions called on President Bush to seek an emergency UN Security Council resolution to authorize "all necessary means," including military force, to protect relief missions in Bosnia-Herzegovina, and to ensure the access of UN and International Red Cross personnel to refugee and prisoner of war camps. These resolutions also urged Bush to consider lifting the UN arms embargo on Bosnia-Herzegovina to permit a flow of arms to Bosnians to fight the Serbs, and to consider establishment of a war crimes tribunal to investigate crimes against humanity allegedly committed by belligerents.

On October 6, 1992, President Bush signed a foreign aid bill which included an amendment authorizing the President to provide U.S. military equipment to Bosnia *if* the UN arms embargo against Bosnia is lifted. The bill also includes $35 million for refugees from the former Yugoslav republics as well as $20 million for food and humanitarian aid.

> *"No crime against humanity by one side excuses the other."*

Seeking Peace

In 1992, Western press sources reported that throughout predominantly Islamic nations, concern grew deeper for the Muslim communities in the former Yugoslavia. A Bosnian leader met with a representative of Saudi Arabia in Texas to appeal for protection. Also, rumors have circulated that Iran, and perhaps other nations, might send volunteers to defend Muslims in former Yugoslavia, if the Europeans or the UN did not succeed in stopping the killing and so-called ethnic cleansing.

On August 26, 1992, the foreign ministers of several industrialized nations and Yugoslavian leaders (of both republics and factions) gathered for a two-day conference on the Balkan War. The Yugoslavian leaders agreed to peace negotiations in Geneva. The one condition of these negotiations was that "territorial gains made by force will not be honored"—making it clear that the partition of Bosnia is unacceptable. The negotiations began in mid-September 1992 and were conducted under the leadership of former U.S. Secretary of State Cyrus Vance and former British Foreign Secretary David Owen. . . .

Mediators of the conference have made repeated requests for Bosnians, Serbians and Croatians to turn over heavy military equipment to the international observers and to cease fire.

No Easy Solution

The tragedy in the former states of Yugoslavia poses difficult questions for the international community, which is only beginning to construct a new global order. The conflicts that have boiled forth in Yugoslavia are deeply rooted in the history of the region. These centuries-old conflicts will not be dissolved in one, or a few, bold military initiatives. It will take, at a minimum, lengthy negotiations among all parties of the former Yugoslavia to resolve these conflicts.

There are groups, organizations, and individuals within the former Yugoslavia who are rejecting warfare and working to ease the sufferings of people. These courageous communities should be supported. Intensive international diplomatic efforts to establish negotiations among all the factions should continue, despite the setbacks.

The suffering in former Yugoslavia is compounded by winter weather. Cyrus Vance joined the UN Commission on Refugees in demanding an increase in humanitarian relief efforts. Vance indicated that food and transport donations were not meeting the overwhelming needs of the region. Increased suffering and continuing warfare have stepped up the pressure on the international community to respond to the Yugoslavian crisis quickly and effectively.

World leaders struggle to determine the next course of action in a region where the UN and other relief agencies cannot deliver boxes of food and medicine to the peoples of Bosnia-Herzegovina. Frustrated by the lack of consensus within the U.S. on policy regarding Yugoslavia, the U.S. State Department chief of Yugoslav affairs, George Kenney, resigned from his post in August 1992. Kenney condemned the U.S. government's approach to Yugoslavia as "classic appeasement" which "gave the green light to Serbia's thuggish leaders to implement their plans for a greater, ethnically pure Serbia" through "genocide." Angered by U.S. policy, which he said involves "cycle after cycle of fruitless negotiation," Kenney proposed the following as elements of U.S. policy: military intervention in Bosnia, halting the flow of supplies to pro-Serbian forces, and the arming of Bosnians.

Humanitarian Intervention

Others, growing alarmed by accounts of human rights abuses, have raised the possibility of "humanitarian military intervention"—that is, a military intervention with a specific humanitarian objective, such as the release of prisoners from detainment camps. Such an international response, proponents say, would not necessarily advocate the aims of any particular faction. Instead, it would seek only to remedy situations of humanitarian concern. But critics believe it is unrealistic to assume that an armed intervention for a humanitarian goal could avoid becoming embroiled in the current crisis. It is more likely that such action would aid the cause of a particular faction and thus lead to full-scale military intervention. This concept of humanitarian intervention, if used, may establish two dangerous precedents. First, it mandates UN or international interference in domestic politics. Second, it provides one party in a civil conflict with the means to draw the international community into a crisis, with a final goal of full-scale international military intervention.

Warnings About Intervention

But Pentagon and other military experts, seeing a region so mired in conflicts within conflicts, warn against external military intervention by the international community. Additional armed conflict would probably only escalate tensions and human suffering. In the event of military intervention, it is not clear which side would be assisted or opposed by international forces. U.S. Army Colonel Richard Haney adds that such military intervention would "mean the immediate loss of effectiveness for peacekeeping forces. . . .

> *"In the states of the former Yugoslavia, crimes against humanity are apparently occurring on all sides of the battle lines."*

Worse, the UN peacekeepers would find themselves in grave danger, since they would increasingly be viewed not as peacekeepers but as foreign occupiers." The use of force by peacekeeping troops gives new meaning to these words.

NATO Should Intervene in the Balkans

by Paul C. Warnke

About the author: *Paul C. Warnke, an attorney in Washington, D.C., served as assistant secretary of defense for international security affairs in the Johnson administration. He was director of the U.S. Arms Control and Disarmament Agency and chief arms negotiator in the Carter administration.*

Where is NATO when we need it? A strong NATO initiative in Bosnia should not be discouraged by defeatist cries that it won't work and that the NATO allies will be dragged into a quagmire—another Vietnam. The time has come to stop running foreign policy by purported historical analogies. The choice is not between "no more Vietnams" and "no more Munichs." This is a different situation and it calls for a new approach. It calls for the North Atlantic Treaty Organization to get tough.

No Obstacles

The slaughter and territorial annexation in the remnants of Yugoslavia have been fueled by the obvious conviction of the leaders of the Bosnian Serbs that no outside force will be used to end their depredations. Up to this point, nothing appeared to block their aspirations for another Serbian republic in eastern and northern Bosnia thoroughly "cleansed" of Bosnian Muslims. Indeed, at least until the May 22, 1993, announcement [of diplomatic sanctions] by foreign ministers of the United States, Russia, Great Britain, France and Spain, there were growing signs of tacit acceptance by Western leaders of the Serbs' preferred final solution.

Yet, when NATO ministers met in Rome in November 1991, they announced that, with the end of the Soviet threat, the real risks to allied security would arise from "the serious economic, social and political difficulties, including ethnic rivalries and territorial disputes, which are faced by many countries in Central and Eastern Europe." The analysis was sound and prescient; unfortunately

Paul C. Warnke, "Justifying NATO's Existence," *The Washington Post National Weekly Edition*, May 31-June 6, 1993. Reprinted with the author's permission.

it appears not to have been intended as a basis for NATO action.

The meeting of U.S., European and Russian foreign ministers provides some basis for hope—though no guarantee—that collective action can be taken to end this tragedy. A failure to do so would, I believe, be extraordinarily short-sighted, inconsistent with European security and with a healthy world economy. Acceptance of the principle of ethnic homogeneity as a criterion for new state-hood would set a dubious and dangerous precedent. Not only would it signal that the world community will look the other way when mini-Holocausts occur, but it could lead to the encouragement of a multitude of mini-states whose whole reason for existence would be a common religion or ethnicity. For exam-ple, the unrest and diversity in the Russian Federation could lead to additional attempted secessions and possibly to an upsurge of greater Russian nationalism.

A case can often be made for self-determination. But certain criteria should be established for recognition of a sovereign entity. These should include, at a minimum, good chances for survival, protection for the rights of minorities and an ability to provide order and the necessities for a decent standard of living. Certainly in today's mobile world, an area's ethnic or religious homogeneity cannot be scored as a plus in the quest for statehood.

There are, of course, no easy or risk-free measures that can be undertaken to end the barbarity and bloodshed in Bosnia. But the powerful industrialized democracies, and the international institutions they control, can be legitimately discredited if they stand aside and fail to make a serious effort.

Thugs Are at Fault

Despite the suggestions that the Bosnian tragedy is the fault of everyone there and the logical culmination of ancient hatreds, there is no reason to believe that most of the Serbian, Croatian and Muslim populations are consumed by a desire to rape, torture and kill one another. As is unfortunately often the case, most of the troops and guns in what used to be Yugoslavia are under the control of thugs, who acquired positions of power during the years of Communist dictatorship.

Nor is there any real reason to believe that the thugs' zeal for ethnic cleansing will stop at the Bosnia-Herzegovina borders. If the Serbian leaders, in particular, come to believe that those who could stop them won't commit the resources needed to do so, the next military excesses may occur in the Albanian-populated enclave of Kosovo in southern Serbia, or the republic of Macedonia, where a polyglot population now appears will-ing to live in peace.

"Collective action can be taken to end this tragedy."

As French Foreign Minister Alain Juppe observed at the May 22 meeting, it is clear that everything still depends on the international community's ability to gather the means necessary to meet the responsibilities outlined in the communique. NATO is the one international institution with an integrated military command that can bring to bear force or the threat of force to end military conflict. As recently as December 1992, the NATO foreign ministers met—with France in attendance—and declared their willingness to support peace-keeping operations under the auspices of the United Nations or the Conference on Security and Cooperation in Europe (CSCE). They also agreed that NATO military authorities should be instructed to plan and prepare forces for such missions. Again, the rhetoric has not been matched by the response.

NATO Deployment for Peace

The traditional NATO reluctance to intervene "out-of-area," if it remains relevant anywhere, certainly should exercise no inhibiting effect in Bosnia. The former Yugoslavia is bounded by NATO countries to the west, to the south and to the east. An expansion of the conflict into other remnants of that shattered land could even find two NATO countries, Greece and Turkey, taking opposing positions.

The disappointing reaction of our European allies to the attempts of Secretary of State Warren Christopher to forge a NATO consensus should not be taken as final, nor should a continued effort to bring NATO into serious engagement be feared as causing an alliance rift. It is, I believe, understandable that some of our European friends questioned whether the prescription then

> *"NATO . . . can bring to bear force or the threat of force to end military conflict."*

advanced by the United States—arming the Bosnian Muslims and attacking Serbian targets—is the best way to bring about peace. But NATO, as the primary European security instrument, can justly be called upon by the United States to come up with a military plan that its members deem more appropriate to meet the crying need for a peaceful solution.

At the foreign ministers' meeting, additional steps were outlined to improve and enlarge the safe havens in Bosnia, to patrol the borders and to prevent the conflict from extending outside the borders of Bosnia-Herzegovina. The United States offered to assist in this effort, but not with ground troops. But none of this in itself is apt to scare the warlords or spare the Bosnian people. There will be no safe havens and no end to the slaughter unless and until significant military forces are introduced into the area. Only NATO can do it. A unilateral American venture is, and should be, out of the question. But the United States should press NATO to design and implement such a plan without delay. The forces would be deployed in a peace-enforcing mission, but with authority to take aggressive military action against any activity that seeks to interfere with that mission. The United States, of course, must do its part as a member of NATO. Russian participation should be encouraged.

The NATO deployment would remain while the contending factions work out whatever compromise arrangements they can all live with. Whatever the starting point, the eventual result would in all likelihood have to be a Bosnian government and military arm that reflect a Muslim majority. Bosnia-Herzegovina has, it must be remembered, received international recognition as a sovereign state, however premature that recognition may have been. If some of its Serbian and Croatian inhabitants don't like living under such a Bosnian government, there are obvious places they can go.

> *"There will be no safe havens and no end to the slaughter unless . . . military forces are introduced."*

There can, of course, be no certainty that strong NATO intervention will do the job. But there is good reason to think that it very well might. Most bullies are cowards and the present aggressors have thus far been in a "no lose" situation. If they are faced with the fact that their continued violations of human rights and international law will cost them heavily, they could well reconsider their present policy.

Bosnia is not Vietnam; NATO intervention there would not involve misguided ideologically driven war. Nor would it replicate the courageous Serbian guerrilla resistance to the Nazi invaders. Serbian and Croatian soldiers are not now fighting for national survival. The security and independence of their own countries is not challenged. The fighting now is about carving up another country.

If NATO fails to act on its 1991 perception of the real threats to European security, this in all probability will not lead to its death and dissolution. Western European leaders will still see it as a useful institution for keeping the United States formally engaged and making it easier for the other Europeans to live with a bigger Germany and a troubled successor to the Soviet Union that is appreciably smaller but still the biggest kid on the block.

But a strong NATO response to the present crisis would more than justify its post-Cold War existence. Lacking such a response, it will limp along, but will no longer be taken seriously as the leading instrument of international or even European security.

Use Military Force to Partition Bosnia

by John J. Mearsheimer and Robert A. Pape

About the authors: *John J. Mearsheimer is a political science professor at the University of Chicago. Robert A. Pape teaches at Air University's School of Advanced Airpower Studies at Maxwell Air Force Base in Alabama.*

Three ideas for peace in Bosnia are now conceivable: the fast-fading Vance-Owen plan [to divide Bosnia into ten separate ethnic provinces]; the European proposal to create U.N.-protected "safe havens" for the Muslims; and the much less discussed concept of partitioning Bosnia into three independent states. There's only one constant: the Western powers want peace in the Balkans and don't want to spend much blood and treasure to achieve it. The debate is therefore governed by a judgment of what will work and how much force will be required to achieve it. Within these constraints, partition is the best option: it is the only plan that doesn't deny the reality of what has happened, does not acquiesce in the decimation of the Bosnian Muslims and has a chance of being enforced without a major military embroilment. . . .

A Partition Plan

A clear partition of Bosnia, while not perfect, is clearly the most feasible solution. Bosnia would be divided into three ethnically homogeneous states. The Croatian and Serbian states would be free to join Greater Croatia and Greater Serbia, respectively; the Bosnian-Muslim state would stand alone as an independent entity. Minority populations trapped behind the new boundaries could move to their new homes under U.N. auspices.

A lasting solution requires that the Bosnian-Muslim state be militarily and economically viable. It must form a single, compact whole; it cannot be a tiny "leopard spot" state. It must be large enough to pose a substantial obstacle to an attacker and to meet the economic needs of its population. The Bosnian-Muslim state should be centered on Sarajevo and cover a large portion of the eastern half

From John J. Mearsheimer and Robert A. Pape, "The Answer," *The New Republic*, June 14, 1993.

of what was pre-war Bosnia-Herzegovina. The northern border should run from Teslic to Tuzla to the western bank of the Drina River near Loznica, along the northernmost mountain ridge before the Pannonian plain. The western border should run from Teslic to Zenica to Konjic. This is mountainous terrain, and the Bosna River serves as a fall-back line of defense. The southern border should run from Konjic along the Neretva River straight to the Serbian border. The Neretva Valley, with its high ridges, is a strong line of defense. The eastern border should run along the present border between Serbia and Bosnia up to Loznica. Most of this border follows the Drina River.

> *"A clear partition of Bosnia, while not perfect, is clearly the most feasible solution."*

The remaining territory of Bosnia-Herzegovina would be divided among the Croats and Serbs. The Croats should get one large chunk of territory on the southwestern border of the new Bosnian-Muslim state. This would include most of the two major areas awarded to them [theoretically] under Vance-Owen. The Serbs should be given the remainder of Bosnia-Herzegovina, which would include the Bihac and the Bosanska Posavina areas. The Muslims of Bihac would move to the new Bosnian-Muslim state, while the Croatians in the small area of Bosanska Posavina would relocate to their new state.

The key territorial trade would be between the Muslims and the Serbs. The Serbs would give up much of their territory in eastern Bosnia in return for Bihac, which the Muslims now control. But the Serbs would still control the southeast and northeast corners of present Bosnia-Herzegovina, and they would have a thirty-five-mile-wide east-west corridor running along its northern border, connecting Serbia proper to the Serbian regions of Western Bosnia and Croatia. Under this plan the Muslims would control about 35 percent (8,000 square miles) of former Bosnian territory; the Serbs, 45 percent (10,500 square miles); and the Croats, 20 percent (4,500 square miles). These percentages roughly reflect the amount of territory each ethnic group controlled in pre-war Bosnia.

Interest in Partition

How readily would the parties accept such a plan? We cannot tell for sure, because partition has not been widely discussed in public by the rival groups, but we can determine something about their attitudes from their past statements and behavior.

The Bosnian Muslims have shown little interest in partition and have instead argued for maintaining the multiethnic Bosnian state that existed in April 1992, before fighting began. This position was perhaps reasonable in the war's early stages. But a multiethnic Bosnia must now have little appeal for the Muslims after their vast suffering at their neighbors' hands. The Croats are likely to accept partition along the lines we propose, as it would offer them much of the territory they were assigned by Vance-Owen, which they quickly accepted. The

Serbs are more likely to balk. Though the plan would help them realize their dream of a Greater Serbia, they would also have to cede substantial territory in eastern Bosnia, including Sarajevo, to the Muslims. This they would likely resist. But if the world powers use enough force and provide sufficient incentives, the Serbs can, we believe, be compelled.

Arguments Against Partition

There are three main arguments against partition. First, some would argue that the military means it requires would escalate rather than dampen the violence in Bosnia. We would answer that violence is just as likely to endure. Greater Serbia, if allowed to preside over its conquests, may well be emboldened by its cost-free expansionism to move on elsewhere. Regrettably, there are times when lives can be saved only by threatening to take lives. Second, some would contend that the population transfer required by partition entails needless injury to innocents. Yet transfer is already occurring. Even Vance-Owen would produce its own population transfers, since minorities would doubtless be driven from areas designated for other groups. Transfer is a fact. The only question is whether it will be organized, as envisioned by partition, or left to the murderous methods of the ethnic cleansers.

"Greater Serbia . . . may well be emboldened by its cost-free expansionism to move on elsewhere."

Finally, some might complain that partition is incomplete because it fails to solve other related Balkan troubles that could produce future wars—most notably the conflict in Serbia's Kosovo region. There's merit to this. The Serbian government has already begun a slowmotion expulsion of Kosovo's 1.6 million Albanians, and signs abound that it plans a more dramatic and complete cleansing soon. Such a move could trigger a general Balkan war involving Albania, Macedonia and perhaps Bulgaria, Greece and Turkey. The West should reiterate that the cleansing of Kosovo will not be tolerated. It might also consider putting Kosovo on the table as it negotiates with Serbia over Bosnia. Freeing the region could be the price for full peace with the West.

Military Solutions

But critical questions remain. How can this settlement be enforced if the Serbs resist? And can it be enforced with an acceptable military cost to the great powers, particularly the United States? We believe the answer to these questions is yes, and that the United States should prepare to lead the alliance into such a strategy.

Two basic military campaigns could be pursued. A "rollback" strategy would use massive military force—supplied simultaneously by Western air forces and Bosnian Muslim ground forces—to win a decisive victory against the Bosnian Serbs and their Serbian supporters. They would be left with no choice but to accept Western demands. "Coercive bloodletting" is a less ambitious strategy. It would use similar means, but wouldn't depend on decisive victory. Instead, it would present the Serbs with the prospect of a costly war of attrition that would continue until they accepted partition.

In theory, air power can be used three different ways: to decapitate an opponent's leadership, to punish an opponent's population or to weaken an opponent's military forces. Of these, only the last stands a chance at being effective, but only if it is applied in conjunction with ground power.

Decapitation—an approach used in Desert Storm—would involve strikes against Serbian leadership in Bosnia and Serbia proper. The strategy has the advantage of requiring relatively few sorties over a few days by precision aircraft (mainly F-117s) against key leadership and telecommunication facilities. Decapitation raids would also cause little collateral damage, given accurate target intelligence. But finding and targeting the key Serb leaders from the air would be very difficult. U.S. troops took days to find Manuel Noriega after the Panama invasion, and they were hunting him on the ground. Furthermore, killing the key Serbian leaders (Radovan Karadzic and Slobodan Milosevic) probably wouldn't moderate Serb policies since extremist currents run strong in both communities. Cutting communication links is also impractical and would have little effect even if accomplished. Bosnian Serb forces simply have too many ways to communicate with their leaders; and this body can fight even without its head.

Aerial Punishment

The second strategy, aerial punishment, would attempt to inflict enough damage on economic targets that Serbian civilians would compel their leaders to withdraw from their occupied lands. While most of Bosnia's economy is already in ruins, the Serbian standard of living could be substantially reduced by a short air campaign. Serbia's meager air defenses would be destroyed first; F-117s, F-111s, F-15Es, F-18s, F-16s, A-6s and Tomahawk cruise missiles would then knock out its electric power grids, oil refineries and food distribution system. In all, several hundred targets would be attacked. With good weather, the campaign might take less than two weeks.

But punishment is unlikely to cause the Serbs to abandon their Bosnian conquests. Air attacks generate more public anger against the attacker than the target. Air power slaughtered British, German and Japanese civil-

> *"A 'rollback' strategy would use massive military force . . . to win a decisive victory against the Bosnian Serbs."*

ians in World War II; threatened Egyptian civilians in the 1970 "war of attrition" with Israel; and depopulated large parts of Afghanistan in the 1980s. In each case, the citizenry did not turn against its government. Moreover, Westerners concerned about the Balkan situation for mainly moral reasons would shrink from using such indiscriminate means against noncombatants. Finally, the opponent most vulnerable to aerial punishment— Serbia proper—is not the opponent the West most needs to coerce. Even if Belgrade agrees to press the Bosnian Serbs for withdrawals, it is not clear that they would obey.

> *"Air attacks generate more public anger against the attacker than the target."*

The third strategy—weakening the Serbian army to the point where Bosnian Muslim ground troops can force its withdrawal—offers the best chance of success. This air campaign might include three sets of targets: the Serbian army in Serbia, the 35,000-man Bosnian Serb conventional army and the 35,000 Bosnian Serb irregulars. Of these three, the Serbian conventional army in Serbia proper is the easiest to track. It is concentrated in bases and armed with heavy weapons that can be found from the air. But destroying this army would only reduce Serbia's ability to *reinforce* its forces in Bosnia; it would do nothing to weaken them directly.

The Bosnian Serb conventional armies present a more important target, and they can be destroyed from the air if conditions are right. Since they seem to operate in small mobile units of about 500 men and are constantly on the move, they need to be forced into a concentration to be made vulnerable. (Air strikes could not destroy Iraqi Scuds in open desert. The odds of finding smaller artillery pieces that can be hidden in forests and mountains are even worse.) How do we do this? Engage them in ground action that forces them to gather in one place. If they fought a large, well-armed land army, they would have to mass in far larger numbers. They would then present a target that could be shattered from the air.

Bosnian Serb irregulars would be more difficult to strike from the air. These forces operate in tiny groups of 100 or fewer and rely on mortars and light arms to do their dirty work. This makes them hard to find and difficult to distinguish from Muslim and Croat fighters. On the other hand, these attributes make them a minor factor in the larger military equation.

Air power, in short, can help compel Serbian withdrawals by damaging the Bosnian Serb regular forces. But all this depends on the Bosnian Serbs facing a powerful, well-armed ground opponent. The Bosnian Muslims, *not* the Western powers, must supply these forces. To do this, the West is going to have to give them heavy weapons and provide training.

Weapons and Training

The Bosnian Muslims have been losing territory for lack of weapons, not troops. The total Bosnian Muslim population exceeds the Bosnian Serb population by at least 300,000. However, the Muslims can now arm only some 50,000 soldiers, while the Bosnian Serbs have 70,000 well-armed troops. What's more, the Serbs have 1,500 artillery pieces, tanks and other armored vehicles. The

Bosnian Muslims have fewer than 50.

Western military assistance to the Bosnian Muslims would equalize the balance. Weapons could be delivered on C-130 transport aircraft; these can use short, primitive airstrips and can therefore operate from a number of fields and roads in Muslim-held Bosnia. The C-130s could deliver light infantry weapons—rifles, mortars, shoulder-launched anti-tank weapons, night vision devices, machine guns, mines—and also heavier weapons, including 105mm and 155mm artillery pieces. When airfields are not available, these weapons could be airdropped. There's no need to use Croatian-held territory to transfer these goods. In a matter of months the Muslims would have 80,000 soldiers armed to the teeth and able to stop a Serbian offensive in its tracks.

Giving the Bosnian Muslims an offensive capability is more difficult for two reasons. First, the Muslims probably would need self-propelled artillery, tanks and armored personnel carriers, which require the giant C-5 transport aircraft, which in turn requires a long landing strip. Muslim-controlled Bosnia has only three such strips—Sarajevo, Bihac and Tuzla—and none is secure from Serbian anti-aircraft fire. So the heavy weapons would have to be brought into Bosnia over Croatian-controlled land routes, and it's likely the Croats would grant passage reluctantly. Second, the Bosnian Muslims have little experience using heavy weapons or conducting offensive operations. It would take a few hundred Western advisers and about two years after we begin arming them for them to become proficient.

> *"The Bosnian Muslims, not the Western powers, must supply [ground] forces."*

Consolidate and Attack

This strategy would take time. The Muslims would require perhaps a year to halt further Serb gains and consolidate their defensive positions before they could move to compel Serb withdrawals. The West should therefore adopt a two-phase plan—protecting Muslim consolidation in the first, compelling Serb withdrawals in the second. The choice between rollback and coercive bloodletting could be deferred until the second phase. In the first phase the West would organize, train and equip the Muslim forces for defensive operations. A fleet of about 100 C-130s would ferry arms to the Muslims, while several hundred fighter and ground attack aircraft stand ready in Italy and on aircraft carriers in the Adriatic to destroy any large Serb offensives. The West would deploy 200 to 400 Special Operations Forces in Bosnia to assist its air operations by serving as ground spotters and to help the Muslims develop a command and intelligence apparatus.

In the second phase, the West would prepare the Muslims for offensive operations and support these from the air. The Serbs now have some 350 main battle tanks, 200 light armored vehicles and 1,000 artillery pieces. A coercive bloodletting strategy could be launched when the Bosnian Muslims have acquired a roughly equivalent ground force. A rollback strategy would have to wait until the Muslims assembled ground forces around twice the combat power of Serb ground forces.

Diplomatic and economic incentives should be joined to these military punishments. As its main reward, the West should offer to recognize Greater Serbia if the Serbs cooperate with the Western program. The Western powers should also promise to lift economic sanctions and perhaps even to help rebuild the Serbian economy.

Peace and Security

Once a peace agreement is signed, populations would have to be moved in order to create homogeneous states. The international community should oversee and subsidize this population exchange. Specifically, the U.N. should establish a Balkan Population Exchange commission, modeled after the League of Nations-sponsored Refugee Settlement Commission, which managed the transfer of more than 1.5 million people between Greece and Turkey from 1923 to 1931. This commission should secure safe passage for immigrants, establish a bank to help them buy and sell property and administer a Balkan Marshall Fund to assist the development of new housing and industry in immigration zones. The commission should have a ten-year mandate: two years for resettlement, eight years for economic development.

How can the long-term survival of the Bosnian-Muslim state be guaranteed? It would inevitably be weaker than its neighbors. Population is a good indicator of latent military power. Allowing for the return of refugees, there are roughly 9 million Serbs, 4.5 million Croats and maybe 1.8 million Bosnian Muslims. There are also some 5.3 million Albanians in the region: of these, 1.6 million live in the Serbian region of Kosovo, 400,000 in Macedonia and 3.3 million in Albania proper. Thus, Serbia would be the strongest state in the region and the Bosnian-Muslim state would be among the weakest.

The NATO powers should therefore undertake to arm it well. They should also issue a security guarantee, promising to intervene with air power if its neighbors attack. NATO should also foster a defensive alliance between the Bosnian-Muslim state, Croatia and Albania. Those states are neither friends of Serbia nor strong enough to check it alone. They should have good reason to ally themselves with the Bosnian Muslims.

This partition plan isn't perfect; and it isn't morally pure. It means transferring hundreds of thousands of civilians from historic homes and countries. It means risking a small number of American lives. But it is the only plan that's realistic about what can be achieved in such a fraught area and idealistic about the principles at stake. And it can be done.

The United Nations and NATO Should Intervene in Kosovo

by Bujar Bukoshi

About the author: *Bujar Bukoshi is an Albanian who was appointed prime minister of the Republic of Kosovo's government-in-exile following 1992 elections, although Serbia controls Kosovo and does not recognize this government. Bukoshi lives in Stuttgart, Germany.*

The deputy head of the United Nations forces in the Balkans, Cedric Thornberry, warned that the crisis in Kosovo, where Albanians comprise 92 percent of the population and the Serbians rule through apartheid, is potentially more dangerous than current fighting in Bosnia-Herzegovina.

The observation may seem strange to some, since international media attention has focused on the atrocities of Serbian "ethnic cleansing" against Muslims in Bosnia.

Brutal Repression

However, for three years human rights leaders have identified Kosovo, a formerly autonomous province and one of the original eight constituent units of former Yugoslavia, as the site of brutal forms of repression of 2.2 million Albanians by a handful of Serbs who control the military.

In 1989, Serbian strongman Slobodan Milosevic revoked Kosovo's autonomous status and launched his "ethnic cleansing" campaign, long before the first Muslim villages were attacked in Bosnia. Since then, the people of Kosovo have lived under a reign of terror, intimidation, abuse, beatings, and killings at the hands of the Belgrade regime, which has imposed martial law on our country.

Serbian authorities have abrogated virtually all of the Albanians' human, civil, and national rights. Martial law has closed Albanian-language schools and the university; severely limited access to health care for Albanians, since

Bujar Bukoshi, "Kosovo's Plea for Help," *The Christian Science Monitor*, June 30, 1993. © 1993 by TCSPS. Reprinted with permission.

Albanian physicians were summarily fired; and led to 80 percent unemployment among Albanians, who were sacked because of their ethnicity. Nearly 300,000 Albanians have been forced to flee Kosovo.

The Serbs have mounted a military buildup with more than 100,000 Serbian troops and heavily armed Serbian police stationed in our country. With the forced removal of Yugoslav President Dobrica Cosic, the hand of the ultra-nationalist hardliners in Belgrade has been strengthened.

> *"NATO troops should be dispatched in sufficient numbers to maintain peace."*

My government has adhered to peaceful opposition to Serbian brutality. We want to be part of the solution, not the problem. However, the patience of our people is not limitless. We must be allowed to pursue our basic rights through freedom and democracy.

Intervention Now

We have asked that the UN immediately deploy an observer mission to Kosovo, coupled with a substantial increase in the number of Conference on Security and Cooperation in Europe human rights monitors now in our country. We need more outsiders inside our country to observe firsthand the degree of repression and brutality. Humanitarian assistance is needed immediately as well.

Furthermore, NATO troops should be dispatched in sufficient numbers to maintain peace as soon as possible. Serbian heavy weapons need to be placed under international control. Serbs already have installed artillery and measured trajectories.

The no-fly zone in force over Bosnia should be expanded to include Kosovo, the roving bands of Serbian paramilitary thugs should be disbanded, and Serbia's practice of colonizing Kosovo by importing Serbs from Bosnia and Montenegro should be ended.

For the longer term, the UN should declare and administer a Trust Territory of Kosovo for a few years. In the absence of any indication that Belgrade is willing to negotiate, Kosovo should be placed under UN protection with the understanding that at the end of the transition phase, the Albanians will exercise their right to self-determination. Under the trusteeship provided for in the UN Charter, Kosovo will be demilitarized while developing close economic and cultural links with its neighbors. The Serbian minority and Serbian cultural and religious monuments will be protected.

Stop Serbian Aggression

A UN trusteeship could be difficult for Serbia to swallow, but it is one of the best solutions to the crisis Serbia has created. Belgrade must accept the fact that its continued rule over Kosovo, in which Serbs comprise only 8 percent of the population, is untenable.

If Serbia refuses to place Kosovo under a trusteeship, the UN Security Council should declare the situation "a threat to international peace and security," while designating our country a safe haven and providing protection for Kosovars by all means necessary, as provided in the UN Charter. Such powers were invoked when Iraq attacked Kurds in southern Iraq, the Khmer Rouge refused to cooperate with the peace settlement in Cambodia, as well as in the difficult situations in Somalia and Bosnia-Herzegovina.

We hope the world community will adopt our approach. Either the world must stop Serbian aggression at the borders of Kosovo, or it will face a very real possibility of a wider Balkan war, which could send shock waves through Europe and Central Asia. Failure to act also would encourage ultra-nationalists elsewhere, such as the former Soviet Union, to engage in "ethnic cleansing."

The citizens of my country are unarmed, defenseless. Their only weapon is a firm commitment to freedom and democracy, with faith that the international community will act morally and courageously if our worst expectations come to pass.

Limited Military Intervention in Bosnia May Be Necessary

by John Roach

About the author: *John Roach is the archbishop of Minneapolis and St. Paul, Minnesota, and is chairman of the U.S. Catholic bishops' International Policy Committee.*

The world has watched with increasing horror as war has brought untold human suffering to the peoples of the Balkans. We and many others have implored the international community to act with greater resolve to stop the slaughter of innocents, to provide aid to millions of suffering people and to help bring about a lasting political solution to this fratricidal war and prevent its spread to other parts of the region.

As our government and the international community appear to be moving closer to making a decision to intervene militarily, I wanted to share with you what we consider to be the critical moral issues at stake in using military force in Bosnia-Herzegovina.

Indifference Is Unacceptable

First, we believe that the United States, with the United Nations and other international bodies, should find effective means of protecting innocent people and bringing about a just and lasting political solution to this dreadful conflict. The parties to the conflict bear the greatest responsibility to reject violence and virulent nationalism and establish a just and peaceful order. But indifference to the tragedy in Bosnia on the part of the United States and the international community is unacceptable.

The international community bears a moral responsibility to intervene, in the words of Pope John Paul, "where the survival of populations and entire ethnic groups is seriously compromised"; "practical indifference or inaction . . . is a

John Roach, "On U.S. Intervention in Bosnia," *Origins*, May 27, 1993. Reprinted with permission.

culpable omission." This moral imperative is warranted by the need to protect the lives and basic rights of the people of Bosnia. But it also is warranted, in the case of the Balkans, by the need to prevent a general Balkan war, to avert a worsening refugee crisis in Europe, to uphold and strengthen international norms and institutions, and to discourage the spread of militant nationalism and ethnic conflicts in other parts of the world. In our judgment, then, the United States has a clear moral as well as national interest in helping to resolve the conflict in Bosnia.

> *"The international community bears a moral responsibility to intervene [in Bosnia]."*

Second, how the United States chooses to intervene in Bosnia raises difficult moral questions. As you know, according to the just war tradition, the strong presumption against the resort to military force may be overridden only if certain strict criteria are met. There must be a just cause, force must be undertaken by a legitimate authority, the intention must be to restore justice and peace and not to seek vengeance, there must be a reasonable probability of success, the comparative justice of the conflicting parties must be weighed, force must be a last resort, the likely overall harm caused by military force must be proportionate to the good likely to be achieved, and particular uses of force must be discriminate and proportionate.

Peace Through Negotiation

These criteria are designed not to facilitate the choice for military means, but to make that choice both difficult and rarely used. A stable and just peace in the former Yugoslavia can be achieved, in the end, only through constructive negotiation and diplomacy, leading to an enforceable and enforced political settlement. Ultimately, success will depend upon a long-term process of political reconstruction that must include replacing aggressive nationalism with a commitment to democracy and basic human and minority rights.

There is no real military solution in the former Yugoslavia. But, as the Holy See has said, governments and the international community have a right and duty to "disarm th[e] aggressor." We are convinced that there is just cause to use force to defend largely helpless people in Bosnia against aggression and barbarism that are destroying the very foundations of society and threaten large numbers of people. The utter disregard for basic human rights and the laws of war, if not clearly confronted, threatens to undermine the legitimacy of international norms and institutions. Increasingly ominous is the possibility that other parts of the Balkans might suffer a similar fate.

Therefore, with the Holy See, we support "timely, measured and firmly executed interventions."

Specifically, we support:

• Implementation, where feasible, of the U.N. Security Council's decision to establish safe havens in Bosnia as a temporary measure to save lives and protect against "ethnic cleansing" until a political solution can be found.

• More concerted measures to protect civilian populations in besieged cities, to protect fleeing refugees and to ensure the delivery of aid to the needy.

• Continued enforcement of economic sanctions.

• Full implementation and enforcement of a political settlement in Bosnia and the cease-fire in Croatia, a step we recognize would probably require the use of U.S. troops.

None of these interventions are free of risks or costs, but in our judgment they are warranted by the gravity of the humanitarian situation in Bosnia.

Limited Military Force

Other military options, such as arming the Bosnian government and air strikes, also raise difficult questions, especially regarding the probability of success, proportionality, and the safety and rights of civilians. Legitimate governments have a right and duty to defend their people, but this right must be exercised in a morally responsible way. Therefore, a decision to lift the arms embargo or intervene militarily in other ways should meet the following criteria:

• Objectives: Force should be strictly limited in its means and objectives, and should be only one part of an ongoing effort to find a just, lasting and comprehensive political solution to the conflict.

• Authority: Force should, if possible, be carried out on a multilateral basis with the authority of the international community.

• Noncombatant immunity: Force must not be directed against civilians.

• Success and proportionality: Military measures should not prolong or widen the war or undermine prospects for a just political solution to the conflict.

• Human rights: Lifting the arms embargo in particular should be conditioned on respect for international norms governing the use of force and other basic human and minority rights on the part of those receiving the arms.

• Humanitarian relief: Force should not further impair the ability of the people of Bosnia to meet their essential needs.

I hope you will examine carefully whether these conditions can be met—particularly with regard to lifting the arms embargo—given the atrocities committed by all sides in this war, the lack of accountability of many of the militias fighting in Bosnia and the likelihood that the war would escalate and widen.

> *"Force should be strictly limited in its means and objectives."*

The conflict in Bosnia-Herzegovina is extraordinarily complex. There are no simple, clear or quick solutions. But the seemingly intractable nature of this conflict is not an excuse for inaction; rather, it reinforces the need for a concerted and sustained commitment of the international community to finding a just solution. The world cannot stand aside as innocent people are destroyed, as aggression shapes a new world, as the hopes of freedom turn into the violence of war.

We support your efforts to find morally appropriate means to create the conditions in which the peoples of the Balkans can live together in peace with justice.

A Clarification

My letter to Secretary Christopher has apparently been misinterpreted in some early accounts as a general endorsement of U.S. military intervention in Bosnia. This misreads the letter and its message, which is an appeal to find effective means to halt the horror in Bosnia and a call to apply strict moral criteria to any use of military force. The letter clearly distinguishes between several limited military measures which we support to protect the innocent and halt the violence (i.e., safe havens, protecting civilians and refugees, enforcing economic sanctions and implementing a cease-fire in Croatia, and a possible overall political settlement) and other measures (i.e., air strikes, lifting the arms embargo) which we believe must still meet stringent moral criteria before they can be used.

> *"There is [not] a true military solution to the crisis."*

We continue to insist the world and the United States cannot turn away from our responsibilities in Bosnia, but our response must be guided by traditional moral criteria (i.e., limited objectives, multilateral authority, strict noncombatant immunity, real probability of success and proportionality, etc.).

As pastors and teachers, our role is to help raise the continuing human and moral consequence of the horror in Bosnia and suggest ethical criteria that ought to guide our nation's response. This letter shares guidelines adopted by the Administrative Board of our conference in March 1993. It rejects the arguments that the United States has no role or responsibility in stopping the slaughter in Bosnia. It also rejects the premise that there is a true military solution to the crisis. Instead, it offers a moral framework for choosing the means to address the grave loss of human life and human rights in Bosnia. Our ethical tradition is neither simple nor easy to apply, but it offers an important resource in assessing the choices facing our nation and world in Bosnia.

Do Not Intervene Against the Serbs

by **Murray N. Rothbard**

About the author: *Murray N. Rothbard is coeditor of the* Rothbard-Rockwell Report (RRR), *a monthly libertarian periodical covering political and social issues.*

There are no excuses left any more. The entire "anti-war Left" has now joined the rest of the rotters on the Respectable Spectrum: liberals, Establishment centrists, Official Conservatives, neoconservatives, and virtually everyone else, in hysterical calls for intervention against the Serbs in Bosnia. It's not because the United Nations is behind the war; on the contrary, the UN is getting as much flak as the US from this "international community" of war-mongers. Why have they "sat it out," they charge, in the face of "Serbian aggression" and expansionism against the poor Bosnian Muslims?

Pressures to Intervene

As usual, there are disagreements about the extent of military intervention demanded; but as usual, the "moderates" are either liars or self-deluders, since timid and moderate first steps will obviously not work, and then the precedent being set and intervention begun, the pressure will become irresistible for ever more accelerated steps, until the maximum pain is inflicted. No-fly zones, air strikes against artillery, all will fail and lead further; and now, the war crowd is beginning to call, *not yet* for bombing Belgrade—the only Serbs they can find and target—but for bombing the "bridges" near Belgrade where supplies are being sent to the Serbs in Bosnia. Bombing Belgrade itself will follow, and when that won't work, which it won't, the Unthinkable will be voiced: nuking Belgrade, using "clean" nukes of course to avoid the fallout's harming other peoples. And when *that* doesn't work, American ground troops—under a UN cover, of course, with half a dozen Brits, Canadians, and Indians thrown in—will be next.

Murray N. Rothbard, "Hands Off the Serbs!" *Rothbard-Rockwell Report*, June 1993. Reprinted with permission.

And one of the reasons none of these measures will work, is because the Serbs are a magnificently gutsy people, a "primitive" folk who don't give a tinker's dam for "world opinion," the "respect of the international community," and all the rest of the pretentious cant that so impresses readers of the *New York Times*. What do the Serbs want? It's very clear what they want, and there is no need for the sort of eternal *kvetching* that Sigmund Freud indulged in about "what do women want?" The Serbs want all the Serbs in former Yugoslavia to be part of a new Greater Serbia being carved out of the ethnic mess in the Balkans. They want a Serb nation, and they don't give a rap for any of the considerations that so intensely motivate Establishment World Opinion, and God bless them for that. World Opinion, in turn, doesn't give a rap for a Serb nation. But why should World Opinion hold sway *anywhere*?

Pro-War Pacifists

Before dealing with the Serbs in depth, let us focus a bit more on the pro-war anti-war movement people whom Harry Elmer Barnes bitterly used to call "the pro-war pacifists." This gang has written an open letter to the UN, President Bill Clinton, and the US Congress (published in *In These Times*, April 19-May 2, 1993). Of course, they are "moderate"; no call, yet for nuking Belgrade. Also, there are the usual Marxoid obeisances to the "democratic opposition in Serbia," an "opposition" generally confined to Belgrade, and virtually nonexistent on the Bosnian front. What they want is the supposedly "even handed" approach of lifting the arms embargo on the Bosnians, so that the Bosnian Muslim government can "defend itself." Sounds fine and balanced on the surface, except that these and similar groups egregiously omit the fact that the UN, prodded by the US, has been cruelly imposing an embargo, not just on arms, but *on everything else*, on the Serbs for many months. I would be all in favor of lifting our arms embargo on the Bosnians *provided that* all international sanctions against the Serbs were lifted as well. But, of course, our pro-war anti-warriors say not a peep about this. Instead, they demand: "vigorous prosecution of war criminals" (who? where? and who's going to do all this, and who will kidnap these "criminals," and how will they get a fair trial and on precisely *what* ex post facto charges?); and "air lifting humanitarian aid, under military protection, to all civilians in need." (You mean like dropping those [parachuted] food mounds?) Furthermore, in addition to denouncing "aggressive Serb expansionism," these bloodthirsty "anti-war" warriors also have the nerve to demand that the US/UN insist that "the Croats cease their aggression in Bosnia." (*What* aggression? The Croats have only occupied Croatian areas in Bosnia, notably Herzegovina in the southern part of that province.) This attack on the Croats shows what these ex-anti-warriors are up to: shilling for the Bosnian Muslim government, which

> *"No-fly zones, air strikes against artillery, all will fail."*

presumes to speak for a non-entity called the "Bosnian nation" and its alleged "territorial integrity," a "nation" that sprang into existence only in 1992.

Never a Nation

Let us emphasize: there is not, and never was, anything called a "Bosnian nation." There was and is a Serbian nation, a Croat nation, and a Slovene nation, each with identifiable longtime national, cultural, and ethno-religious characteristics. There is no more a "Bosnian nation" than there is a "nation" of North Dakota. Bosnia is simply a geographical entity, in which have lived three very different, clashing, and mutually antagonistic nations: the Serbs, the Croats, and the "Bosnian" Muslims. These are three nations slugging it out in one small territory. . . .

But what about us at RRR? Haven't we, too, flip-flopped in the opposite direction? Aren't we former anti-Serbs now born again as pro-Serbs?

Not quite. To recall those dear dead days months ago: the United States, along with the UN, and all Received Opinion, including leftists/liberals/Centrists/ Official Conservatives/ and neocons, were all fanatically pro-Serb, calling for the old Wilsonian-Rooseveltian "guarantee of the territorial integrity of 'Yugoslavia,'" and therefore bitterly hostile to all national secessionist movements, including the Croats and Slovenes. The Croats, in particular, were constantly smeared by Received Opinion as being "Nazis."

> *"The UN . . . has been cruelly imposing an embargo, not just on arms, but* **on everything else,** *on the Serbs."*

We at RRR, on the other hand, always Out of Step with Received Opinion, recognized from way back that "Yugoslavia" is not, and never has been, a nation, that it was born of the rotten Victors' Peace imposed by the Entente Powers (redubbed the "Allies" Britain, France, and the US) at Versailles and in other dictated settlements after World War I. Yugoslavia was a geographical expression which served only as a mask for Serbian imperialism and dictatorship over the other peoples incarcerated into that expression: notably the Croats and the Slovenes.

For the problem with the Serbs was, and still is, that while yearning for the perfectly acceptable ideal of a Greater Serbia, that they have not been exactly reticent or scrupulous in avoiding expansion of the Serbs' unwelcome embrace to the Croats etc. in the Balkans.

So we at RRR were always, and still are, staunchly opposed to "Yugoslavia" or any of its pomp and works.

The Ethnic Land-Grab

But now that Yugoslavia has fallen apart, and has collapsed into its constituent peoples and nationalities, the situation is very different. The Serbs seem to have abandoned the goal of a Greater Yugoslavia, and have moderated their demands into the perfectly reasonable one of a Greater Serbia. And the guerrilla warfare on the ground has, more or less, sorted it all out, as it always does: with each nationality getting more or less its own ethnic areas. Much of Croatia in the hands of Serbian guerrillas and incorporated into the Republic of Krajina is ethnically Serb; the Slovenes have ethnic Slovenia, etc.

Bosnia, with its ethno-religious mixture of villages and populations, is particularly difficult to sort out, but even Bosnia now enjoys rough ethno-religious justice with the Croats running the Croatian areas of Herzegovina, the Serbs running their areas, and so on. The Bosnian Muslims have less territory than the others because most of the Muslims are concentrated in the large Bosnian cities, such as Sarajevo.

And so rough ethnic justice has come to Bosnia, and it will sort itself out provided that the blankety-blank US/UN combo keeps its hands off. If the Bosnian Muslims get a bit less than their quota, so what? The main problem now in former Yugoslavia is not the Serbs but the pretensions of the Bosnian Muslim government to run and dominate *all* of Bosnia-Herzegovina. It is the Muslims and their shills in "world opinion" who keep bleating about the "territorial integrity" of this non-existent nation, an "integrity" that didn't even exist before 1991. It is the Muslims and their shills who refuse to agree to the "cantonization" of Bosnia, a process that that area sorely needs. The Vance-Owen plan [to divide Bosnia into ten separate ethnic provinces] was only a feeble step in that direction, for it insisted on preserving the powers of a central Bosnian (Muslim) government. Instead, the only hope of genuine peace and justice is to destroy "Bosnia" and to allow this non-country to be divided completely into its constituent parts.

No Ethnic Cleansing

What is really incomprehensible is the intensity of the flip-flop on the Serbs from the serried ranks of Received Opinion. The Serbs . . . are Serbs, and always have been, with their vices and virtues. The Serbs are a constant factor; they want a Greater Serbia, as much as they can get, but are willing in the end to settle for Serb lands. And so are all the other nationality groups in the area. But what about the dread term "ethnic cleansing," repeated like a mantra in every news item in the West for months? Well, in the first place, the Serbs didn't say "ethnic cleansing"; they used some Serbo-Croat phrase and that doesn't sound so bad. Serbs

> *"Yugoslavia was a geographical expression which served only as a mask for Serbian imperialism."*

have recently claimed mistranslation; that what they really meant is "ethnic transfer." And it makes sense: the Serbs don't want to exterminate clashing peoples; they just want them *out* of predominantly Serb areas, out of Greater Serbia.

And let us not forget that it has been the sainted Bosnian Muslim troops who have done their darndest to prevent UN workers from getting Muslim civilians out of Srebrenica and other Muslim towns; they want the Muslim civilians staying there in mortal danger, to keep world pressure on for these towns to become part of Muslim Bosnia. *All these clashing groups perform ethnic transfer/cleansing when they can get away with it.*

> *"It is the Muslims and their shills who refuse to agree to the 'cantonization' of Bosnia."*

And what about the mass rapes, which have brought Left Feminists screaming into the kill-the-Serbs camp? Well, I don't want to disillusion any tender souls, but almost *all* victorious troops through history commit systemic rapin' and lootin' of the vanquished. It's called the "spoils of war," and will continue to exist, despite Received Opinion, so long as war exists. Trying to *expand* the war, as the Establishment is doing, will only prolong and expand the looting and raping. And yes, it hasn't only been the *Serbs* who have committed these crimes, believe me; all the groups do it, and it's just that the Serbs have been better fighters in this civil war and so have had more occasion to indulge in this time-honored practice.

Americans Misunderstand

American meddling is made even more futile by the fact that it is impossible for Americans to understand, not only these fierce rivalries, but the tremendous sense of *history* they all possess. How can Americans, who have no historical memory whatever and scarcely remember when Ronald Reagan was president, possibly understand these peoples of the Balkans, to whom the great 15th century battle against the invading Turks is as real, nay *more* real, than yesterday's dinner? To the Serbs and the Croats, the Bosnian Muslims are not the "gentle people" lionized in Western propaganda. The Bosnian Muslims are not only still reviled as traitors selling out to the hated Turks, but in addition, the very quality of their devotion to Islam is in question. For the Bosnian Muslims were once the hated Bogomil heretics, a Manichaean heresy with horrifying implications, and there is much evidence that the Muslims still practice their Bogomil rites in secret, engraving its symbols on their tombstones. The Bogomils were what Ayn Rand followers wrongly believe all Christians to be: believers that the world of matter and the flesh are pure evil created by Satan, whereas the spirit is good and created by God. As for the Nazi question, the Serbs tried to be as much "pro-Nazi" as the Croats (a minority) but weren't trusted by the Germans, whereas the "gentle" Bosnian Muslims enlisted in proportionately far greater numbers in the Waffen SS than did the Croats or Serbs. So let's stop romanticizing the Bosnian Muslims. Let them take their chances on their own.

So what to do about Bosnia? What to do about the Serbs? The answer, as repugnant as it is to this meddling age, is to stay the Hell out. Let the peoples of

America's Military Should Not Intervene in the Balkans

by John McCain, interviewed by Major Garrett

About the authors: *John McCain is a Republican senator from Arizona and a member of the Armed Services Committee. McCain is a former naval aviator who was a prisoner of war in Vietnam for more than five years. Major Garrett is a reporter for the* Washington Times *daily newspaper in Washington, D.C.*

Garrett: You oppose limited U.S. military involvement in the Balkan civil war. Tell us what you hope will be the result of following the policy you support. What do you hope U.S. action or inaction will have accomplished?

McCain: I hope the result would be the civil conflict in what was Yugoslavia that has been going on for at least 700 years will be at a very low point, that the boundaries will have been stabilized, and that sanctions, embargoes and other measures will bring about a dramatic reduction in the slaughter. That's what I hope would happen. I am by no means convinced that that would be the case.

Historical Comparisons

Garrett: Many analysts have compared this conflict to Vietnam, the peace-keeping mission in Lebanon and World War II. From your perspective, which is the best historical comparison and what does it suggest about the likely success or failure of an active U.S. role to resolve the conflict?

McCain: You should not overdraw comparison to any war because there are unique aspects of this conflict that do not apply. But I would suggest that probably the closest analogy would be the Beirut situation.

There were different religions and different sects battling each other with incredible ferocity and the United States, motivated by the purest of ambitions, inserted "peacekeeping" forces into the region without the ability to beneficially affect the outcome of the situation, and 241 young Marines lost their lives. It has the elements of Beirut only magnified by a factor of a thousand.

I don't think that anything is going to wipe out the ethnic and religious [hos-

John McCain, interviewed by Major Garrett, "The Bosnia Question," *The Washington Times*, May 16, 1993. Reprinted with permission of the Washington Times Corporation.

tility] that exist all over what was once Yugoslavia. Our goal should be to minimize and then control that conflict as much as possible. I say that with the greatest reluctance, but until somebody comes up with a better idea, that one, I think, should be pursued.

No one has a corner on the market of horror, disgust, dismay and repugnance over what has happened. The question returns again and again: What is a viable option to beneficially affect the situation, not just one that makes us feel good for a short period of time?

Questions of Arms and Intervention

Garrett: Secretary of State Warren Christopher has strongly suggested lifting the arms embargo. Do you support this? If not, why not? If yes, do you fear U.S. enemies such as Libya, Iraq and Iran would become suppliers to the Muslims, thereby heightening the religious antagonisms?

McCain: I reluctantly support the proposal, but I have few illusions as to the efficacy of such a policy to beneficially affect the situation. I think its effect would be marginal and, yes, I think there is some risk of Islamic fundamentalist nations being involved. More importantly, we must recognize that the kind of support the Bosnia Muslims are seeking will ratchet up the level of combat, with an ensuing increase in civilian casualties, at least in the short run. One British diplomat said it levels the killing field.

> *"[The conflict] has the elements of Beirut only magnified by a factor of a thousand."*

Garrett: Some say the Serbian attacks on Muslims amount to modern genocide. No one disputes the Serbs have committed the most egregious violations of human rights, but it's equally true atrocities have been perpetrated by all three sides. Does the United States have a moral responsibility, separate from its national security interests, to stop genocide? If so, how far should we be willing to go to stop them? If not, how does this policy square with our rhetorical support for human rights the world over?

McCain: The United States has a clear moral imperative, just as we had in Somalia. But the question, the recurring question must be asked: Can we beneficially affect the situation through military intervention, and if so, how? It is my firm belief that air strikes alone will not resolve or help the situation. That view is shared by Gen. Norman Schwarzkopf, Gen. Colin Powell and every military expert that I know. We may reach a point where moral imperatives combined with U.S. vital national security interests warrant military intervention. If so, I believe the only viable option is the use of ground forces assisted by U.S. air power. I would hope that those ground forces would be European. I think the Europeans have much more at stake, and I think they have a greater responsibility. It might be pleasant for us to hold the Europeans' coat for a change, instead of them holding ours.

Garrett: Some argue the United States has a larger stake in the Balkan conflict than meets the eye. They fear a wider conflict could distract and possibly engulf other European nations, thus prolonging the European recession and shrinking valuable U.S. export markets. Are these fears justified and are they sufficient to involve the United States militarily in the conflict?

McCain: That may be the case. But it sounds a little bit to me like the much-discredited domino theory. For us to enter into a virtually insoluble military situation based on fears of expansion of the conflict is not an appropriate course of action. There are scenarios where the United States' vital national security interests are at stake, such as a war between Greece and Turkey. In my view, that is an unlikely scenario. Our European friends don't seem to share this domino theory. Otherwise, I think they would be much more eager to be involved.

> *"To enter into a . . . military situation based on fears of expansion of the conflict is not . . . appropriate."*

America's Interests

Garrett: Does the United States have a strategic interest in rolling back the Serbian territorial gains in the former Yugoslavia, and is that a militarily achievable objective?

McCain: We have a moral interest in rolling back the Serbian gains. At the same time, I have seen no militarily viable option that would achieve that goal without a massive infusion of ground troops into the area. And even at that point, our young men and women in the military may have some difficulty differentiating friend from foe. Fundamentally, it's a civil war. They dress alike. They are fighting one another in various areas. Identification of who is on our side and who isn't is somewhat difficult.

Garrett: Does the United States have a strategic interest in containing the Balkan civil war within the boundaries of the former Yugoslavia?

McCain: If you view the United States' strategic interest as avoiding civil conflict anywhere in the world, then yes. But we also have an interest in Azerbaijan, Armenia, Sudan, Tibet, Sri Lanka and Cambodia. The last time I looked at the map, there were 28 places in the world where a civil conflict was going on. Yes, we have a strategic interest in stopping every one of those. The question is, do they require military intervention? . . .

I'm concerned about the definition of what a U.S. peacekeeping role [in Bosnia] would be. The American people should know what their young people are going to be over there doing and how great is the risk to their lives. I mean, one scenario is that everybody says, "OK, we've all signed this [Vance-Owen peace] agreement and we all trundle back into the places where Mr. Cyrus Vance and Mr. David Owen have told us to be," and everything is fine. There is a much more likely scenario where the Serbs are incredibly reluctant to give up what in their view they gained at the cost of a considerable sacrifice.

Garrett: Isn't it true that the Serbs have achieved most if not all of their military objectives? If so, what is the point of involving the U.S. military at this point? And what, then, is the value of the Vance-Owen peace treaty [to divide Bosnia into ten separate ethnic provinces]?

McCain: As much as I hate to say it, it might be necessary for possibly a significantly modified Vance-Owen [agreement] that would recognize to some degree the territorial gains of the Serbs. I understand the profound distaste we would have for that because they gained it through clearly unlawful and illegal means. Possibly that recognition, that type of thing should be considered. I believe at some point the Serbs' territorial ambitions will be realized.

Garrett: You're saying as repugnant and displeasing as it might be, it might be better for all involved to cut their losses?

McCain: As repugnant as it is to possibly recognize at least some territorial gains which are clearly not within the boundaries of the Vance-Owen plan, I say that, fully understanding we would validate the use of force for territorial gain. But as much as I hate to do that, it wouldn't be the first time in history.

Foreign Military Intervention Would Fail

by Misha Glenny

About the author: *Misha Glenny is an award-winning correspondent in Central Europe for the British Broadcasting Company. He is the author of* The Fall of Yugoslavia: The Third Balkan War.

More than ever, the options open for an international response to the Bosnian war are extremely limited. As the Russian foreign minister, Andrej Kozyrev, put it: "There is no best option. We are choosing between bad and worse—or very, very bad, as a matter of fact. Let us not forget that the First World War started exactly in Sarajevo. There is unfortunately very much potential for a bigger Balkan war, which should be avoided by all means, and there is potential also for an international crusade, be it Muslim or Christian or whatever." As long as there is no consensus among the four major outside powers with interests in the region (the US, Russia, the European Community, and Turkey), no policy for intervention can succeed.

Arming the Muslims

Since it took office, the Bill Clinton administration has said that it has been considering "all options except the sending of US ground troops to Bosnia." These boil down to lifting the arms embargo on the Bosnian government or selective air strikes against Bosnian Serb artillery positions, or both. Although the first policy is supported by some influential members of the Clinton administration as well as a caucus of developing world countries at the UN and among the Islamic states, carrying it out would be extremely difficult. After the embargo is lifted, just how would the Muslims receive more arms? The Croats control all land routes from the Adriatic to the Bosnian forces and Croatia's president, Franjo Tudjman, has prevented weapons from reaching them. It is inconceivable that Tudjman would allow new weapons to reach Bosnian government forces. Therefore, arms could reach Sarajevo, Gorazde, Bihac, and Tuzla only by air and, as we know from the food drops to Zepa and Srebrenica, this is a difficult policy to carry out. Food reached some of the besieged enclaves only because the Serbs agreed not to fire on the trucks carrying it. Planes carrying weapons into Bosnia would become targets for Serb forces and most probably Croat forces as well. The forces flying in those weapons would be at war with the Serbs and Croats.

Let us assume for the moment that it were possible to supply weapons to the Muslims. What would be achieved by that? In the first instance, it would mean a sharp increase in the fighting in Bosnia-Hercegovina. If the Muslims received sufficient weapons, they would try to push back the Serbs in eastern Bosnia. If their behavior toward Croats in Zenica is anything to go by, they would commit the kind of atrocities to which their people in the region have been subjected by the Serbs. Is the assumption behind this move—so attractive as an expression of indignation—that it will force the Serbs to the peace table? Is it to punish the Serbs? To stop the Serbs from committing atrocities? To drive the Serbs out of eastern Bosnia never to return? We do not know because nobody in the Clinton administration has actually articulated what it hopes to achieve in the Balkans.

The Vance-Owen Peace Plan

Indeed while the Clinton administration has been strong on rhetoric and declarations, it has failed badly when it comes to working out a policy. Inheriting a muddled and evasive US position from George Bush, President Clinton began his term with strong words about the unacceptability of Serb actions in Bosnia and an attack on the Vance-Owen plan [to divide Bosnia into ten separate ethnic provinces] for "legitimizing ethnic cleansing," and "justifying aggression." The administration then spun a cocoon around its Bosnia policy. Three weeks later, the butterfly emerged—And lo! it hardly differed from the Vance-Owen plan— except, that is, for Warren Christopher's remark that the new map of Bosnia-Hercegovina suggested by Vance and Owen was unacceptable. It is time to scotch a persistent myth about the Vance-Owen plan. It does not legitimize ethnic cleansing. On the contrary, it punishes the Serbs by taking away 60 percent of the territory they have conquered militarily. It demands of the Serbs that they hand back Srebrenica, the key towns of eastern Bosnia, Zvornik, Foca, Visegrad, and other places they have "ethnically cleansed." It provides for a UN force to supervise the agreement once it is signed.

"Planes carrying weapons into Bosnia would become targets for Serb forces and most probably Croat forces as well."

The Croats and the Muslims have signed the Vance-Owen plan (maps and all) because, whatever their reservations, they believe it to be in their best interests to do so. The Serbs feel it discriminates against them precisely because it forces them to take so many territorial losses. For all its blustering about the inadequacies of the Vance-Owen plan, the Clinton administration has come up with nothing else in its place. It has succeeded in doing one useful thing—appointing Reginald Bartholomew as a special envoy to Yugoslavia; and Mr. Bartholomew has, in fact, been busy in Zagreb and Belgrade trying to persuade all sides to agree to the scheme that has been the object of so much contempt—the Vance-Owen plan.

Air Strikes

Since the Serbs will not agree to it, should the international community instead bomb them into accepting it? In response to this question, three things must be considered. First, are effective strikes possible on the terrain of Bosnia-Hercegovina? Secondly, will the Bosnian Serbs (and indeed Serbians inside Serbia) retreat when they realize that a punitive UN or US force has military superiority? Thirdly, will the Russians stand by and accept such a move?

The Western military leaders, such as Colin Powell, who have commented on the feasibility of bombing the Serbs into submission have not been confident about it. The senior NATO commander, General John Shalikashvili, counseled caution. "Bombing limited targets, for instance, artillery positions," he said, "is more difficult than people think and there is also no guarantee that such an act would bring a party to the negotiating table." This means that bombing risks further inflaming the situation on the ground for no real purpose other than an understandable but misguided desire for retribution—retribution that may also kill civilians.

The idea that the Serbs are inveterate cowards is most frequently propagated by exhausted journalists, like myself, who have been traumatized by taking cover so often from Serbian shells. However, the history of the last two centuries would tend to favor the private assessment of Cyrus Vance's tireless deputy, Herbert Okun. He maintains that "the Krajina and Bosnian Serbs kill without compunction and die without complaint." General Ratko Mladic, the commander of Bosnian Serb forces, has promised to lay waste large parts of the northern Balkans in the event of air strikes against his forces. Having talked at length with the man and observed his handiwork in several parts of the Kninska Krajina and Bosnia, I take his threats seriously.

> *"Bombing limited targets, for instance, artillery positions . . . is more difficult than people think."*

And the Russians? There is much empirical evidence to suggest that most ordinary Russians care not a fig for the Serbs, concerned as they are with chronic problems of their own. President Boris Yeltsin appeared to confirm this on April 27, 1993, when he announced that he would not supply arms to Serbia in the event of outside military intervention. So it does not appear that air strikes against the Serbs would break the delicate spirit of cooperation which has emerged between Washington and Moscow. However, the foreign minister, Andrej

Kozyrev, has warned that no action should be taken without first seeking the approval of the Russians.

Widening the War

If I am right on just one of the cautionary points I have raised, then the kind of military intervention being proposed may result in the escalation of the war in an appalling fashion. The UN and its officers on the ground in Bosnia and Croatia are firmly opposed to the action. The most senior civilian UN official in the former Yugoslavia, Cedric Thornberry, has said, "I am totally skeptical of the idea of quick, clean, Rambo-like, clinical strikes. All that's going to do . . . is solidify [Serbian] opposition and possibly widen the war."

I would add one element that could make an all-out Balkan war between the different religious and national communities explode—the military interference of great powers. An experienced diplomat who shuttles between New York, Belgrade, Zagreb, and Sarajevo described an American intervention as potentially "the Tonkin Gulf of the Balkans." So far as the northern Balkan war is concerned, such intervention would almost certainly mean an end to the negotiations which have successfully frozen the conflict between Croats and Serbs in Croatia. It would also mean the withdrawal of the UN forces now delivering humanitarian aid. The great problem with the bombing that has been proposed is that it has no clear

> *"One element . . . could make an all-out Balkan war . . . explode—the military interference of great powers."*

political policy that it wishes to reinforce—it is instead an expression of moral indignation, which is quite justified, masquerading as policy. Field Marshal Richard Vincent, the chairman of the NATO military committee, has explained the difficulties of such a policy: "The military out there are a means to an end, not an end in themselves. If we go out on the basis that we are an end in ourselves, we will be there halfway through the next century."

So what is left? Not much. The United Nations is trying to establish the principle of a safe haven around Srebrenica which would protect not the Bosnian army but the city's civilian population. By the end of April 1993 there were almost 150 Canadian soldiers in Srebrenica. Representatives of the UN in Zagreb are keen to expand this number and to turn the town into a model safe haven. They want to concentrate next on Gorazde and Zepa, the other two threatened Muslim enclaves in eastern Bosnia. The plan would then be expanded to include other communities, of which most would, of course, be Muslim although some Serb and Croat areas should have similar treatment. The people inside the havens should be disarmed but assured of protection.

In order to carry this out, the UN would have to send many more troops into Bosnia, at first as many as thirty to fifty thousand. Their mandate would have to be strengthened: UN troops should be given the right to return fire when they

234

are protecting civilians and shipments of aid. After the first safe havens are established, UN battalions should secure the major roads so that humanitarian supplies can pass unhindered. The final stage of such a UN operation, which would lead to a gradual demilitarization of Bosnia, would be to secure Bosnia's borders. This would protect the republic from the illegal transfer of weapons and other military supplies from Serbia and Croatia. So far as protecting life is concerned, the Americans, the Russians, the European Community, and the United Nations all now support the principle of safe havens. It is time to carry out a policy which they all agree on and which just may save them from sinking into the Bosnian quagmire.

Even after the Bosnian Serb parliament had rejected the Vance-Owen plan, Greece and Russia, two countries friendly to Serbia, were urging Slobodan Milosevic to force [Bosnian Serb leader] Radovan Karadzic into signing the Vance-Owen plan. If Milosevic is serious about his support for the United Nations proposal (which remains the only policy being offered), he should start imposing the sanctions on the Bosnian Serbs and stop greasing the wheels of their war machine. Otherwise the Bosnian Serbs may take Serbia and large areas of the Balkans into an unholy war which will dwarf the current conflict.

This offers no solace, I know, to the millions of victims of the Serbo-Croat war in Croatia and the Serbo-Muslim-Croat war in Bosnia-Hercegovina. But we also have a responsibility to the millions of Croats, Serbs, Muslims, Albanians, and Macedonians who are now more than ever endangered—not to mention the UN troops who have through good fortune so far escaped the ravages of a full-scale conflagration in southeastern Europe.

Chapter 5

How Can Ethnic Conflict Be Prevented?

Chapter Preface

Few nations today are ethnically homogenous and many are grappling for solutions to ethnic conflicts and crises. While some governments seek quick solutions through brute force, many first consider diplomatic and other peaceful strategies. Indeed, although some ethnic conflicts may never be completely resolved, many nations have successfully avoided or ended serious ethnic violence through peaceful economic, political, and social means.

Such options are frequently applied to ethnic trouble spots by the United Nations, the world's largest peacekeeping body. For example, one of the UN's goals is to use diplomacy to prevent violence from breaking out. In July 1992, the UN sent a team on a fact-finding mission to Moldova, a former Soviet republic southwest of Russia and Ukraine, where armed Russian residents had begun fighting troops of the newly independent country. UN undersecretary general of political affairs Vladimir Petrovsky credits the team with bringing both sides together in negotiations and ending the violence.

In other conflict areas, UN goals include promoting democracy and disarmament. In its largest—and perhaps most arduous—operation ever, the UN sent twenty-two thousand troops and civilians to Cambodia in 1992 to attempt to disarm and keep peace between Cambodian and rebel Khmer Rouge armies. The UN also supervised Cambodia's first-ever elections and is attempting to build a democracy where none has existed before.

However, as the UN's success in Moldova shows, plans to prevent conflict cannot succeed unless ethnic groups are committed to peace. As evidenced by continued fighting in Cambodia, the former Yugoslavia, several former Soviet republics, and other troubled regions, the intransigence of some ethnic warlords and the refusal of ethnic factions to coexist peacefully have shattered many cease-fire agreements and peace plans. The viewpoints in this chapter discuss how nations and ethnic groups can prevent conflict and work toward lasting peace.

Collective Security Can Prevent Ethnic Conflict

by Madeleine K. Albright

About the author: *Madeleine K. Albright is the U.S. ambassador to the United Nations.*

If you were to search for one term that best describes the challenge confronting the new era, it is "collective security." Every day we witness this challenge of collective security on television—some call it the "CNN effect"—and hear of it on the broadcasts of National Public Radio. Aggression and atrocities are beamed into our living rooms and cars with astonishing immediacy. No civilized human being can learn of these horrid acts occurring on a daily basis and stand aloof from them. But then, few of us want to respond alone. Collective security offers a means both to respond to these injustices and to protect our vital interests. But we have a long way to go before collective security becomes a truly workable system. . . .

Defining Collective Security

Let's start with a modern definition of collective security. What sets this concept of international order apart from others at the close of the 20th century? First, we need to understand that collective security is not another term for alliance. An alliance requires of each of its members that they respond if any alliance member is attacked from outside the alliance, typically by a common enemy. The North Atlantic Treaty Organization is the most successful alliance in history. The common enemy of the United States and Western Europe was the Warsaw Pact.

In a system of collective security, the enemy is a threat to regional or international peace and security. That threat can originate anywhere in a region or, if the collective security system is international in its reach, anywhere on the globe. Any nation within the regional or international system that commits aggression, imperils the peace, or grossly exceeds the bounds of civilized behav-

Excerpted from Madeleine K. Albright, "Building a Collective Security System," *U.S. Department of State Dispatch*, May 10, 1993.

ior violates the norms of that collective security system and is subject to enforcement action. No nation is excluded from the responsibility of maintaining
peace and security regardless of where, within its collective security system, the
threat originates. Nor are the responsibilities of membership in a collective security system avoided because of the
ideological character of a government, its grievances against other
governments, or its military power.

> *"Collective security is a . . .*
> *potent weapon for deterring*
> *aggression and maintaining*
> *international peace."*

Collective security can be triggered
another way. A threatened nation, exercising its inherent right of collec-
tive self-defense, can call on others for help. Collective security is the institutional way in which other nations respond to defend a nation under siege. If it
works properly, collective security is a far more potent weapon for deterring aggression and maintaining international peace and security than is the traditional
right of self-defense standing alone.

When the League of Nations was created after World War I, the collective security system that emerged was fatally flawed. The League covenant did not
outlaw war. Its members simply pledged, rather than obligated themselves, to
confront aggression. No real institution of collective security was created that
could organize enforcement actions. The most powerful enforcer, the United
States, never joined the League. The reason lay in an unfortunate and, I would
argue, avoidable breach that occurred between President Woodrow Wilson and
the Senate. If we have learned anything from the League days, it is that collective security requires a new kind of partnership between the executive and leg-
islative branches of not only this government but also others.

UN Peace-Keeping

After World War II, the new United Nations tried again to establish a collective security system. The UN Charter represents a best-efforts basis in 1945 to
establish the fundamental principles and organization precepts of collective security. But before those principles and precepts could be tested and refined, the
alliances of the Cold War gridlocked world politics and controlled the world's
military arsenals. Many provisions of the UN Charter and organs of the United
Nations, for all practical purposes, faded away. Scholars and policy-makers
alike wrote the obituaries on Chapter VII, the enforcement provisions, of the
charter and on the Military Staff Committee. Do you even recall any serious
discussion of collective security as late as the 1980s? Anyone who professed
the wisdom of realpolitik derided collective security as the phantom of a Wilso-
nian age long since departed.

Yet the idea of collective security was kept alive during the Cold War by the
evolution of a concept more intriguing than anyone dared imagine. It was UN
peace-keeping. Nowhere in the charter is "peace-keeping" identified or explic-

itly authorized. But it emerged by sheer invention during the earliest years of the United Nations, particularly as a tool to monitor cease-fires and assist in efforts to achieve the peaceful settlement of disputes. Dag Hammarskjold, the UN Secretary General during the 1950s, pioneered the concept when he played a critical role in establishing the first peace-keeping force in response to the Suez [Canal] crisis of 1956. Through the years, the Security Council and the member states of the United Nations have learned much about working together to maintain international peace and security through the instrument of peace-keeping. The record is by no means devoid of superpower rivalries and less-than-successful missions. But the lessons derived from four decades of UN peace-keeping are now guiding us into a new era of collective security.

America's Stake in Collective Security

I want to focus on this new era of collective security. What does collective security have to do with American security? Plenty. In the aftermath of the Cold War, the security of the United States is no longer defined by the size and strength of our nuclear arsenals and military deployments on the front lines of the Iron Curtain. President Clinton has spoken often of this nation's security being defined by the strength of our economy, the adaptability of our armed forces to the new threats of the 1990s, and the spread of democratic government in the world.

> *"[Peace-keeping] emerged by sheer invention during the earliest years of the United Nations."*

The security threat to America—a threat that only collective security can ultimately manage—is a world where weapons of mass destruction proliferate and ethnic and regional conflicts trigger massive refugee flows, enormous economic dislocations, unacceptable human rights atrocities, environmental catastrophes, and the senseless killing and maiming of millions of civilians. That world has already arrived. Unless we face up to it and create the institutions and resources necessary to share the burden of restoring international order, the United States will stand exposed to an endless raid on its resources, its goodwill, its soldiers, and, finally, its territorial integrity or the territorial integrity of its allies.

Anyone in this country who thinks that what occurs in Bosnia or Somalia or Cambodia is too distant to concern Americans—or has nothing to do with US security—has a very narrow view of economics, politics, and morality and has not learned the lessons of history. The costs of these conflicts are staggering, and, ultimately, we end up paying large shares of those costs.

Economic Costs of Inaction

Consider for a moment the enormous expense of responding to massive refugee migrations triggered by ethnic or interstate conflicts. Hundreds of billions of dollars are required to restore collapsed economies and rebuild devastated towns and cities. What will it cost the international community to restore the Bosnian economy someday? The Somali economy? The Cambodian economy? Consider the impact on regional and international trade each time an ethnic conflict flares up and disrupts thousands of commercial relationships. Not only are existing trading relationships broken, but potential trade and investment is killed

> *"Consider the impact on regional and international trade each time an ethnic conflict flares up."*

off. The loss of potential business alone—for American companies and individuals—has to be a staggering figure.

I do not know of any study that really calculates what ethnic and regional conflicts cost Americans or the American economy. But common sense tells you that when trade is shut down with a defiant regime like the one in Belgrade or the Gulf war erupts with repercussions throughout the world economy, there are economic impacts that can stretch all the way to Main Street, USA. How many California businesses have lost business—real or potential—because of the miserable state of affairs in Cambodia? How many New York companies have lost business because of the conflicts in the Balkans or in the Middle East? How much business is being lost today because of conflicts in India, Africa, or Haiti or regional threats on the Korean Peninsula or from Fidel Castro's regime on Cuba?

When you start to add up the loss of ongoing and potential business, trading, and investment opportunities for Americans because of proliferating armed struggles in this decade, the cost must be colossal. I might suggest that it would be an interesting study for the Congress to undertake. Far more immediate and calculable are the millions and billions of dollars—and thousands of American soldiers—that the United States commits when it launches a massive military intervention to restore peace and security and, in some cases, reverse the failure of a society like Somalia. If we let anarchy or ethnic conflict fester too long, if we permit either to spin out of control, the cost will always be much higher in the end to restore order. The burden will always be more unilateral. The cost of preventive measures applied collectively and early to quell a society's self-destructive instincts will always be much cheaper. I share Secretary of State Warren Christopher's belief "that millions spent now on preventive diplomacy and peace-keeping can save hundreds of millions of dollars later in defense and international relief."

Political and Moral Costs

The political cost of ignoring far-off conflicts also mounts with each passing day. Much of our credibility as a superpower—if, indeed, we want to remain one—will depend upon our ability to influence and bring pressure to bear on

241

the belligerents of the post-Cold War world. Our nuclear arsenal means nothing to the Bosnian Serbs or the Khmer Rouge. The most effective way we bring our influence to bear on these conflicts early and effectively is through the instruments of collective security. The petty tyrants and defiant warlords have to know that they stand alone, that the world community speaks with one voice and acts collectively to thwart their ambitions. If the United States acts unilaterally to stop them, then they have found their propaganda tool—their so-called imperialist enemy to fight. Alternatively, if defiant rulers know that the United States has withdrawn from world politics and thus crippled collective security, they will pursue their ambitions unchallenged.

Finally, the moral consequences of these conflicts are inescapable. American values simply will not permit us to stand aloof from massive human suffering, whether caused by natural or man-made sources. Nor do the fundamental principles set forth in the UN Charter or in international human rights treaties permit us to ignore the plight of so many others. Yet, we cannot possibly implement these principles alone. Nor should we. Collective security offers a means by which to share the burden and provide the opportunity for millions of innocent human beings to live in peace. In particular, the United Nations needs us, and we need it to reach and then implement multilateral strategies. There simply is no other way.

If there is one overall theme that I want to stress, it is that collective security has broadened in theory and practice to encompass far more than military remedies to keep the peace. We know that collective security is a potent means to impose tough economic sanctions on defiant regimes, be they found in Baghdad or Belgrade. The success of sanctions is often debated, but there is no doubt that they are becoming a means by which the international community can act in unison and thwart the designs of aggressor regimes.

A Humanitarian Agenda

Collective security has increasingly become an essential ally in many humanitarian relief operations. Increasingly, we are fusing peace-keeping and peace-enforcement operations with the delivery of humanitarian assistance to civilian populations trapped in the hostilities. That is a mission best done through collective means. These are missions that must be undertaken for the sake of common humanity. The international community must be organized to respond quickly and effectively to get humanitarian aid delivered when and

> *"The petty tyrants and defiant warlords have to know that they stand alone."*

where it is needed. There will be many instances when the United States need not participate on the ground, but we will need to support the organization that undertakes the mission. That kind of support is, increasingly, an integral element of collective security. The work of UNPROFOR [UN Protection Force] in Croatia and Bosnia represents how a peace-keeping force can provide critical support in trying to get humanitarian aid through belligerent lines. Our intervention in Somalia under UN authority shows how a Chapter VII operation can be essential in saving millions from starvation.

Another dimension of collective security today is state-building operations. There is simply no way the United States or any other nation could unilaterally undertake the rescue of failed societies. But a viable

> *"Collective security is a potent means to impose tough economic sanctions on defiant regimes."*

collective security system can provide authority and, when necessary, military muscle to achieve democratic aims that are unquestionably in our best interests. The United Nations has become an agent in support of democratic change in Namibia, the Western Sahara, Haiti, El Salvador, Angola, Mozambique, Cambodia, and Somalia. In each of these cases, UN peace observer, peace-keeping, or enforcement operations have facilitated or will soon help in building democratic governments. The work is by no means finished in some of these countries, and there have been setbacks. But the role of a modern collective security system in facilitating democracy has been and will continue to be essential.

A further dimension of collective security is its vital role in protecting human rights, particularly the rights of ethnic minorities and other groups of peoples. Atrocities continue with maddening frequency in our time. Bosnia stands out starkly. At the United Nations, I hear of atrocities in other parts of the world on an almost daily basis. The only realistic way of dealing with this tragic proliferation of human rights injustices is through a system of collective security.

Preventive Diplomacy

In all of these dimensions of collective security, we need to focus much more attention on what regional organizations can accomplish in their own backyards. We also need to improve regional abilities to take care of the victims of regional conflicts.

President Clinton and Secretary Christopher have spoken often of the need to develop better instruments of preventive diplomacy. We desperately need to prevent ethnic disputes, in particular, from spinning out of control—as they did in the former Yugoslavia. I want to stress that collective security must be complemented by preventive diplomacy if the system of collective security is not to be overwhelmed. [UN] Secretary General Boutros Boutros-Ghali reinforced this in his 1992 report, "An Agenda for Peace." We would be deluding ourselves if we thought that collective security is only the convening of Security Council meetings and the marshalling of armies to restore international peace and security. It first and foremost must be the determined application of diplomacy to prevent armed conflicts and humanitarian catastrophes. If preventive diplomacy falters, then subsequent steps may include non-military instruments of persuasion, followed, if necessary, by military action. But the Clinton Administration is committed to preventive diplomacy as the linchpin of collective security.

Finally, I want to speak about some of the other initiatives that will be required to strengthen collective security in the years ahead.

The United States and other member states of the United Nations need to establish a much sounder basis for financing and budgeting peace-keeping operations. The current system is inefficient, lacks transparency and accountability, and does not provide an adequate basis for rapid response to fast-breaking peace-keeping needs. In addition, the distribution of financial responsibilities is so outdated that it does not spread the burden equitably among member states.

An Overtaxed System

On the operational side, our concerns are equally serious. Since 1988, we and our Security Council colleagues have tasked the United Nations with peace-keeping missions of enormous size and complexity and extraordinarily difficult goals. On a per-mission basis, the cost of peace-keeping has increased as a reflection of these new and ambitious assignments. Yet, despite the fact that the UN has some 90,000 blue helmets in 13 missions, the resources available to lead and manage them have hardly grown at all. Indeed, the peace-keeping system is now so overstretched that, I must tell you, we are at a point of dangerous and unprecedented stress. It will, therefore, be a top US priority to work with the UN Secretariat and key peace-keeping contributors to ensure that the UN is equipped with a robust capacity to plan, organize, lead, and service peace-keeping activities. In this regard, we welcomed the Russian proposal to convene a Security Council ministerial in May 1993 in order to give a strong impetus to peace-keeping reforms.

There is also much work to be done in creating a UN military capability to engage in combat operations. There are plans under discussion that seek to strengthen the UN's ability to respond forcefully and in a manner that spreads the burden of military enforcement among many nations. This will be one of our greatest challenges in building a collective security system. Congress will be the critical partner as we explore the options. I expect [Congressional] subcommittees, in particular, will be deeply involved in this important exercise.

> *"A further dimension of collective security is its vital role in protecting human rights."*

A third challenge to collective security is how we keep the Russian government fully engaged as a partner in peace-keeping and enforcement operations. As you well know, Moscow is experiencing a severe shortage of foreign exchange. Russia now has surpassed the United States as the largest debtor at the United Nations. In short, it is finding great difficulty in paying its bills. UNOSOM [United Nations Operation in Somalia] II, [a] phase of the UN's operations in Somalia, was almost jeopardized because of Russia's shortage of funds to pay its peace-keeping assessment. So we need to work very hard with the Russians and other major or influential contributors to peace-keeping to strengthen the capabilities of the United Nations and various regional bodies. . . .

Not a day passes without the United States' being called upon to take the lead at the United Nations, whether it be to preserve or restore the peace, uphold the rule of law, save the environment, or rescue failing societies. If the previous era was one of containment, the new era is one of engagement in a global agenda of immeasurable complexity and diversity. The United States cannot possibly rise to this challenge without a viable system of collective security that lifts some of the burden from our shoulders and provides a means for us to lead other countries in truly collective responses to the tragic conflicts of the new era. I believe that is our responsibility as a superpower, and we must not shirk from it.

Disarmament Can Prevent Ethnic Conflict

by Michael Renner

About the author: *Michael Renner is a senior researcher for the Worldwatch Institute, a Washington, D.C., research organization that studies global and environmental problems.*

The term "war" still conjures up an image of massed armies clashing on the battlefield. But this kind of war is now largely a thing of the past. The vast majority of violent disputes today (and quite likely of tomorrow) are of a different nature: civil wars in which the fighting is not limited to a delineated battlefield, and in which the distinction between combatants and non-combatants is blurred. In fact, of the more than 30 major armed conflicts active in 1992, none was unambiguously of the classical country-against-country variety, and only four displayed some of its characteristics. Analysts are now more concerned with the distinctions between "state-control" conflicts (armed groups fighting to topple a government and replace it with their own) and "state-formation" conflicts (armed groups fighting to secede from a state or to gain greater autonomy within it).

The Threat of War

Still, although wars of the inter-state variety are less common, they have not become extinct; new ones could well be ignited in coming years. The fighting in the former Yugoslavia could spark a much wider Balkans conflagration; the Middle East remains a powderkeg despite intensive negotiations; and China has unresolved territorial disputes with some of its neighbors. Relations between India and Pakistan, between the two Koreas, and between Russia and some of its neighbors (Ukraine, Georgia, and the Baltic states) remain strained or uneasy. . . .

Western television audiences have become tragically familiar with the "ethnic cleansing" of Bosnia and the "killing fields" of Cambodia; Somalia and Lebanon have become synonymous with death and destruction. But there are many more places where no TV cameras and few outside observers are present

From Michael Renner, "Critical Juncture: The Future of Peacekeeping," *Worldwatch Paper* 114, May 1993. Reprinted with permission of the Worldwatch Institute, Washington, D.C.

to provide an eyewitness report to the world. These may seem "remote" (of no "strategic" interest), or have hard-to-pronounce names, but the suffering is no less real, and the destruction no less horrendous. There is fighting among Armenians and Azerbaijanis; Georgians, Abkhazians, and Ossetians; Hutu and Tutsi; Tamils and Sinhalese; Kashmiris and Indians; Karen and Burmese. These and other clashes involve communal violence

> *"The millions of innocents caught in the fighting are the inevitable losers."*

or they pit government and opposition forces against each other in fierce political and ideological struggles. In short, for every Sarajevo there is a Dushanbe [Tajikistan], for every Beirut a Bor [Sudan]. In countless locations like these, no matter who wins the battle, the millions of innocents caught in the fighting are the inevitable losers. . . .

Reducing Available Weapons

If war is to lose its legitimacy as an acceptable instrument in the conduct of human affairs, the still feeble norms against the use of force need to be reinforced, and global institutions that can promote peaceful conflict resolution need to be bolstered. Among the key components of an alternative system are a shift from offensive weapons and strategies to ones that can defend but not attack, and a strengthening of international peacekeeping and peacemaking capacities. But if peacekeeping and peacemaking are to succeed, they need to be accompanied by meaningful barriers against the production, possession, trade, and use of armaments. There is, in short, a symbiotic relationship between international peacekeeping and disarmament.

Unrestrained production and trading of arms has resulted in enough accumulation of weapons around the world to ensure that fighting, once it breaks out, can continue for a long time. Spending an estimated $30 trillion (in 1990 dollars) for military purposes since World War II, the world's nations have acquired a collective arsenal of unprecedented lethality. In 1992, they had either deployed or stockpiled some 45,000 combat aircraft, 172,000 main battle tanks, 155,000 artillery pieces, more than 1,000 major surface warships, and about 700 military submarines. Added to these are tens of thousands of light tanks, armored vehicles, helicopters, mortars, missiles, and smaller naval vessels. Assault rifles, machine guns, and other small arms, meanwhile, are far too abundant to keep track of. Although the bulk of these armaments (and especially the most sophisticated pieces of weaponry) are found in the Northern industrialized countries, many developing countries, particularly those in Asia and the Middle East, have built substantial military machines of their own. Few of them produce weapons domestically, but a huge arms trade keeps them well-supplied. Since 1960, at least $1 trillion worth of arms crossed international borders, much of it going to the Third World.

Although armaments are often just a symptom of unresolved deeper conflicts, there are three reasons why curbing their availability is nevertheless crucial. First, the proliferation of arms frequently does gain a momentum of its own. Governments argue that they simply want to maintain a balance of power with their adversaries, but they are unlikely to be satisfied with an equilibrium. In a heavily armed world, each adversary is likely to see its opponent's capabilities and intentions through the lens of a worst-case scenario, and therefore be more inclined to build up its own military muscle. There is usually no agreement on what constitutes true parity, and the result is an imbalance that drives an escalating arms race—such as that being waged between India and Pakistan, for example.

Weapons Fuel Conflicts

Second, the ready availability of arms often means that governments rely on them to settle disputes with other governments or domestic opponents—if not by their actual use, by threatened use—rather than on the admittedly difficult compromises without which lasting political solutions and a stable peace are impossible. In both the Israeli-Arab struggle and the terminated civil war in El Salvador, for example, the steady infusion of arms from politically interested suppliers kept conflicts fueled for years.

> *"The ready availability of arms often means that governments rely on them to settle disputes."*

Third, limiting arms is essential because where they are ubiquitous—as they are in many countries—the outbreak of hostilities tends to have much more devastating consequences than if they were less widely available. Somalia is a case in point. Large amounts of arms were supplied during the Cold War, first by the Soviet Union and then by the United States, each in its efforts to draw the country into its sphere of influence. In the civil war that broke out in 1991, Somalia's infrastructure has been destroyed, its economy collapsed, and government authority disintegrated. Status and power now are obtained at gunpoint, with armed factions ruthlessly competing for spoils. Keeping or imposing peace in such a situation is fraught with difficulty. . . .

The spread of conventional weapons is, as their name suggests, nearly universal. And while nuclear arms have the potential to wipe out all of humanity, it is of course conventional arms that are the stock of conflicts. Yet, little progress is in sight with regard to constraints against their manufacture, trade, and use.

Some headway has been made with the 1990 CFE [Conventional Forces in Europe] Treaty. Signed by the members of the North Atlantic Treaty Organization (NATO) and the now-dissolved Warsaw Pact, it established equal limits on the numbers of battle tanks, armored vehicles, artillery pieces, combat aircraft, and helicopters that the states in the area—reaching from the Atlantic to the Ural Mountains—may deploy. Implementing the treaty means that one of the most militarized regions of the world will need to weed out its immense arsenals. Even so, large numbers of arms, particularly the most sophisticated kinds, will remain on the continent. The treaty, in any event, does not erect any hurdles to continued weapons modernization.

The limitations of the CFE Treaty notwithstanding, the European experience stands in striking contrast with the situation in many other regions, particularly the Third World, where numerous unresolved conflicts continue to fuel arms races. An important step toward defusing these would be to curb the flow of arms across borders. The Third World currently accounts for about 60 percent of world arms imports, and most of these countries depend almost entirely on imports for equipping their armed forces. Fewer weapons imports would likely improve the level of trust among opponents and provide an opening for peaceful settlement. In the few instances where developing countries possess a significant domestic arms manufacturing capacity, import restraints would need to be matched with production restraints.

No Current Restraint

Throughout the past half-century, attempts to curb the international arms trade have been unsuccessful. In keeping with the traditional balance-of-power approach, virtually all governments assert that arms transfers—especially their own—can help create stability in relations among countries. The decline in arms exports that has occurred since the mid-1980s is a result not of political restraint but of dire economic conditions: many developing countries cannot afford to continue their buying binge. This means a reversal of economic fortunes could revive the flow of weaponry. Thus, while the end of the Cold War creates an opportunity to remove the link between arms exports and big-power influence peddling, ideological factors are now often replaced by economic considerations. As domestic military procurement budgets shrink in East and West, many arms producers see their best hope in aggressively pursuing export markets. In the absence of adequate programs to convert weapons production facilities to civilian use, this pressure will continue.

A number of countries have adopted national arms export regulations, with relatively little constraining effect. The few international attempts to curb arms exports remain halfhearted. For instance, the largest arms exporters—the United States, Russia, China, the United Kingdom, and France—have been talking about restraining arms sales. But to date they have only produced vaguely worded statements, the interpretation of which has been

> *"Fewer weapons imports would likely improve the level of trust among opponents."*

left to each government. For example [according to defense researcher Susan Willett,] they endorsed transfers "conducted in a responsible manner."

Although supplier restraint is crucial, controls are unlikely to work in today's buyer's market without comparable commitments by recipient nations. Whether on a bilateral or regional basis, self-imposed quantitative ceilings on weapons imports would yield a mutual reduction of tensions—and economic burdens. An even better approach, however—since some countries have the capability to produce arms domestically and hence rely less on imports—would be to prohibit the deployment of specific weapons systems, or to establish weapons-free zones. To date, however, there has been a conspicuous lack of recipient initiatives.

Registering Arms Sales

Greater transparency about arms transfers and other military matters can help build the confidence among governments needed to reduce arms. An encouraging initiative in this regard is the effort to establish an international arms trade register. A December 1991 U.N. General Assembly resolution asked all governments to voluntarily submit, on an annual basis, information concerning transfers of major weapons systems. Data for the calendar year 1992 have been made available. Initially, at least, the register includes only a small number of items and the reporting requirements are not highly detailed. No distinctions are made, for example, about the technical sophistication of weapons. And the 1992 *SIPRI Yearbook* comments that the register "will not report on those areas of the arms trade about which least is known—deliveries of small arms, components, sub-systems and arms production technologies and dual-use items."

"Self-imposed quantitative ceilings on weapons imports would yield a mutual reduction of tensions."

Over time, these shortcomings may be corrected; the register's scope could be expanded when it comes up for review. One possibility is to include arms production—an idea favored by many developing countries. To make the system effective, national reporting will need to be made mandatory, with international inspectors verifying data submitted. The register could then become, in time, a tool not just to monitor arms flows but to curb them. However, governments will need to grow comfortable with a voluntary approach first—and to be persuaded that the reporting does indeed serve a useful purpose. As such confidence takes hold, the scope and authority of the register can be gradually broadened.

True demilitarization can only occur with international agreements that impose strict limits on military arsenals. Such agreements, in turn, can only be concluded and implemented if there is confidence that all nations will adhere to the terms.

Democracy Can Prevent Ethnic Conflict

by Benjamin R. Barber

About the author: *Benjamin R. Barber is the Walt Whitman Professor of Political Science and director of the Whitman Center for the Culture and Politics of Democracy at Rutgers University in New Brunswick, New Jersey. He is the author of* Strong Democracy *and* An Aristocracy of Everyone: The Politics of Education and the Future of America.

Escalating internecine warfare in a Europe that was supposedly undergoing an uneventful process of "democratization" in the east and forging a single European political and economic entity has brought a predominantly American debate into global relief. Multiculturalism has become a haunting specter for Europe and the world beyond. Hence, although political correctness, a preoccupation with race and gender, and controversies over the academic canon—along with the generic focus on multiculturalism that gives rise to them—may still generate more rhetoric in the United States than elsewhere, the pertinence of the debate to other continents is finally becoming apparent.

Multicultural Nations

England, France, Germany, and other continental nations were once relatively homogenous. They were nation-states in the nineteenth-century sense, with a shared language, culture, history, and religion. Today, they are increasingly fractious and disintegrative—multicultural with a vengeance. The language of tribes has become commonplace in international politics, as books by Daniel Patrick Moynihan and Joel Kotkin make clear. The United Kingdom has absorbed large and increasingly unassimilable populations from its former colonies: nearly a million Hindus and almost two million Muslims, who, when they are not being abused by their hosts, are warring with one another.

Since the Second World War, France has accommodated over five million citizens from the Maghreb [Northwest Africa], along with many others from

From Benjamin R. Barber, "Global Multiculturalism and the American Experiment," *World Policy Journal*, Spring 1993. Reprinted with permission of the World Policy Institute, New York.

French West Africa and the West Indies. But the French are no longer sure that their historical commitment to civic assimilation can work in the face of a resurgent, and often angry, Muslim culture whose adherents are no longer willing to be integrated into a France for which they have lost respect.

Germany is in tumult. Its immigration policies resulted in a volume of immigrants that has led to widely reported skinhead excesses, including the murder of foreigners and the resurgence of several varieties of neo-Naziism. The scale of these activities in Germany is reminiscent of the radical polarization that destroyed Weimar [Germany's post-World War I republic] and the weak-state response for which its pallid and legalistic constitution was notorious. It is not clear that Germany can even absorb its "cousins" from east Germany as "natives," let alone the flood tide of immigrants from further east.

> *"[European nations] are increasingly fractious and disintegrative—multicultural with a vengeance."*

Even Switzerland, Europe's traditional standing tribute to sustained multicultural nationalism, is at risk, its Francophone and Germanic populations angrily divided over the new relationship to Europe. In the autumn of 1992, a substantial majority of German-speakers, aligned against any deepening of the relationship to the new Europe, outvoted, and thereby outraged, the French-speakers, nearly 80 percent of whom had voted to strengthen the European connection. While the dismantling of the Helvetic Confederation (founded in 1848 in its modern form) is not at hand, Switzerland's troubles bode well neither for Swiss multiculturalism nor for a united Europe.

With such strife-ridden former nations as the Soviet Union, Afghanistan, Yugoslavia, Liberia, and Czechoslovakia offering their own peculiar pathogenic alternatives to American multicultural development, the experience of the United States as an embattled but relatively successful multicultural society cries out for careful attention in Europe. . . .

America's Constitutional Faith

Underlying America's multicultural paradox is a Tocquevillean dilemma that is universal. Alexis de Tocqueville noted that free liberal societies were likely to nourish a diversity that could undermine the social cohesion on which they depended for their stability. The nineteenth-century alliance of nationalism and liberalism had after all brought together two contradictory principles inclined to work in contrary directions—a nationalism that fostered uniformity, and a liberty that encouraged diversity. To the extent that societies were defined by an integral nationalism, they became hostile to liberty. Yet, at the same time, free societies more than most others needed unity and cohesion, which their liberty tended to deny them (or, when unity arose out of religion or nationalism, which liberty undermined).

America faced this dilemma early on, seeking a surrogate for religion in new civic beliefs—what [U.S. Supreme Court] Justice Hugo Black later called constitutional faith (*Verfassungspatriotismus* is the term used by Jurgen Habermas). Because—as with so many so-called peoples elsewhere today—Americans then were divided by private religious faith, by race and gender, by class and ethnic origins, they could have no faith in common other than a faith in the commons: a fidelity to the Constitution as a set of broad principles uniting them under shared democratic and legal processes. Whereas in places like the former Yugoslavia, private faith has become a public identity subject to civic repression, the American constitutional faith is faith in a civil society that, precisely because it separates public from private, permits private differences and private freedoms to flourish without jeopardizing the political commons.

To be sure, the actual story of America has often failed to live up to, and has frequently even contradicted, its constitutional aspirations. As Judith Shklar wrote in her remarkable book, *American Citizenship*, "from the first, the most radical claims for freedom and political equality were played out in counterpoint to chattel slavery, the most extreme form of servitude." Yet even where constitutional faith has been bad faith, it has offered a promise of unity in an otherwise vast and diversified republic of continental extent. The quarrels over multiculturalism today are not new: when Arthur Schlesinger, Jr., worries that the celebration of difference may occlude a fragile unity, he only rehearses nineteenth-century anxieties about America's capacity to absorb wave after wave of non-Wasp immigrants.

> *"[American] civil society . . . permits private differences and private freedoms to flourish."*

Constitutional Faith Abroad

Is it possible, then, that America's constitutional faith proffers a solution to Europe's recidivist tribalisms? Is there an equivalent of constitutional faith for India or Nigeria or Yugoslavia or Somalia that would pull the tribes off each other and nurture a framework for political unity? In America, constitutional faith has lost its novel artificial look. It has become conventional. Like an old shoe, it fits comfortably and its wearers need not examine too carefully how it was cobbled. But beyond American shores, constitutional faith has to be manufactured afresh each time a fractious nation-state tries to keep from flying apart. In the absence of a history of commitment to common civil practices, such an aridly secular faith is unlikely to draw much fealty. For what is its substance to be? Who is the "we" in Europe's or India's or Russia's "we the people"? Are the common principles exclusively commercial and technological, as Eurocrats in Strasbourg and Brussels often intimate? Or is there a potential civic element as well? For example, democracy? . . .

There may be a form of constitutional faith that responds to the new tribalism, but it will not be a faith simply borrowed lock, stock (rock?), and barrel from America or Switzerland or some other successful multicultural society. Civic faith depends, in part, precisely on its adaptability to the circumstances and conditions of particular peoples at particular historical moments. Attempting to paper over the fissures in the former Yugoslavia by importing an American civic ideology is no more likely to succeed than attempting to prop up its democracy by importing American party institutions. Technology transfer sometimes works; institution transfer almost never does. Democratic institutions succeed because they are molded to the landscape in which they are to be grounded and planted in the soil of a well-established civil society. This has been the lesson of all political theory from Charles Montesquieu and Jean-Jacques Rousseau to James Madison and Tocqueville, both of whom demanded a *new* science of politics for a new society.

Honoring Differences

Nonetheless, there are several formal principles involved in establishing a successful civil society that are relevant. A constitutional faith pertinent to nations comprising rival ethnic fragments requires a civic ideology in which difference itself is recognized and honored. This is the secret of Switzerland's remarkable multicultural, multiconfessional success: Italian, though the language of only a tiny minority of Swiss, remains a national language; Raeto-Romansch, though spoken by only a few tens of thousands in Graubuenden, is an official language of that canton.

Second, the honoring of difference must be accompanied by some territorial or geographical expression of it, ideally through federal or confederal institutions. Partition destroys a civil society; federation preserves it while acknowledging the relative autonomy of the parts. The Cyrus Vance/David Owen solution for Bosnia and Herzegovina tries to find its way between partition and federalism, in a situation that manifests the worst-case scenario: where there are hostile ethnic groups intermingled in populations that are not geographically discrete and nearly impossible to disentangle other than by relocation (a euphemism for expulsion). The Vance/Owen plan multiplies the number and reduces the size of confederal units to a point where every small ethnic neighborhood has some autonomy. This finally cannot work unless a society is carved into units the size of a town street or three or four adjacent houses or apartments! In the case of Bosnia and Herzegovina, the difficulties are overcome by giving Muslims the short end of the stick, a

> *"The honoring of difference must be accompanied by some territorial or geographical expression of it."*

politically prudent but morally dubious solution at best. In any case, solutions that do no more than try to keep rival groupings apart do not so much deal with, as yield to, bigotry and hatred. Bloody as the American Civil War was, it was fought in the name of union, not dissolution.

Furthermore, in the American case, separation has always been a short-term tactic that belongs to a long-term strategy of integration. The parts are honored so as to strengthen their tie to the whole and demonstrate that the ideology of the whole represents not the hegemony of one group but a (potentially) genuine inclusiveness. Unless working together is seen as crucial to the survival of the parts, they will inevitably come to view themselves as diasporas of some other (perhaps invisible) blood nation whose reconstruction will come to be seen as the only avenue to preservation. Unhappily, the antagonism of one group may actually ignite a defensive separatist identity in some other group that had previously seen itself as assimilated. Thus, Bosnian and Croatian Muslims, secularized and assimilated into Yugoslav life, have only become self-consciously Islamic and separatist in the face of continuing aggression by their erstwhile fellow citizens and neighbors.

> *"Bloody as the American Civil War was, it was fought in the name of union, not dissolution."*

The Promise of a Confederation

Federalism is probably too aggressive and centralist a solution for countries as fractured as Croatia or Afghanistan. Confederalism may be more promising. *The Federalist Papers* have been required reading for foreign nationals seeking an American solution to their multicultural difficulties for some time, but I would offer the Articles of Confederation as a far more relevant model. Article III would seem to provide a relatively modest framework for holding rival nations like the Czech Republic and Slovakia or Serbia and Croatia together. It provided for the full autonomy of the member-states and honored their independence, but it also declared that "the said states hereby severally enter into a firm league of friendship with each other, for their common defense, the security of their liberties, and their mutual and general welfare, binding themselves to assist each other against all force offered to, or attacks made upon them, or any of them, on account of religion, sovereignty, trade, or any other pretense whatever."

Article IV provided that the "free inhabitants" of each state "shall be entitled to all the privileges and immunities of free citizens in the several states, and the people of each state shall have free ingress and regress to and from any other state, and shall enjoy therein all the privileges of trade and commerce." Similar provisions held together the Helvetic Confederation from 1291 to 1800, when Napoleon tried in vain to impose a unitary constitution on the recalcitrant cantons. The splintered factions of many a ruptured nation could do worse than reconceive themselves in terms of a "firm league of friendship."

The problem remains what to do with minorities *within* each confederal region. Initially, in the most volatile regions where, as in Bosnia and Herzegovina, deeply hostile groups are inextricably mingled, some form of external intervention will probably be required: a security shield that protects them from fratricide while they labor to establish a civil society. The shield need not necessarily be provided by the United Nations, which has had a mixed record in its peacekeeping efforts. A coalition of forces (NATO, for example) or a powerful neighbor (Russia in Serbia, the United States in Haiti) may do the job. It certainly seems unlikely that the redrawing of maps can bring peace to Armenia or the former Yugoslavia or Sudan in the absence of armed enforcement. Even America failed to secure its multiculturalism in a setting of tolerance until it had engaged in a bloody civil conflagration.

Yet, the presence of foreign peacekeepers, even where effective in the short term (and it often is not), cannot do more than buy time and establish a provisional setting for long-term internal solutions. The American Civil War set the stage for a reconstruction that failed to pay off on the promise of justice. The proof, ultimately, is in the internal, noncoercive settlement.

Some still think there is hope in economics, but markets, while they may attenuate the sharpness of internecine divisions, do little to soften hatred or reduce the sorts of deep-seated bigotry that lead to tribal warfare, ethnic cleansing, or genocide. Germany's economic miracle and its leadership in the Common Market did not translate into immunity against domestic violence or against the rage aimed at foreigners. The integrating forces of McWorld [author's term for "one commercially homogenous global network" of nations] operate best where there is relative tranquility and social order. They are no substitute for internal reconciliation.

Democracy as a Civil Religion

Where the social order has broken down, there is no recourse but to a civil religion of reciprocal rights and mutual respect. Such a civic faith cannot be contrived from scratch but must emerge out of civil institutions like public schools, common customs, and a shared civic consciousness—the very institutions that have failed to take root in so many of eastern Europe's disintegrating states. Such institutions crosscut cleavages and allow people to think of neighbors separated from them by ethnic or religious background as sharing other objectives and ends—the common values arising out of, for example, trade-union or parent-teacher association or political-party membership. Difference needs not only to be offset against common membership but understood as a claim *to* common membership ("as African Americans, we deserve equal respect and equal treatment before the law!"), rather than as an argument for separation ("as Croatians, we deserve a country of our own!"). In America, difference has served to legitimize inclusion; in Europe it has too often served to rationalize exclusion. Our civic

> *"It certainly seems unlikely that the redrawing of maps can bring peace . . . in the absence of armed enforcement."*

faith in "we the people" as a formula for inclusion has much to do with whatever success we Americans have had.

Most important of all in establishing a viable constitutional faith, however, is democracy. Democratic institutions put flesh on the bones of civic identity. They turn mutual respect into a set of political practices. More than anything else, it has been the absence of democratic institutions in Russia, Yugoslavia, Afghanistan, Somalia, Liberia, Czechoslovakia, and all the other disintegrating multicultural nations that has aided and abetted tendencies to ethnic fragmentation and national dissolution. By the same token, it has been America's and Canada's and Belgium's and Switzerland's democratic practices that have held together peoples and civic cultures that have, on their own, been only slightly less vulnerable to the siren call of ethnicity than the Yugoslavs or the Afghans.

Democracy First

As strategy, this suggests a need to set new priorities: put democracy first as the foundation of civil society, and resistance to fragmentation may follow. Ethnicity is unlikely to create a form of democracy that can contain and limit its negative effects; democracy can create a form of ethnicity that is self-limiting. When rights are taken seriously and perceived as defining individuals and groups, it is easier to attach them to minority ethnic groups under pressure and to persuade majority ethnic groups that their own identity, expressed as exclusion, is in violation of their civil faith.

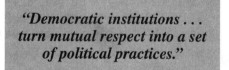

"Democratic institutions . . . turn mutual respect into a set of political practices."

Putting democracy first means treating it as a way of life, not just as a set of institutions. When membership in the community is rooted in democratic political practice, ethnic and religious traits grow less crucial in forging a public identity. The American separation of church and state not only protects the state from religion, it protects religion from the state and from rival religions. Separating the public from the private, liberal democracy actually enlarges the space for the exercise of private religious beliefs and ethnic customs, while insulating against their potential public consequences—intolerance, for example.

Ethnicity is a healthy expression of identity that, however, like a healthy cell, is susceptible to pathologies that turn the growth mechanism against itself. The resulting cancer destroys not only the body around it (the larger nation) but the cell itself (the ethnic entity). Democracy seems to be ethnicity's immunological key: the source of its normalcy and capacity to control its own growth so as to make it compatible with the growth of other cells and, hence, the basis for its ability to participate in the building of a stable body politic. The time may have come for those states around the globe falling into warring pieces to stop worrying about keeping the parts together and to start thinking about how to make the parts democratic, to recognize that the true source of America's measured and all too partial, but still significant, success as a multicultural society is its democratic civic faith.

A genuinely democratic Bosnia and Herzegovina and a genuinely democratic Serbia might not only cease to make war on Muslims or Croats but might discover in their democratic ideals and practices sufficient common ground to re-fashion a confederation that would permit renewed civic coexistence. If the democratic solution sounds improbable, think of the "realistic" solutions currently being debated—whether expulsion, partition, U.N. trusteeship, or foreign intervention—and consider how improbable it is that they will succeed in restoring sanity, let alone stability, to peoples caught up in the spreading global fires of ethnic jihad.

Empowering Ethnic Groups Can Prevent Ethnic Conflict

by Jack D. Forbes

About the author: *Jack D. Forbes is a professor of native American studies and anthropology at the University of California in Davis. Forbes is the author of* Columbus and Other Cannibals.

A great many national, ethnic, and language groups do not possess their own sovereign states. Many do not even control local units of government or, if they do, these units may be devoid of genuine authority. A large number of such groups are divided by inter-state boundaries and are prevented from exercising ethnic unity.

Much of the world's warfare and unrest arises from a failure to find means, short of war, for resolving the problems of stateless nationalities, linguistic minorities, and ethnic groups. One has only to list the locations of current or recent wars: Yugoslavia, Turkey, Iran, Iraq, Israel-Palestine, Northern Ireland, Nigeria-Biafra, Uganda, Georgia, Zimbabwe, Somalia, Eritrea-Ethiopia, Sudan, Sahara, Chad, Azerbaijan, South Africa, Timor, West Papua, Mindanao, Guatemala, Spain, Corsica, Angola, Namibia to realize the human and material cost of thwarted ethnicity.

Addressing Ethnic Unrest

Unfortunately, the breaking up of the great modern European empires has failed to solve this problem. Most independent states in the Americas possess boundaries which cut across ethnic groups; modern Africa is especially notable for its arbitrary, counter-ethnic borders; few of the states of Eastern Europe or the successor states of the Soviet Union are composed of a single ethnic group.

An obvious answer for the problems of ethnic minorities and stateless nationalities is, of course, war or armed rebellion. But most modern states possess the

Jack D. Forbes, "Cross-Boundary Sub-States." This article, revised in 1993, first appeared in *Plural Societies*, vol. 15 (1984), pp. 255-64. The revised version is reprinted here from *Global Visions: Beyond the New World Order*, edited by Jeremy Brecher, John Brown Childs, and Jill Cutler (Boston: South End Press, 1993), pp. 233-38 and from *Z Papers*, vol. 2, no. 2 (April/June 1993), pp. 23-25. Reprinted with permission.

military for inflicting devastation on and ultimately suppressing rebellions. Few states will voluntarily allow an ethnic minority to secede or allow a neighboring nationality to have so much as an inch of state territory. Some means short of war or armed violence must be found to defuse explosive minority situations and to provide some degree of unification and meaningful self-determination for stateless nationalities and other groups divided by international boundaries.

Everyone understands that a given state may contain within its external boundaries units of government which exercise their authority separate from that of the central state. In some federal states, the subordinate units possess constitutionally guaranteed powers; in other states, the separate powers are derived from ancient charters; in still others, the central government possesses all authority but delegates power to local units.

In most instances, such local units—be they provinces, republics, cantons, states, counties, cities, or boroughs—exist only within the territory of a given state. But it is also possible for bi-state (or non-state) institutions to exist and function on both sides of an international boundary. Such crossover institutions or territories have existed in the past, and a few exist today.

Limited Sub-States

Before the rise of the modern nation-state there were many examples of dual sovereignties, trans-state units, and limited sub-states. In pre-Cortés Mexico, for instance, the Triple Alliance (the so-called Aztec Empire) acquired general suzerainty over a vast area, but each local city or region was essentially left to manage its own internal affairs. The Triple Alliance was not a highly centralized empire, but accommodated a great deal of diversity.

This pattern was also common in the case of many early empires in the Middle East and has been a form often used by later colonial systems as well (e.g., indirect rule or leaving local governments intact but with limited functions). The Turkish (Ottoman) Empire sometimes allowed religious communities to possess their own courts, legal systems, and local communal governments. Other examples existed during the era of the Holy Roman Empire, as when the King of England controlled lands on the continent as a vassal of the King of France. At times the King of Scotland also ruled as King of England. Such concepts as multiple jurisdictions, dual sovereignties, and limited sub-states may be even more common outside of the European region, and especially among folk people, with flexible and democratic political systems.

> *"Bi-state (or non-state) institutions [can] exist and function on both sides of an international boundary."*

Current examples of dual sovereignty and overlapping jurisdictions, both formal and unofficial, range from very limited cooperation across international boundaries (as in the rights of Sami people to herd reindeer across Norwegian,

Finnish, and Swedish boundaries) to informal quasi-states such as those of the Guajiro people (Colombia and Venezuela) and the Shan states (Burma and Thailand).

In the United States, the Native American nations (tribes) continue, for the most part, to possess a certain degree of officially recognized sovereignty. (They have been called domestic dependent nations.) Certain Kickapoo people possess dual-citizenship status (Mexico, United States), as do the Akwesasne Mohawk Nation (with reservations on both sides of the U.S.-Canadian border). Certain Native American people possess the right, guaranteed by the Jay Treaty of 1794, to cross the U.S.-Canadian boundary without observing customs formalities.

Potential Applications

Cross-boundary sub-states provide a possible way of addressing the needs of groups that have been parceled up among other nations. For example, in North America and northwestern Siberia, the Inuit (Eskimo) people share a common heritage and have common problems, but they are divided among the United States, Russia, Canada, and Greenland. At present, Inuit delegates can come together to discuss common problems, but they possess no unified official apparatus.

> *"Native American nations (tribes) continue . . . to possess a certain degree of . . . sovereignty."*

There are certain functions of government which could be turned over completely to an Inuit governmental authority of multi-state character, such as education, including all elementary and secondary schools as well as an Inuit language center of higher education; communications, including Inuit-language radio and television; environmental regulation, for example, pollution from oil spills; authority over marriage, the structure of the family, the inheritance of personal property, and other matters often left to provincial authority; and all powers of taxation currently possessed in the region by any existing provincial authority.

Such areas are basic to any ethnic group. Who, for example, should control schools for Inuit children? Who will develop curriculum? Who will determine which of the three or more competing orthographies should be used for the writing of the Inuit dialects? Will Inuit students always be forced to attend higher-education facilities operated in Russian, English, French, or Danish and controlled by outsiders? Who will determine whether an Inuit family shall have only a monogamous character? Who will decide how tax laws affect the structure of Inuit society? Alien nationalities should not be conceded authority over a different nationality in such areas as education and family life, even though they possess state power.

The establishment of such an Inuit limited-authority sub-state would require agreement between the United States, Canada, Russia, and Greenland. Such an agreement might involve phases, or it might be limited initially to a single objective, for example, control over pollution.

The O'odham (Papago) people are similarly divided by the U.S.-Mexican border. Such divided peoples should be able to develop agencies which extend across the border in order to protect traditional lands, water holes, and springs, and also to control education, health, and other aspects of social living.

> *"Alien nationalities should not be conceded authority over a different nationality."*

Such an approach may be relevant to some of the most intractable ethnic conflicts. For example, if a Kurdish-language university existed, it might well serve Kurds from any geographical setting. Similarly, an agency designed to further Rom (Gypsy) culture and history might have no fixed geographical territory or service area.

Overlapping Jurisdiction

Another application of this approach might be in Northern Ireland. In Northern Ireland there are two major populations, both of which are also found in the Irish Republic in different proportions. At present the British government possesses total control over the region, but Irish sovereignty can be said to also exist, based on the former unity of Ireland both as an independent country and as a unified British colony for over four centuries.

Under the limited-authority sub-state approach, overlapping jurisdiction would be introduced (by agreement) into Northern Ireland. Areas and institutions of an Irish character would be combined in a jurisdiction articulated with the Irish Republic, while areas and institutions of a Unionist or British character would be articulated with Great Britain. Neutral zones might also exist. In a way, it would represent a partitioning of Northern Ireland, but not in a total sense and not in a permanent manner. Both British and Irish sovereignty would be recognized for all of Northern Ireland; all Northern Ireland residents would be granted dual citizenship (in the United Kingdom and the Irish Republic); all citizens of Northern Ireland would be entitled to vote in all appropriate Irish and British elections, and dual representation would exist in both the Irish and British parliaments.

Agreements would also have to include provisions for economic development in all zones, for free trade with both Britain and the Irish Republic, and for the protection of minority rights. The Irish Republic might well have to offer guarantees of complete separation of church and state in order to satisfy the fears of non-Catholic religious groups.

The entire arrangement could be seen as a gradual transition to some form of Irish unity acceptable to all parties. The present contract between the United Kingdom and the People's Republic of China over the future of Hong Kong, which anticipates that for at least half a century Hong Kong will exist as a limited sub-state under Chinese sovereignty but with a distinctive local system and a British presence, provides a possible model.

New Opportunities

In many parts of the world, the local community, tribe, city, or province often has a juridical existence prior to that of any modern state. A case can be made for a common law transmission of unsurrendered sovereignty by such units. Many states will resist this doctrine, since such rights would fall outside of existing constitutional law and limit central state power. But in the case of many indigenous groups in North America, the Pacific, and elsewhere, such prior status has provided the basis for successfully asserting at least limited group rights.

Emerging forms of international integration also open new opportunities for groups divided by national boundaries. For example, the proposed North American Free Trade Agreement (NAFTA) between Canada, the United States, and Mexico provides a possible framework in which tribal groups could insist upon the right to develop unified cross-state institutions across the Mexican, U.S., and Canadian borders.

The evolution of the European Economic Community and other organs of Western European unification also offer an opportunity for innovations with regard to ethnic minorities. In theory, as the region becomes more politically unified, the possibility of self-determination should be enhanced, since regional security will no longer require that the Basques, Alsatians, Bavarians, Bretagnes, Welsh, Scots, Sami, and other groups be denied their own specific membership in the union. At a certain stage, it should make no difference if Corsica, for example, enters the union as a part of France, as a new member, or as a sub-state with an intermediate status. Scotland could both be a member of the union and retain certain ties with the United Kingdom (such as sharing the same monarch with England and Wales).

> *"International integration ... open[s] new opportunities for groups divided by national boundaries."*

So far, the unification of Western Europe is almost entirely a coming together of sovereign states and not of nationalities or ethnic groups. It is not yet clear whether its constitutional evolution will ultimately guarantee that sub-units, regions, and nationalities can enter the union on their own, rather than only as parts of existing supranational states.

Absolute sovereignty and the absolute separation of sovereign states are, in many ways, serious obstacles to problem solving in relation to ethnic issues. Divided ethnic groups are not always well served when local units stop at international boundaries. What we are talking about, in essence, is a way that such units can become trans-state entities. By abandoning ideas of exclusivistic and centralized states, we may be able to find ways to solve ethnic clashes without recourse to violence.

Intergroup Dialogue Can Prevent Ethnic Conflict

by Harold H. Saunders

About the author: *Harold H. Saunders is the director of international affairs at the Kettering Foundation, a public policy research organization in Washington, D.C. Saunders served as deputy assistant U.S. secretary of state under Henry Kissinger, assisting in Middle East peace negotiations.*

Many nongovernmental organizations, from elementary and secondary schools through labor organizations and environmental groups, are creating institutions to teach the philosophy, skills, and techniques of negotiation and mediation in a wide range of circumstances. They have done so on the theory that teaching individuals and groups to think of resolving differences by discussion rather than by force opens the door to a different way of behaving in situations of impending conflict. In some instances, conciliation commissions are being established involving individuals with such training in formally established social institutions charged with responsibility for stepping in and trying to resolve conflict peacefully in its earliest stages.

In many deep-rooted conflicts, however, the parties are not ready to meet in mediation and negotiation; in fact, the problems that bring them into conflict cannot even be framed in ways subject to mediation and negotiation. The purpose of this essay is to suggest an additional approach that can be used as a complement to the more traditional approaches in such conflicts.

Changing Conflictual Relationships

Resolution of ethnic and national conflict requires a broad array of approaches and instruments used in widely varying circumstances. UN Secretary-General Boutros Boutros-Ghali, in *Agenda for Peace* issued in June 1992, reviewed in some depth the more traditional work of preventive diplomacy, peacemaking, and peacekeeping. Then he added a significant fourth concept—"post-conflict peace-building." If we are to focus on either the prevention of vi-

From Harold H. Saunders, "A Political Approach to Ethnic and National Conflict," *Mediterranean Quarterly* 4 (1): 16-23. Copyright Duke University Press, 1993. Reprinted with permission of the publisher.

olent conflict or the building of constructive relationships in a postconflict environment, a political—as contrasted to a negotiated—approach to conflict is essential. That is the dimension of conflict resolution that needs to be added to current practice.

If we are to add to traditional thinking about interstate relations a dimension of focusing on intrastate, intergroup relationships, we then need to think about a political process for changing conflictual relationships. The emphasis is on the *politics of changing relationships*, because if we are including in our thinking relationships between whole bodies politic, then we must think of politics in the original meaning of the word—what happens when people in community organize themselves to deal with their problems. The question becomes how one can understand the political processes through which groups interact and ways of changing the dynamics of a destructive interaction.

Ongoing Group Discussion

One approach that has been found increasingly useful over the past two decades, from the Arab-Israeli arena to the Soviet-U.S. relationship, has been to form a small dialogue group of individuals from both sides of a conflict, each member reflecting a significant perspective in his or her community. Through regular meetings among the same participants with a cumulative agenda over time, groups have become virtual laboratories within which members probe the dynamics of the relationship and, over time, transform that group almost into a microcosm of the relationship itself. As their capacity to talk and think together deepens, members can design scenarios of actions that can be taken in both bodies politic to change perceptions and to create a sense that change in the relationship is possible. Because of their standing in their communities, members can even stimulate larger organizations in each body politic to carry out such a scenario.

For example, in 1981 a group of Soviet and American citizens who had participated in the Dartmouth Conference exchanges between the two countries since 1960 decided to form two small task forces. These would meet between plenary sessions and probe two areas where détente had foundered—arms control and regional conflicts. The Dartmouth Conference Regional Conflicts Task Force met first in August 1982, and in 1992 it passed its tenth anniversary and its twentieth meeting. (The arms control task force has met sixteen times.) The experience has, in retrospect, produced a model of a process of cumulative dialogue that proved to

> *"One approach . . . has been to form a small dialogue group of individuals from both sides of a conflict."*

be an experience in the gradual transformation of the Soviet-U.S. relationship.

As one looks back over the record of that experience, it is possible to describe a process that developed through five stages. The question now is whether that process—developed in dialogue between representatives of two countries that led adversary military camps in a nuclear standoff—can provide a useful example of such dialogue for other "mortal enemies."

To speak in terms of stages in a process is somewhat artificial, because any group of individuals will move back and forth in a systematic dialogue as feelings ebb and flow and as it tackles new issues, but there is some explanatory value in presenting the experience this way. Once the process has been developed through experience, defined, and transferred to other groups, they may be able to telescope these stages so as to move more quickly to the more productive phases of the dialogue.

Beginning of Dialogue

First is a period of *precipitating a decision to engage in dialogue*. It requires identifying individuals on both sides of a conflict who believe that the existing situation hurts their group's interests and judge that governments are not likely to pay adequate attention to the situation before it does major damage. Individuals may take serious risks in becoming part of such a dialogue, because members of their communities will see them as "traitors talking to the enemy." Normally, they will need some kind of political permission from their communities, but occasionally some individuals will courageously brave disapproval to engage.

> *"[Participants] need to put out on the table for discussion the problems . . . and hopes in the relationship."*

Secondly comes a period at the beginning of a dialogue when participants begin *exploring their relationships together*. They have to learn to talk with each other analytically rather than polemically. They need to put out on the table for discussion the problems, grievances, irritants, fears, and hopes in the relationship. In effect, they are mapping the relationship. Since their focus is on the relationship rather than on technically defined issues, they will normally need to keep all significant elements of the relationship in view at the same time. They will also need to identify a few problems that, if discussed in depth, will lead those in the discussion toward probing some of the underlying interests and interactions at work in the relationship. At the end of this stage, they will settle on a small number of such problems to probe in greater depth so as to understand more fully how the relationship works and how it might be changed.

Thirdly, as they begin *discussing in increasing depth* these particular areas of the relationship, they will come to understand more clearly the deeper-rooted impediments to a more constructive relationship that would serve each party's interests better. At some point in this portion of the dialogue, they will reach a moment when they begin to see the capacity to change the relationship. As they begin to think that way, a transformation in the relationship begins because the group as a whole begins to focus on a problem which both parties have an interest in dealing with constructively.

The fourth stage is a period of *thinking together to identify specifically the obstacles to a more constructive relationship and how to remove them.* Since some steps for removing those obstacles can be taken only when one side is assured of a positive response by the other, it becomes necessary to lay out a sequence of interacting steps in a design that is sometimes called a "political scenario" because it be-

> *"They become a microcosm of the relationship itself and develop the capacity to think of ways of changing it."*

comes a plan of steps arranged almost like the scenes of a play. As members work through this stage together, they actually experience the constraints and political pressures that affect leaders in each of their bodies politic. In one sense, they become a microcosm of the relationship itself and develop the capacity to think of ways of changing it by consulting their own experience.

In the fifth stage, if the group actually comes up with a plan that can be implemented, they have the option of *acting together* in some way either to bring about implementation of that scenario or to put it in the hands of governments or other organizations in the community who have the capacity to act. If they are to remain a safe space where individuals can continue to monitor their relationship and explore ways of further changing it, they may want to design action but stay out of the work of implementation itself.

These stages are not intended for rigid emulation. They are presented to illustrate that such a group can systematically probe the dynamics of a destructive relationship and actually design ways to change it to make cooperation possible.

The Situational Dynamics of Dialogue

One must pay close attention to whether a situation is ripe for such an approach. It may be difficult to bring individuals together when violence is only a distant prospect, but the effort may be rewarded because the opportunity to head off violence may be great. Experience in the Israeli-Palestinian arena suggests that this approach also is possible at a time when violence is in remission and the parties are considering ways out of a destructive deadlock. If some individuals have had earlier experience in dialogue, it may even be possible, as was the case during the Lebanese civil war, for discussion to continue during fighting and pave the way for the day when fighters will become exhausted and conclude that no one party can impose its way through force. In the case of Lebanon, ideas discussed in such small groups ultimately provided some of the content of the Taif accords that brought the fighting to an end.

Where there is no such capacity for dialogue across the lines of conflict, it may be necessary to wait until exhaustion sets in. During these periods, the more traditional efforts of third-party peacemakers may be the only approach that has a chance of working, and the only useful techniques may be those of trying to negotiate the terms of a cease-fire and/or an immediate postviolence relationship. Once the fighting stops, a broader dialogue may be possible in designing postconflict relationships.

This approach of small-group dialogue can profit from much of the thinking that lies behind new approaches to mediation, negotiation, and conciliation as techniques of conflict resolution. Such training predisposes individuals to engage in dialogue rather than tests of force. The approach presented here is intended to add a significant political dimension to that thinking. In some significant instances, establishment of centers of conflict resolution or conciliation commissions is a significant and needed step toward changing how people deal with each other, but they may still lack important dimensions—the capacity to probe deeply into the causes of conflict and to design ways of reducing them over time when parties to a conflict are not yet ready for mediation and negotiation.

Time itself is a critical ingredient in this approach—one not widely accepted by participants or by the foundations funding these programs. There is a fundamental difference of views among those dealing with these problems today. One school of thought wants measurable achievements in dealing with conflicts within a finite period of time. In that context, the only achievements that can normally be expected are lists of the number of training sessions held, institutions established, and specific agreements mediated. In a world of longstanding deep antagonisms between peoples, this may leave outside the scope of attention those areas of work that cannot be quantified in such a way.

Valuable Experience

What I am speaking of is captured more in the experience, for instance, of the more than three decades of Soviet (now Russian)-U.S. dialogue in the Dartmouth Conference exchange between citizens of the two countries. It is found in more than two decades of experience in various Israeli-Palestinian meetings and workshops. In each case, a small group of individuals meeting together over time became the core in their bodies politic for rethinking a conflictual relationship. It is not possible to prove such a statement through quantifiable means. One can only note that virtually all of those who wrote the articles and speeches, constituting the "new political thinking," with Soviet president Mikhail Gorbachev and foreign minister Eduard Shevardnadze in the late 1980s were veterans of two or three decades of continuing dialogue with people in Western Europe and the United States. Additionally, one can note in the Israeli-Palestinian context that most of the Palestinian and a few of the Israeli delegates in the official negotiations of 1992 were veterans of such dialogues. If an interim agreement looking toward an ultimate peace between the two peoples is reached, it

> *"Once the fighting stops, a broader dialogue may be possible in designing postconflict relationships."*

will have been shaped in significant ways in nonofficial dialogue that complemented the official peace process and then virtually merged into it. These processes take time.

The focus of dialogue in such groups is not the technically defined options for dealing with technically defined problems that are normally found on the agendas of officials when they talk. When citizens outside government come together in public groups they are able, in a creatively designed process of dialogue, to discuss the deeper interests that they have in a relationship, the factors in the relationship that block them from achieving these interests, and the ways of changing that relationship. They probe the reasons for historical animosities, they experience each other's pictures of the conflict, they rehumanize each other, and they understand each other's historical grievances in the relationship. Having probed each other's experience, fears, hopes, and perceptions, they can see ways of changing them. These are subjects not normally found on the agendas of government.

It is not inconceivable to construct a strategy for change built around such groups. What has happened in the Israeli and Palestinian bodies politic—not by any one person's design—is that groups in dialogue have proliferated over a period of more than a decade so that there is in effect a critical mass of people who have already worked through the problem of changing the relationship between the two peoples. Reflecting on that experience, one

"[Dialogue groups] have the capacity to influence thinking in their communities."

can see the possibility of deliberately building from an initial dialogue group to spin off one group after another until the number of individuals involved in such experiences has grown to the point where they have the capacity to influence thinking in their communities in significant ways. Such a strategy is itself the product of more than a decade's experience in this work. That strategy, too, would take time to work itself out, but it seems to have greater promise of producing lasting change than does relying only on training individuals in the skills of mediation and negotiation.

Proposals for Dialogue

The purpose of this essay is not to prescribe a specific course of action. . . . It is rather to propose that, when and where possible, groups deeply engaged in these conflicts seriously consider finding a few individuals from each party who will come together quietly to begin a process of understanding how the conflictual relationship might be changed.

This also poses a challenge for groups and nations in the "neighborhood" of these conflicts. Many of them have intimate historical interactions with groups in the new areas of conflict; they have a familiarity with the dynamics of these groups that others farther away may not have. It may be their unique contribution to help members of communities in conflict to come together in dialogue. Greece and Turkey as well as the Greek and Turkish communities on Cyprus have a chance to resolve differences surrounding the Cyprus conflict in this way. Numerous groups form minorities in central Europe, and—apart from Yugoslavia—there is an opportunity to begin work before conflict breaks out. Throughout the states that have grown from the former Soviet Union, there are pressing needs to deal with impending conflict between groups and between states.

Why am I, as a citizen of the so-called one remaining superpower, writing this essay for an audience of citizens from smaller and supposedly less powerful countries? I believe that large and small powers alike—citizens outside as well as inside government—may gain new appreciation of what each can contribute to the resolution of conflict in a world where such resolution is no longer within the capability of governments alone. The needs, even in this area, are practically infinite. Governments, with all of the other problems that beset them in the areas of political and economic reform, are not likely to be able to give the intimate attention that is needed to deal with all conflicts. If that attention is to be provided at all, it is more likely than not to be provided by nongovernmental groups. That is why I call attention to the potential of a peace process that is within the capacity of citizens to initiate and conduct.

Ethnic Conflicts Around the World Snapshot: September 1993

Africa

Egypt Radical fundamentalists intent on creating a Muslim theocracy founded on Islamic law, or *sharia*, threaten Egypt's secular government with bombings in Cairo and assassinations of government officials. Since December 1992, military courts have sentenced to death more than twenty-five fundamentalists for violent antigovernment acts.

North Africa Several North African governments, particularly that of Algeria, face threats of coups by fundamentalist Muslim groups. In Algeria, a 1992 military coup prevented the freely elected Islamic Salvation Front, since banned, from coming to power. In response, fundamentalists blew up an airport terminal and assassinated Algeria's president. In 1993, a former prime minister was also assassinated. Algeria has sentenced to death more than one hundred fundamentalists.

South Africa Despite the scheduling of first-ever multiracial elections and the establishment of government goals to abolish apartheid (South Africa's official policy of discrimination), violence between black South Africans and whites, known as Afrikaners, continues. Right-wing whites seek to retain apartheid. Violence between black tribespeople and residents of black townships also mars South Africa's path to democracy.

Sudan Christians in southern Sudan are violently opposed to the imposition of *sharia* by the Islamic north. The continuing religious civil war has killed or displaced hundreds of thousands of Sudanese.

Asia

Afghanistan Thousands have been killed in civil war among competing guerrilla factions of majority Pushtuns and minority Tajiks and Uzbeks.

Armenia and *Azerbaijan* South of the Caucasus Mountains, Christian Armenia and Muslim Azerbaijan, former Soviet republics, are at war over the Armenian

271

enclave of Nagorno-Karabakh in Azerbaijan. Since fighting began in 1988, approximately three thousand people have been killed. Gains by Armenian forces in 1993 prompted concerns that Iran, Russia, and/or Turkey could intervene in the conflict.

Georgia Since 1990 this former Soviet republic north of Armenia has been fighting against the secession of South Ossetia and Abkhazia, both autonomous regions. Peace accords between parties have repeatedly collapsed.

India The 1980s and 1990s have been marked by increased violence among majority Hindus and minority Muslims and Sikhs. In recent years, ethnic conflict has been responsible for the deaths of thousands of Indians, including two prime ministers.

Sri Lanka Tamil rebels seek an independent homeland on this island off India's southeast coast. Ethnic fighting between ruling Sinhalese and minority Tamils has killed more than eight thousand people and forced two hundred thousand Tamils into refugee camps. In 1993, Sri Lanka's president was assassinated during a May Day rally, allegedly by a Tamil suicide bomber.

Tajikistan In 1992, pro-communist forces ousted a coalition government of Islamic fundamentalists, nationalists, and democrats. More than twenty thousand people have been killed as communists and Muslims vie for control of this former Soviet republic.

Europe

Bosnia and Herzegovina and *Croatia* Ethnic warfare among Orthodox Christian Serbs, Roman Catholic Croats, and Muslim Bosnians in these newly independent nations has killed hundreds of thousands of civilians and forced millions more to flee their homes. Although UN peacekeepers have occupied both republics, fighting has spread and the North Atlantic Treaty Organization (NATO) has threatened to intervene.

Germany Neo-Nazi assaults against African, Turkish, and other immigrants numbered more than two thousand in 1991 and 1992. The widespread violence prompted Germany to toughen its asylum law, which had previously granted asylum to virtually all immigrants.

Northern Ireland Roman Catholics and Protestants regularly exchange violence in this perennial conflict area. Catholics and the Irish Republican Army (IRA) seek freedom from Great Britain, which has directly ruled Northern Ireland since 1972. However, two-thirds of the population are Protestants who remain loyal to Britain. IRA rebels not only have targeted British soldiers in Northern Ireland, but also have set off bombs in London and attempted to assassinate British leaders.

Middle East

Iraq Immediately after the Persian Gulf War, Kurds in Iraq's mountainous north and Shia Muslims in the south sought to capitalize on Saddam Hussein's defeat and overthrow his regime. The rebellions were quashed. The United States and its allies have imposed no-fly zones in northern and southern Iraq to prevent further Iraqi air attacks on these minorities.

Israel Since its founding as a nation in 1948, Israel has been directly involved in six wars or invasions with its Arab enemies. During the Persian Gulf War, Iraq attacked Israel with Scud missiles, damaging neighborhoods in Tel Aviv and eliciting Israel's vow to retaliate. In August 1993, Israel sought to end its long conflict with Arabs by agreeing in principle to withdraw from occupied territories in the Gaza Strip and West Bank and to grant Palestinians there limited autonomy.

Lebanon Periodic raids and rocket attacks by Iranian-funded Hezbollah ("Party of God") guerrillas from south Lebanon threaten Israeli settlements in Galilee. Retaliating against the bombing deaths of eight soldiers in south Lebanon in 1993, Israel launched its largest attack on south Lebanon since it invaded the nation in 1982. Exchanges of heavy rocket attacks forced more than one hundred thousand Israelis into shelters and forced a substantially higher number of Lebanese to flee. Hezbollah vowed to continue raids and rocket attacks until Israel withdraws all forces from south Lebanon.

South America

Brazil Miners and indigenous tribes in Brazil's interior clash as miners increasingly encroach upon tribal lands. In 1993, miners attacked a reservation and used machetes to kill scores of Yanomamis, who are considered South America's largest unassimilated tribe. It was the worst Indian massacre in Brazil since 1910.

Peru Communist rebels known as *Sendero Luminoso*, or Shining Path, seek the overthrow of Peru's government. These Maoist guerrillas are also fighting to control the Ashaninka forest people, trying to force them to abandon their language, customs, and political autonomy. In 1993, a rebel rampage through seven villages killed sixty-three Ashaninkas.

United States

Detroit Two white police officers were convicted in 1993 of second-degree murder in the fatal beating of motorist Malice Green. City officials feared that civil disturbances would erupt if the pair were acquitted.

273

Los Angeles The April 1992 acquittal of police officers charged with beating black motorist Rodney King ignited three days of rioting and racial violence that left more than fifty people dead and more than two thousand injured. Looters also ransacked or burned many small businesses, both black- and Korean-owned. In 1993, the police officers were tried in federal court on charges of violating King's civil rights; two of the officers were convicted and sentenced to thirty-month prison terms. Residents had feared that a second acquittal would spark more racial violence, especially in light of the possible conviction and harsher sentencing of black defendants then on trial for beating white trucker Reginald Denny during the riots. Also in 1993, federal agents arrested white supremacist skinheads who were accused of plotting to assassinate Rodney King, blow up a black Methodist church, and kill Jewish rabbis with mail bombs.

New York In 1993, federal agents arrested New York-area Muslims and charged them with bombing the World Trade Center. Agents also uncovered a related plot to bomb UN headquarters and assassinate Egyptian president Hosni Mubarak. A federal indictment charged that the Muslims' terrorist campaign dated back to the 1990 murder of Rabbi Meir Kahane, founder of the radical Jewish Defense League. Also in 1993, a state report was issued criticizing police response to three days of rioting between blacks and Hasidic Jews in the Crown Heights section of Brooklyn in August 1991. The riots began after a car driven by a Jewish man accidentally struck two black children, killing one of them.

Bibliography

Books

Saïd K. Aburish	*Cry Palestine: Inside the West Bank.* Boulder, CO: Westview Press, 1993.
Rabia Ali and Lawrence Lifschultz	*Why Bosnia? Writings on the Balkan War.* Stony Creek, CT: Pamphleteer's Press, 1993.
Peter Alter	*Nationalism.* New York: Edward Arnold, 1989.
J. Bowyer Bell	*The Irish Troubles: A Generation of Violence, 1967-1992.* New York: St. Martin's Press, 1993.
Zbigniew Brzezinski	*Out of Control: Global Turmoil on the Eve of the Twenty-First Century.* New York: Macmillan, 1993.
Janusz Bugajski	*Nations in Turmoil: Conflict and Cooperation in Eastern Europe.* Boulder, CO: Westview Press, 1993.
John Bulloch and Harvey Morris	*No Friends but the Mountains: The Tragic History of the Kurds.* New York: Oxford University Press, 1992.
Carnegie Endowment for International Peace	*The Other Balkan Wars.* Washington, DC: Brookings Institution, 1993.
John Coakley, ed.	*The Social Origins of Nationalist Movements: The Contemporary West European Experience.* Newbury Park, CA: Sage Publications, 1992.
John Feffer	*Shock Waves: Eastern Europe After the Revolutions.* Boston: South End Press, 1992.
Robert I. Friedman	*Zealots for Zion: Inside Israel's West Bank Settlement Movement.* New York: Random House, 1993.
Misha Glenny	*The Fall of Yugoslavia: The Third Balkan War.* New York: Penguin, 1992.
Liah Greenfeld	*Nationalism: Five Roads to Modernity.* Cambridge, MA: Harvard University Press, 1993.
Paul Hainsworth, ed.	*The Extreme Right in Europe and the USA.* New York: St. Martin's Press, 1992.
Morton Halperin and David J. Scheffer	*Self-Determination in the New World Order.* Washington, DC: Carnegie Endowment for International Peace, 1992.
Helsinki Watch	*War Crimes in Bosnia-Hercegovina.* New York: Human Rights Watch, 1993.

Bibliography

Human Rights Watch	*"Foreigners Out": Xenophobia and Right-Wing Violence in Germany.* New York: Human Rights Watch, 1992.
Human Rights Watch	*Struggling for Ethnic Identity: Czechoslovakia's Endangered Gypsies.* New York: Human Rights Watch, 1992.
Mark Juergensmeyer	*The New Cold War? Religious Nationalism Confronts the Secular State.* Berkeley: University of California Press, 1993.
Robert D. Kaplan	*Balkan Ghosts: A Journey Through History.* New York: St. Martin's Press, 1993.
Anto Knezevic	*An Analysis of Serbian Propaganda.* Zagreb, Croatia: Domovina TT, 1992.
Gail W. Lapidus and Victor Zaslavsky	*From Union to Commonwealth: Nationalism and Separatism in the Soviet Republics.* New York: Cambridge University Press, 1992.
John Lukacs	*The End of the Twentieth Century and the End of the Modern Age.* New York: Ticknor & Fields, 1993.
Branka Magas	*The Destruction of Yugoslavia.* London: Verso, 1993.
Kanan Makiya	*Cruelty and Silence: War, Tyranny, Uprising and the Arab World.* New York: Norton, 1993.
Sebastian Mallaby	*After Apartheid: The Future of South Africa.* New York: Random House, 1992.
Donald E. Miller and Lorna Touryan Miller	*Survivors: An Oral History of the Armenian Genocide.* Berkeley: University of California Press, 1993.
Daniel Patrick Moynihan	*Pandaemonium: Ethnicity in International Politics.* New York: Oxford University Press, 1993.
Benjamin Netanyahu	*A Place Among Nations: Israel and the World.* New York: Bantam Books, 1993.
Jehuda Reinharz and George L. Mosse	*The Impact of Western Nationalisms.* Newbury Park, CA: Sage Publications, 1992.
James Ridgeway	*Blood in the Face.* New York: Thunders Mouth Press, 1991.
Kumar Rupesinghe, Peter King, and Olga Vorkunova, eds.	*Ethnicity and Conflict in a Post-Communist World: The Soviet Union, Eastern Europe, and China.* New York: St. Martin's Press, 1992.
Mark Thompson	*A Paper House: The Ending of Yugoslavia.* New York: Pantheon Books, 1993.
Susan L. Woodward	*Balkan Tragedy: Chaos and Dissolution After the Cold War.* Washington, DC: Brookings Institution, 1993.

Periodicals

| Anonymous | "A Voice from the Bosnian Whirlwind," *Refugee Reports*, May 31, 1993. Available from American Council for Nationalities Service, 95 Madison Ave., 3d Floor, New York, NY 10016. |

276

Peter Applebome	"Skinhead Violence Grows, Experts Say," *The New York Times*, July 18, 1993.
Michael Barone	"The Triumph of American Nationalism," *The Public Interest*, Spring 1993.
Andrew Bell-Fialkoff	"A Brief History of Ethnic Cleansing," *Foreign Affairs*, Summer 1993.
Robin Blackburn	"The Break-Up of Yugoslavia and the Fate of Bosnia," *New Left Review*, May/June 1993.
Janice Broun	"Worse Yet to Come? Kosovo and Macedonia," *Commonweal*, January 1993.
George Bush	"Resolving Global Conflicts and Disarmament," *Vital Speeches of the Day*, October 15, 1992.
Chronicles	Special issue on nationalism in Eastern Europe, August 1993. Available from the Rockford Institute, 934 N. Main St., Rockford, IL 61103-7061.
Harold M. Cubert	"The Militant Palestinian Organizations and the Arab-Israeli Peace Process," *Terrorism and Political Violence*, Spring 1992. Available from Frank Cass & Co., Gainsborough House, Gainsborough Rd., London E11 1RS, England.
Daedalus	Special issue on nationalism, Summer 1993. Available from 136 Irving St., Cambridge, MA 02138.
F.W. de Klerk	"Progress with Reform: Honest Negotiation," *Vital Speeches of the Day*, November 15, 1992.
Slavenka Drakulic	"Women Hide Behind a Wall of Silence," *The Nation*, March 1, 1993.
The Economist	"Little Local Wars?" March 13, 1993.
Thomas Emmert	"The Serbs, Forever on the Battlefield of Kosovo," *The Washington Post National Weekly Edition*, June 21-27, 1993.
Mahmud A. Faksh	"Withered Arab Nationalism," *Orbis*, Summer 1993.
Brian Hall	"A Holy War in Waiting," *The New York Times Magazine*, May 9, 1993.
Thomas Harrison	"The Betrayal of Bosnia," *Z Magazine*, July/August 1993.
Gertrude Himmelfarb	"The Dark and Bloody Crossroads: Where Nationalism and Religion Meet," *The National Interest*, Summer 1993. Available from Dept. NI, PO Box 3000, Denville, NJ 07834.
Llewellyn D. Howell	"Ethnic Conflict Threatens International Stability," *USA Today*, July 1993.
Josef Joffe	"The New Europe: Yesterday's Ghosts," *Foreign Affairs*, 1992/93.
Bill Keller	"South African Commandos: Vigilant, or Vigilante?" *The New York Times*, July 14, 1993.

Robin Knight, Eric Ransdell, and Paul Brandus	"Home Sweet Homeland," *U.S. News & World Report*, July 26, 1993.
Cardinal Franjo Kuharic	"Appeal to Croats and Muslims: Stop Fighting Each Other," *Origins*, June 3, 1993. Available from Catholic News Service, 3211 Fourth St. NE, Washington, DC 20017-1100.
Jeri Laber	"Bosnia: Questions About Rape," *The New York Review of Books*, March 25, 1993.
Walter Laqueur	"Danger on the Far Right," *U.S. New & World Report*, June 21, 1993.
Catharine A. MacKinnon	"Turning Rape into Pornography: Postmodern Genocide," *Ms.*, July/August 1993.
Branka Magas	"The Rise and Fall of Vance-Owen," *Against the Current*, July/August 1993.
Marguerite Michaels	"Voting with Their Guns," *Time*, August 16, 1993.
Charles Moore	"Ireland Must Fight the IRA Too," *The Wall Street Journal*, March 9, 1992.
Ms.	"Dispatches from Bosnia and Herzegovina: Young Survivors Testify to Systematic Rape," January/February, 1993.
Bruce W. Nelan	"Europe Slams the Door," *Time*, July 19, 1993.
New Perspectives Quarterly	Special issue on German nationalism and identity, Winter 1993.
New Politics	Special section on nationalism and self-determination, Summer 1993.
The New Yorker	"The Choices in Bosnia," January 25, 1993.
Barry Newman	"Flooded by Refugees, Western Europe Slams Doors on Foreigners," *The Wall Street Journal*, July 8, 1993.
Conor Cruise O'Brien	"The Patriot Game," *National Review*, April 26, 1993.
Off Our Backs	"Serbia's War Against Bosnia and Croatia," special section, May 1993.
Milan Panic	"The Yugoslav Crisis," *Vital Speeches of the Day*, July 15, 1993.
William Pfaff	"CSCE Should Act to Solve the Tragic Fighting in Bosnia," *Liberal Opinion Week*, July 19, 1993. Available from PO Box 468, Vinton, IA 52349-0468.
Jyoti Punwani	"India: Searching for Answers in the Wake of Religious Violence," *Ms.*, July/August 1993.
Tom Reiss	"Strange World of Germany's Neo-Nazi Youth," *The Wall Street Journal*, December 17, 1992.
Susan Hoeber Rudolph and Lloyd I. Rudolph	"Modern Hate," *The New Republic*, March 22, 1993.

Salman Rushdie	"The Struggle for the Soul of Islam," *The New York Times*, July 11, 1993.
Peter Schneider	"Neo-Nazi Violence: Stop It Now, Explain It Later," *Harper's*, June 1993.
Momcilo Selic	"Letter from Serbia: Notes from the front, Part II," *Chronicles*, July 1993.
Social Education	Special issue on teaching about genocide, February 1991. Available from 3501 Newark St., Washington, DC 20016-3199.
Tad Szulc	"Cyprus: A Time of Reckoning," *National Geographic*, July 1993.
Jasminka Udovicki	"Yugoslavia's Wars: Notes on Nationalism," *Radical America*, February 1993.
James M. Wall	"A Love of Destruction: The Balkan Disease," *The Christian Century*, March 17, 1993.
Stuart Weir	"In Iraqi Kurdistan: Living Short, with Dignity," *New Politics*, Winter 1993.
Robert W. White	"Comment: British Violence and British Injustice in Undemocratic Northern Ireland," *Terrorism and Political Violence*, Autumn 1992.
Albert Wohlstetter	"The Way Out," *The Wall Street Journal*, July 2, 1993.
Stanley Wolpert	"Resurgent Hindu Fundamentalism," *Contention*, Spring 1993.
World Press Review	Special section on Hindu-Muslim violence, April 1993.

Organizations to Contact

The editors have compiled the following list of organizations that are concerned with the issues debated in this book. All have publications or information available for interested readers. For best results, allow as much time as possible for the organizations to respond. The descriptions below are derived from materials provided by the organizations. This list was compiled at the date of publication. Names, addresses, and phone numbers of organizations are subject to change.

American Protestants for Truth About Ireland (APTI)
104 E. Main St.
Lansdale, PA 19446
(215) 362-3888

APTI is concerned with the protection of human rights of all people in Ireland. APTI publishes a monthly newsletter, *Northern Ireland Human Rights Review/Advocacy Letter.*

Americans for a Safe Israel (AFSI)
147 E. 76th St.
New York, NY 10021
(212) 628-9400

AFSI provides information on the Middle East conflict "based on the belief that a strong Israel is vital to American security interests." It publishes the monthly *Outpost* and books and pamphlets.

Anti-Defamation League of B'nai B'rith (ADL)
823 United Nations Plaza
New York, NY 10017
(212) 490-2525

The league's goal is to stop the defamation of Jewish people and to secure justice and fair treatment for all citizens alike. The ADL promotes better interfaith and intergroup relations, counteracts antidemocratic extremism, and strengthens democratic structures and values. It publishes the newsletter *ADL on the Frontline News* ten times a year and several quarterly publications, including *Dimensions* and *Middle East Insight.*

Campaign for Peace and Democracy (CPD)
PO Box 1640
New York, NY 10025
(212) 666-5924

The campaign is a network of peace activists, feminists, and social activists who advocate democracy, disarmament, and social justice throughout the world. CPD publishes the magazine *Peace & Democracy News* twice a year.

Center for War/Peace Studies (CW/PS)
218 E. 18th St.
New York, NY 10003
(212) 475-1077

The center conducts studies on various global problems, including ethnic conflicts. It advocates arms control and disarmament, seeks a Middle East peace settlement, and works to move the world beyond violent conflict and toward international cooperation under law. The center publishes the quarterly newsletter *Global Report: Progress Toward a World of Peace with Justice.*

Council on Foreign Relations
58 E. 68th St.
New York, NY 10021
(212) 734-0400

The council specializes in knowledge of foreign affairs and studies the international aspects of American political and economic policies and problems. Its journal *Foreign Affairs*, published five times a year, includes analyses of current ethnic conflicts around the world.

Human Rights Watch (HRW)
485 Fifth Ave.
New York, NY 10017-6104
(212) 972-8400

HRW comprises groups and individuals who promote and monitor human rights worldwide. It evaluates the human rights practices of governments according to standards set by international laws and agreements. HRW serves as an umbrella organization for affiliated regional groups such as Asia Watch, Middle East Watch, and U.S.-Helsinki Watch Committee. Each group publishes periodic newsletters and reports.

Irish National Caucus (INC)
413 E. Capitol St. SE
Washington, DC 20003
(202) 544-0568

The caucus is an independent lobbying group in Washington, D.C., concerned with the protection of human rights in Northern Ireland. It advocates nonviolence and a lasting peace in Ireland, free from British rule. INC publishes the monthly newsletter *Irish Lobby.*

Kurdish Heritage Foundation of America
345 Park Pl.
Brooklyn, NY 11238
(718) 783-7930

The foundation includes American Kurds, human rights advocates, academics, and others who seek to inform Americans of the efforts of the Kurdish people to retain their ethnic identity. Articles on the history and plight of the Kurds are available in the foundation's semiannual *Kurdish Studies: An International Journal* and the quarterly newsletter *Kurdish Life.*

281

Palestine Solidarity Committee
PO Box 372, Peck Slip Station
New York, NY 10272
(212) 505-1992

The committee seeks to create solidarity between Americans and the Palestinian and Lebanese people. It opposes U.S. intervention in the Middle East and supports the Palestine Liberation Organization as the sole legitimate representative of Palestinians. The committee publishes a newsletter that covers issues of Palestinian rights, the Israeli peace movement, and the U.S./Israeli role in the region.

Project on Ethnic Relations (PER)
One Palmer Square, Suite 435
Princeton, NJ 08542
(609) 683-5666

The project is a research organization that studies ethnic relations in the new European democracies. It seeks the peaceful resolution of ethnic conflicts there, in part by encouraging mediation and negotiation. Publications include conference reports and the quarterly *Project on Ethnic Relations Bulletin.*

U.S. Committee for Refugees (USCR)
1025 Vermont Ave. NW, Suite 920
Washington, DC 20005
(202) 347-3507

The committee, the public relations arm of the American Council for Nationalities Service, is an information and advocacy center that communicates to Americans the plight of the world's millions of refugees. It monitors American policy and legislation on refugees. Its publications include the quarterly *Issue Papers* and the monthly *Refugee Reports.*

U.S. Department of State
Office of Public Communications, Public Information Service
Bureau of Public Affairs
Washington, DC 20520
(202) 647-6575

The Department of State advises the president in the formulation and execution of foreign policy. It fosters democratic movements throughout the world and supports the rights of many ethnic groups to seek independence. Its weekly *U.S. Department of State Dispatch* includes reports and testimonies on various ethnic conflicts around the world and texts of United Nations resolutions.

White Aryan Resistance (WAR)
PO Box 65
Fallbrook, CA 92088
(619) 723-8996

WAR is a white supremacist organization that promotes the advancement and protection of the white race in America and abroad. WAR believes that armed conflict against nonwhites is justified only to protect living space, food, and the gene pool of the white race. It publishes the monthly tabloid *WAR* and has books, cassettes, and videotapes available on white supremacy, Adolf Hitler, and Jews, among other topics.

Index

Index